Democracy in Crisis

REACTING TO THE PAST is an award-winning series of immersive role-playing games that actively engage students in their own learning. Students assume the roles of historical characters and practice critical thinking, primary source analysis, and argument, both written and spoken. Reacting games are flexible enough to be used across the curriculum, from first-year general education classes and discussion sections of lecture classes to capstone experiences, intersession courses, and honors programs.

Reacting to the Past was originally developed under the auspices of Barnard College and is sustained by the Reacting Consortium of colleges and universities. The Consortium hosts a regular series of conferences and events to support faculty and administrators.

NOTE TO INSTRUCTORS: Before beginning the game you must download the game materials, including an instructor's guide containing a detailed schedule of class sessions, role sheets for students, and handouts.

To download this essential resource, visit https://reactingconsortium.org/games, click on the page for this title, then click "Game Materials."

Democracy in Crisis

WEIMAR GERMANY, 1929–1932

ROBERT GOODRICH

BARNARD

The University of North Carolina Press

Chapel Hill

ISBN 978-1-4696-6554-2 (pbk.: alk. paper)

ISBN 978-1-4696-6555-9 (ebook)

Cover illustration: Historical cartoon of the Weimar Republic as a "republic without republicans," by Thomas Theodor Heine, published in the German magazine *Simplicissimus* on March 21, 1927. Courtesy Wikimedia Commons. Heine was an illustrator for the satirical Munich magazine *Simplicissimus*, for which he appropriated the stylistic idiom of Jugendstil and the graphic qualities of Henri de Toulouse-Lautrec, Aubrey Beardsley, and Japanese woodcuts. The illustration, "They carry the company's letters: But who carries its spirit?" appeared in *Simplicissimus*. The popular and influential magazine was in large part defined by his artistic style, and included contributions by George Grosz, Käthe Kollwitz, and John Heartfield. The magazine's content took a strong stand against extremists on the left and on the right. But conservatives in particular denounced it as an example of what they perceived as the Republic's libertine and degenerate culture. Heine was especially targeted as a Jew. While Heine and the magazine pilloried every aspect of the Republic, they generally did so from a pro-Republic point of view. The characters portrayed in this particular graphic show the awkward coalition necessary to support the new Republic. Given the hostility of the social groups to each other, the caricature implies that the Republic is less than stable. The characters were easily identifiable to Germans in the 1920s. From left to right:

1. The Catholic clergyman is the Centre Party and Christian democracy
2. The professional urban middle class is the liberal DDP, DVP, and WP
3. The soldier is the national conservative Reichswehr and the DNVP
4. The urban worker is the Marxist KPD and SPD
5. The poor farmer/peasant is the agrarian CNBP and the DBP
6. The bourgeois capitalist is the DDP, the DVP, or the DNVP
7. The indescript citizen is just about anyone in the middle, such as the CSVD or WP
8. The man with the swastika armband is an SA member from the NSDAP

Contents

Illustrations

Abbreviations

POLITICAL ORGANIZATIONS

BVP — Bavarian People's Party (conservative Bavarian Catholic separatists)

CNBP — Christian National Farmers' League (conservative Protestant small farmers)

CSVD — Christian Social People's Service (conservative Protestant corporatists)

DBP — German Farmers' Party (democratic secular small farmers)

DDP — German Democratic Party (democratic liberals)

DHP — German-Hanoverian Party (conservative Hanoverian particularists)

DNVP — German National People's Party (national conservative elites)

DVP — German People's Party (conservative liberals)

KPD — German Communist Party (pro-Bolshevik Marxists)

NSDAP — National Socialist German Workers' Party (fascists)

RLB — National Agrarian League aka Agrarian League (national conservative big landowners)

SA — Storm troopers (*Sturmabteilung*), aka Brownshirts, the NSDAP paramilitary

SPD — German Social Democratic Party (anti-Bolshevik Marxists)

WP — Economic Party of the German Middle Class aka Economic Party (conservative middle-class liberals)

X — Centre Party (broad-based Catholic corporatists)

German Language and Pronunciation

Many German terms are traditionally retained in the original. However, German can be difficult. If you know a few rules and if you can spell it, you might be able to pronounce it, though, since German spelling is phonetic. German is more guttural and consonantal than English: *d* and *t* and *b* are pronounced hard; all syllables are pronounced fully (no silent vowels). The best way to figure it out is to go to an online guide with audio examples. Unfortunately, German also creates complex nouns, adding multiple words together, making pronunciation even more challenging. Words such as *Bildungsbürgertum* or *Katastrophenpolitik* challenge the non-native speaker beyond any phonetic problems.

1

Introduction

Democracy in Crisis takes place in the **Reichstag** (parliament) of Germany's highly democratic republic after World War I (WWI). You are (mostly) delegates to the Reichstag representing over a dozen different factions, mostly organized in political parties. Your task is to shape Germany into your character's vision by passing or preventing legislation, or, if that fails, perhaps by resorting to other means—violence, bribery, demagoguery, obstructionism.

> **Reichstag** (Imperial Diet, or Diet of the Realm) may refer to the building or the constitutional assembly. The term has ancient roots in the Holy Roman Empire of the German Nation in the Middle Ages.

Each character is closely identified with a specific ideology, or, perhaps better stated, with a holistic *Weltanschaung*—an overarching perception of reality and the framework of ideas and beliefs through which your character interprets the world and interacts with it.

Democracy in Crisis explores how a liberal democracy responds to extreme pressures including ideological extremism, populist demagoguery, partisan gridlock, economic dislocation, **revanchism** and **irredentism**, constitutional crisis, political violence, entrenched special interests, and corruption. These pressures all converged in Germany after WWI. The results were not positive.

> **Revanchism** and **irredentism** both refer to the desire and attempts to reverse the outcome of war (in this case, WWI) and recover lost territory or historically claimed territory.

The Big Issues: The Limits of Democracy

What happens in democratic societies where democracy fails to produce working majorities or promote the interests of citizens?

By the twentieth century, Western societies had developed holistic ideologies promoted by well-organized political parties that drew broad layers of the citizenry into the political rituals of mass society. These ideologies did not remain mere abstractions; instead, millions fought for them by rallying to their platforms, symbols, and personalities as forms of mass participatory political culture emerged. All of the major ideologies of the twentieth century clashed openly in post–WWI Germany during the so-called Weimar Republic (1919–33).

Under the burdens of a global capitalist crisis, national humiliation, and the unraveling of prewar consensus, traditional German parties struggled to provide viable answers.

Each party promoted a specific ideology and pulled Germans in different directions, often refusing to compromise with or even recognize other parties. As the conservative Austrian scholar Erik von Kuehnelt-Leddihn wrote in 1943:

> Catholic Centrists wanted to create conditions in Germany which would make it easier for the individuals to save their souls; Socialists denied the existence of souls and divided people into classes; the German Nationalists were interested in language and culture; while the National Socialists put the main stress on race.
>
> Whereas some looked at pocketbooks, others at the pigmentation of the skin or the index of the skull, fruitful discussions became impossible. When the speaker of one party indulged in his oratory, the others walked out. It was not worthwhile to listen to somebody's opinion when you knew that his premises were all wrong. The grim determination to silence the unconvincible enemy by execution or imprisonment already existed prior to 1933 in many parties.[1]

In short, Germans often regarded those who disagreed with them as either ignorant fools or charlatans who misunderstood or distorted the most basic nature of society and therefore could only reach absurd conclusions totally at odds with reality. Opponents became enemies and traitors. This logic dictated that one's opponents should have no role in political life. Statements of principle mattered more than the pragmatic concessions essential to democracy. The numerous political parties reflected and reinforced this fractured reality inside the Reichstag.

Compromises, which were essential because no party possessed a stable parliamentary majority, alienated the parties' purist ideologues, opening the door to radical alternatives that did not fit into a liberal democratic concept. As Germans viewed every social, cultural, diplomatic, legal, economic, and constitutional issue through these different ideological lenses, every issue became a matter of principle and identity—compromise became defeat.

Perhaps, had the only issue been one of ideology, the Republic might have survived, but the Republic's birth had been painful, and the ensuing years offered little respite. Germans were stunned by their loss in WWI, angered by the Versailles Treaty, and confused by the new domestic realities. Fueled by conspiracy theories, revanchism and reaction simmered at a near boil.

Special interests created additional instability by finding ways to subvert democracy through extra-parliamentary means, including political violence. Severe economic hardship exacerbated already pronounced economic dislocations in both industry and agriculture. And Germans argued over definitions of citizenship and, in particular, who deserved civil rights: Jews? Those of African descent? The handicapped? Political dissenters?

As a result, one of the distinct aspects of the Republic was its lack of any political discursive commonality. Almost every member of the Reichstag was part of the *Bildungsbürgertum* (a term roughly meaning the educated professional middle class), who shared a common cultural fluency grounded in the Western Christian and German cultural traditions, but little else held them together aside from citizenship. In fact, they bitterly disagreed over the meaning of even the most basic political and cultural terms. German society had become "siloed"—a single nation in which separate subcultures sought to avoid influences from the others.

What to Call the Weimar Republic

"Germany" is the universal translation of *Deutschland* (literally, Land of the Germans). Before 1871, it referred only to a cultural region. In 1871, it became synonymous with the Kaiserreich but excluded German-speaking areas (Austria-Hungary, Switzerland, and many borderlands). Germans referred to the Republic as *das Deutsche Reich*, usually translated as "the German Empire." *Reich*, however, has broad connotations, so the name is usually left as the *German Reich*. The word "realm" captures the same meaning but is rarely used. The common form in English remained "Germany." Only Nazis called it the "Weimar Republic," and then derisively. For game purposes, we use "Germany" or "the Republic" to avoid confusion.

BASIC FEATURES OF REACTING TO THE PAST

This is a historical role-playing game. After a few preparatory lectures, the game begins and the students are in charge. Set in moments of heightened historical tension, it places you in the role of a person from the period. By reading the game book and your individual role sheet, you will find out more about your objectives, worldview, allies, and opponents. You must then attempt to achieve victory through formal speeches, informal debate, negotiations, and conspiracy. Outcomes sometimes differ from actual history; a debriefing session sets the record straight. What follows is an outline of what you will encounter in Reacting and what you will be expected to do.

Game Setup

Your instructor will spend some time before the beginning of the game helping you to understand the historical context for the game. During the setup period, you will use several different kinds of material:

- The game book (what you are reading now), which includes historical information, rules and elements of the game, and essential historical documents.
- A role sheet, which provides a short biography of the historical person you will model in the game as well as that person's ideology, objectives, responsibilities, and resources. Some roles are based on historical figures. Others are "composites," which draw elements from a number of individuals. You will receive your role sheet from your instructor.

Familiarize yourself with the documents before the game begins and return to them once you are in role. They contain information and arguments that will be useful as the game unfolds. A second reading while *in role* will deepen your understanding and alter your perspective. Once the game is in motion, your perspectives may change. Some ideas may begin to look quite different. Those who have carefully read the materials and who know the rules of the game will invariably do better than those who rely on general impressions and uncertain memories.

Game Play

Once the game begins, class sessions are presided over by students. In most cases, a single student serves as some sort of presiding officer. The instructor then becomes the GM (the "game master" or "game manager") and takes a seat in the back of the room. Though they do not lead the class sessions, GMs may do any of the following:

- Pass notes
- Announce important events
- Redirect proceedings that have gone off track

Instructors are, of course, available for consultations before and after game sessions. Although they will not let you in on any of the secrets of the game, they can be invaluable in terms of sharpening your arguments or finding key historical resources.

The presiding officer is expected to observe basic standards of fairness, but as a fail-safe device, most games employ the "podium rule," which allows a student who has not been recognized to approach the podium and wait for a chance to speak. Once at the podium, the student has the floor and must be heard.

Role sheets contain private, secret information that you must guard. Exercise caution when discussing your role with others. Your role sheet probably identifies likely allies, but even they may not always be trustworthy. However, keeping your own counsel and saying nothing to anyone is not an option. In order to achieve your objectives, you *must* speak with others. You will never muster the voting strength to prevail without allies. Collaboration and coalition building are at the heart of every game.

Some games feature strong alliances called *factions*. As a counterbalance, these games include roles called *indeterminates*. They operate outside of the established factions, and while some are entirely

neutral, most possess their own idiosyncratic objectives. If you are in a faction, cultivating indeterminates is in your interest, since they can be persuaded to support your position. If you are lucky enough to have drawn the role of an indeterminate, you should be pleased; you will likely play a pivotal role in the outcome of the game.

Game Requirements

Students playing Reacting games practice persuasive writing, public speaking, critical thinking, teamwork, negotiation, problem solving, collaboration, adapting to changing circumstances, and working under pressure to meet deadlines. Your instructor will explain the specific requirements for your class. In general, though, a Reacting game asks you to perform three distinct activities:

Reading and writing. What you read can often be put to immediate use, and what you write is meant to persuade others to act the way you want them to. The reading load may have slight variations from role to role; the writing requirement depends on your particular course. Papers are often policy statements, but they can also be autobiographies, battle plans, newspaper articles, poems, or after-game reflections. Papers often provide the foundation for the speeches delivered in class. They also help to familiarize you with the issues, which should allow you to ask good questions.

Public speaking and debate. In the course of a game, almost everyone is expected to deliver at least one formal speech from the podium (the length of the game and the size of the class will determine the number of speeches). Debate follows. It can be impromptu, raucous, and fast paced. At some point, discussions must lead to action, which often means proposing, debating, and passing a variety of resolutions. GMs may stipulate that students must deliver their papers from memory when at the podium, or they may insist that students begin to wean themselves from dependency on written notes as the game progresses.

Wherever the game imaginatively puts you, it will surely not put you in the present. Accordingly, the colloquialisms and familiarities of today's college life are out of place. Never open your speech with a salutation like "Hi guys" when something like "Fellow citizens!" would be more appropriate.

Always seek allies to back your points when you are speaking at the podium. Do your best to have at least one supporter second your proposal, come to your defense, or admonish inattentive members of the body. Note-passing and side conversations, while common occurrences, will likely spoil the effect of your speech; so you and your supporters should insist upon order before such behavior becomes too disruptive. Ask the presiding officer to assist you. Appeal to the GM as a last resort.

Strategizing. Communication among students is an essential feature of Reacting games. You will likely find yourself writing emails, texting, attending out-of-class meetings, or gathering for meals. The purpose of frequent communication is to lay out a strategy for achieving your objectives, thwarting your opponents, and hatching plots. When communicating with fellow students in or out of class, always assume that they are speaking to you in role. If you want to talk about the "real world," make that clear.

Controversy

Most Reacting games take place at moments of conflict in the past and therefore are likely to address difficult, even painful, issues that we continue to grapple with today. Consequently, this game may contain controversial subject matter. You may need to represent ideas with which you personally disagree or that you even find repugnant. When speaking about these ideas, make it clear that you are speaking *in role*. Furthermore, if other people say things that offend you, recognize that they too are playing roles. If you decide to respond to them, do so using the voice of your role and make this clear. If these efforts are insufficient, or the ideas associated with your particular role seem potentially overwhelming, talk to your GM.

When playing your role, rely on your role sheet and the other game materials rather than drawing upon caricature or stereotype. Do not use racial and ethnic slurs even if they are historically appropriate. If you are concerned about the potential for cultural appropriation or the use of demeaning language in your game, talk to your GM.

Amid the plotting, debating, and voting, always remember that this is an immersive role-playing game. Other players may resist your efforts, attack your ideas, and even betray a confidence. They take these actions because they are playing their roles. If you become concerned about the potential for game-based conflict to bleed out into the real world, take a step back and reflect on the situation. If your concerns persist, talk to your GM.

Skill Development

A recent Associated Press article on education and employment made the following observations:

> The world's top employers are pickier than ever. And they want to see more than high marks and the right degree. They want graduates with so-called soft skills—those who can work well in teams, write and speak with clarity, adapt quickly to changes in technology and business conditions, and interact with colleagues from different countries and cultures. . . . And companies are going to ever-greater lengths to identify the students who have the right mix of skills, by observing them in role-playing exercises to see how they handle pressure and get along with others . . . and [by] organizing contests that reveal how students solve problems and handle deadline pressure.

Reacting games, probably better than most elements of the curriculum, provide the opportunity for developing these soft skills. This is because you will be practicing persuasive writing, public speaking, critical thinking, problem solving, and collaboration. You will also need to adapt to changing circumstances and work under pressure.

COUNTERFACTUALS

While every character is a historical personage, they all represent composite interests. Additionally, a few of the characters were not in the Reichstag in 1929, although they were party officers and elected later; others did not remain in the Reichstag until the end of 1932 (Hermann Müller, for example, died in 1931 after a gallbladder operation). Some offices are distributed ahistorically to ensure that the proper party is represented.

Some of the documents included here were published shortly after 1929, which is when the game begins, but they represent general ideas well known in 1929, and no document is from later than 1932. All come from the immediate context. Similarly, the chronology of the agenda items may not correspond precisely to the historical sequence.

The game reduces the Weimar Constitution's complexity, especially by eliminating the Republic's bicameralism and the role of the individual states historically represented in the Reichsrat (the Imperial Council). This institution represented the German traditions of **particularism** and **federalism**. Similarly, the Reichstag had a complicated internal structure that has been simplified. The president of the Reichstag has been renamed "Speaker" to avoid confusion with the Reich president. The cabinet portfolios have been reduced, and while the historical cabinet of 1929 included all of the parties in the game's initial cabinet, the personalities and portfolios are not necessarily the same.

Particularism refers to the long tradition of regional loyalty above national loyalty. The Republic institutionalized these loyalties via **federalism**, a system of government that unites states within an overarching political structure that allows a degree of local sovereignty. Both the Bavarian People's Party (BVP) and the German Hanoverian Party (DHP) were particularist parties.

Similarly, several small parties are integrated into larger Indeterminates; these small parties failed to have representation at some point in 1929 to 1933, and included the following:

Conservative People's Party (added to CNBP)
German Country People (added to CNBP)
People's Justice Party (added to CSVD)
Reich Party for Civil Rights and Deflation
   (added to CSVD)
Saxon Peasants Party (added to CNBP)
Thuringian Agricultural League (added to RLB)

CHALLENGES TO ROLE PLAYING DEMOCRACY IN CRISIS

Antisemitism and Nazi Discourse

Antisemitism is the race-based hostility or prejudice against Jews. The increasingly preferred scholarly spelling is "antisemitism," without a hyphen or capitalization.[2]

Ban on Nazi Symbols and Slurs
This game specifically prohibits the following:

1. Racist and ethnic slurs, specifically Nazi terminology that renders Jews and others as sub-humans, such as "vermin"
2. Nazi symbols or variations thereof, including
   The swastika
   The greeting "Heil Hitler" or "Sieg Heil"
   The fascist or "Hitler" salute
   Uniforms or Nazi-like dress meant to simulate Nazi uniforms

In reacting games, you compete with other students, in character, to advance your character's intellectual goals. In trying to "win," your character often advocates offensive ideas. But you must compete intellectually while being respectful to your classmates, even while criticizing the beliefs and goals of opposing characters. Any use of racist language in the game threatens that respectful behavior. The power of certain words and symbols is entirely emotional, not intellectual. All characters in this game have strong, serious intellectual arguments to make. You should make them, but you may not personalize criticism of an idea by making a personalized attack on a fellow student; instead, you must try to discredit your opponent's ideas using your character's reasoning (based on your primary documents).

If you feel that a classmate has personalized issues of the game into hostility toward you or anyone else, please speak to your instructor immediately in private.

Antisemitic Ideas in the Game
Every faction has a document on your character's stance on antisemitism. However, the game master will decide if and how to integrate the topic. During game preparation, the GM will announce one of three options regarding antisemitism as a topic.

OPTION 1: Basic game. Antisemitism is integrated as a mandatory topic and treated as any other, as written in the game book. Appropriate warnings, especially for how Nazi characters should play this issue, are in the character sheets.

OPTION 2: Hybrid approach. Antisemitism is integrated as a mandatory topic but treated differently. Rather than Nazi and related characters presenting their views directly, everyone is directed to historical documents that are to be read in class as part of the debate during game play. Once debate has opened, it will proceed as follows:

- The GM instructs the class to read the National Socialist German Workers' Party (NSDAP) handout. NSDAP characters do *not* speak from the podium or floor on the topic. The handout counts as their participation.
- All other characters present their views normally by engaging with the NSDAP text.
- Those in support of the NSDAP will do the same as the NSDAP, except that they will have a party-specific document on the issue for the class to read. The GM provides these handouts as the characters are recognized by the Speaker of the Reichstag.

OPTION 3: Elimination. Antisemitism is entirely eliminated. It is replaced as a mandatory agenda item by "eugenic sterilization" following the same schedule as antisemitism.

Playing a Nazi Role
In *Democracy in Crisis* you will confront fascist ideas that nearly all Americans find abhorrent, deeply offensive, or at the least controversial. You may be expected to play a character who advocates these ideas. Most challengingly, students playing Nazis

must come to terms with a deliberately inflammatory discourse, especially in regard to antisemitism.

If, after reading your assigned role and thinking it over, you believe that you cannot play it, contact your instructor in private, explain your position, and request a different role sheet.

Most importantly, let your instructor know if, at any point, you are facing emotional obstacles. The goal of the game is to learn, which can only happen in an emotionally (and of course physically) safe environment. We can expect discomfort when confronting atrocity, but drawing the line between discomfort and true suffering that prevents learning, while not always easy, is what we, as a class, will undertake together.

Confusing Terms for Contemporary Americans

The political vocabulary in the United States has developed separately from much of the rest of the world. As a result, many terms that have one meaning in the United States can actually have an opposite meaning in the game's European context. The game remains as true as possible to the labels of Germany in 1929. You will be confused if you do not carefully read this manual and take careful note of these terms. Importantly, you must read the primary texts to grasp how these concepts were understood and applied. A few of the most important and misused terms include:

Liberal: In the United States, liberalism has developed since around 1920 to be associated with social spending, a large proactive regulatory government, and, more narrowly, with the Democratic Party. However, in Europe, liberalism is associated with a combination of support for parliamentary democracy and an unregulated market. Liberal parties are, therefore, generally hostile to regulatory government and social spending. Think about "liberal" in the context of the classical liberal thought of Locke, Smith, and Mill.

Republican: In the United States, this term refers almost exclusively to the Republican Party and its agenda (which in Germany would be termed liberal—see above). Yet, in Germany, "republican" referred to any party that identified with parliamentary democracy (i.e., the Constitution of 1919 and the Republic). Thus, socialists, liberals, Christian democrats, and conservatives are all republican.

Conservative: In the United States, we associate this term with the Republican Party. However, in Germany, conservatism was an eclectic concept that could include anything from restorationist monarchists to nationalist liberals. About the only thing they agreed on was a strong sense of nationalism and, for many, a nostalgia for the social and cultural norms of the deposed Kaiserreich, rural Germany, and past greatness, combined with opposition to socialism in any form.

Democratic: In the United States, this term is narrowly associated with the Democratic Party. In Germany, though, the Democrats were the German Democratic Party (DDP), a left-leaning liberal party (again, in the German sense of liberal) that supported the Republic and civil liberties but opposed economic regulation. They were thus republican in the German sense.

Socialist: Today, "socialist" can refer to anything including capitalist China, totalitarian North Korea, democratic Sweden, the U.S. Democratic Party, or, most confusingly, Hitler. In Germany, too, its meaning depended entirely on context. It was usually used exclusively for the Social Democratic Party (SPD), to contrast them with the Communists. However, it could apply to both the SPD and the German Communist Party (KDP) as "Marxist" parties. Furthermore, many conservatives, especially monarchists, lumped the SPD, KPD, and NSDAP together as socialist.

Communist: In the United States, communism is intimately associated with the Cold War and the Stalinism of the Soviet Union and its ideologically associated states. It is viewed overwhelmingly negatively, as a form of totalitarian dictatorship hostile to the United States. In Germany after 1918, it was used much more precisely to distinguish the KPD from the SPD (socialist or social democratic). It was explicitly linked to the USSR and a Leninist-type revolution and was synonymous with "Bolshevik."

Marxist: This term included both the socialists and the communists, who both claimed ideological descent from Karl Marx. However, socialists and communists rejected each other completely, each accusing the other of being hostile to the true meaning of Marxism. But non-Marxists frequently lumped socialism, communism, and Marxism together (along with Bolshevism).

Nationalist: In the United States, the term "nationalist" fell out of favor after the world wars as it became associated with chauvinism, xenophobia, demagogic populism, jingoism, war, and genocide. In Germany in 1929, however, it was still widely accepted as a term of loyalty to the German state and people—the equivalent of "patriot." With the notable exception of the KPD, every party considered itself nationalist, though they disagreed on what it meant, with definitions ranging from simple pride in the German cultural legacy to virulent racism.

National Socialist: In the United States, we prefer the more generic label "fascist" or "Nazi," which we apply to just about any party, person, or policy with which we disagree, to the point that it has lost all analytic meaning and become clichéd. In Germany, though, Nazi refers exclusively to the party of Hitler (NSDAP) and its policies, which were dramatically distinct from and implacably hostile to most other political parties, especially the Marxists. "Nazi" began as a slang acronym for NAtionalsoZIalistische (National Socialist) as a counterpart to "Sozi" for the Social Democrats.

To make matters worse, Germans did not agree on labels either. One of your goals will be to control the terms of debate in the Reichstag, to convince others that the way your character thinks and defines others is correct.

For example, the Right and many moderates referred to both the SPD and KPD as Marxist, often making no distinction between them. Yet the SPD and KPD bitterly opposed each other. The KPD referred to both the NSDAP and SPD as "fascist," though they refined this concept by stating that the SPD was "social fascist." The SPD, for its part, joined every other party in denouncing the KPD as "Bolshevik," but conservatives and liberals often characterized certain NSDAP and SPD polices as "Bolshevism," such as land reform being "agro-Bolshevism."

To confuse the matter more, the Left and moderate parties simply referred to those on the right collectively as "the Right" or "antidemocratic" or "conservative." But the Right was split between **völkisch** and national conservatives. The right-wing DNVP had several tendencies—some were *völkisch*, others national conservative. Many national conservatives, even some with *völkisch* ideas, existed in the moderate Centre Party, which supported the Republic; others in the anti-Republic DNVP and elsewhere looked for completely different solutions such as a restoration of monarchy or a military dictatorship.

Völkisch referred to an eclectic set of ideas that positioned the *Volk* (an ethnic/racial national group) as the center of history and identity, idealized the mystical connection of people to the land, and strove for a national rebirth on this basis.

In short, use caution with even the most basic labels. Place emphasis on how you describe your own party and others. Controlling how the issues are defined in the public sphere is not mere semantics; it goes to the heart of power.

MAPS

Treaty of Versailles Territorial Revisions (1919)

Part II of the treaty dealt with the "Boundaries of Germany" (fig. 1). It contained only four articles (27–30) out of a total of four hundred and forty. The brevity, however, was utterly disproportionate to the consequences—both tangible and psychological—to Germans. No German political party accepted the territorial changes as legitimate or permanent, and recovery of ceded territories considered historically and culturally German became a central goal across the political spectrum.

German nationalists were irredentists and demanded the return of all ceded territories including Schleswig (ceded to Denmark); Alsace-Lorraine (ceded to France); Eupen-Malmedy (ceded to Belgium); West Prussia and Posen (ceded to Poland); Upper Silesia (ceded to Poland and Czechoslovakia); Danzig (administered by League of Nations); and Memel (annexed by Lithuania in 1923).

The Polish Corridor (land ceded to Poland: West Prussia, Posen, and Danzig) was especially contentious. No German politician accepted its annexation. The appropriation of German farmland by Poland and de-Germanization of the region, as allowed by Versailles, kept the issue at a constant boil.

French troops occupied the Rhineland and Saarland, with a promise to withdraw in 1930 if the Young Plan were ratified, though these areas would remain demilitarized.

Pan-German nationalists demanded the creation of a Greater Germany that included Austria (Versailles forbade Austria from joining Germany) and the Sudetenland (German-speaking areas of Czechoslovakia)—see fig. 2.

German Racial and Cultural Territory (1925)

Albrecht Penck's map (fig. 2) graphically conceptualized the notion of Lebensraum, especially in the "German East," with its ideological, even mystical link between the German peasant and the soil. His map subordinated states, as merely transitional administrative units, to *völkisch* territory—defined by where a *Volk* settled (*Volksboden*) and where their cultural influence held sway (*Kulturboden*). Earlier geographers and politicians had emphasized the notion of German-speaking peoples, but Penck supported claims for certain prized territories, especially where Polish was spoken. This made it possible to claim not only lost territories but even areas outside prewar Germany by pointing to their German cultural character, however spurious. Penck's maps were extremely popular, and variations were especially common in schoolbooks.

Dark areas (*Volksboden*) were presumably racially German based on primary language.

Gray areas (*Kulturboden*) were appropriate for colonization and Germanization due to significant German cultural influences.

The presence of German "islands"—isolated pockets—presented potential bastions for future expansion in the East to create a future contiguous area of German *Volksboden* stretching to Russia and the Balkans.

Pan-Germanists believed that Germans had been denied self-determination and demanded that all lands with a German-speaking majority (not just those ceded in Versailles) be integrated into a Greater Germany.

German States and Prussian Provinces (1929)

Prussia dominated the other German states (fig. 3). It occupied almost two-thirds of Germany, and the Prussian police force was larger than the military. Its eastern provinces were the homeland of the **Junkers**.

The **Junkers** were the Protestant, landowning aristocratic elites, especially of eastern Prussia, who dominated state and military affairs even after the collapse of the Kaiserreich.

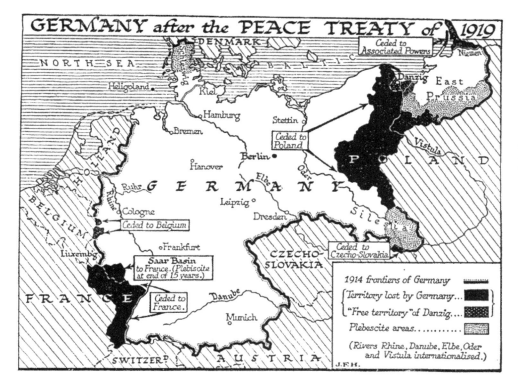

FIGURE 1 Treaty of Versailles territorial revisions (1919).

James Francis Horrabin, "Figure 1075: Map of Germany after the Peace Treaty of 1919," in *The Outline of History: Being A Plain History of Life and Mankind*, by H. G. Wells (London: Cassell, 1920), 384.

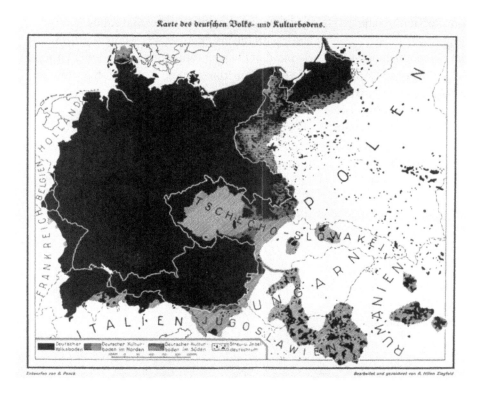

FIGURE 2 German racial and cultural territory (1925).

Albrecht Penck, "Deutscher Volks- und Kulturboden," in *Volk unter Völkern: Bücher des Deutschtums*, vol. 1, ed. Karl Christian von Loesch and Arnold Hillen Ziegfeld (Breslau: F. Hirt, 1925), 62–73.

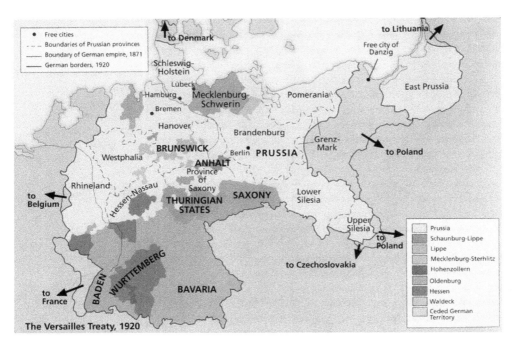

FIGURE 3 German states and Prussian provinces (1929).

"Germany in 1919, Territorial Losses," Active History (University of Saskatchewan and Huron University College), 9 July 2018, http://activehistory.ca /2018/07/24040 /germany-in-1919 -territorial-losses-wlu -edu/.

Yet a pro-Republic coalition (SPD, Centre, DDP) had ruled Prussia since 1918. "Red" Berlin, Hamburg, and the industrialized Ruhr area of the Rhineland and Westphalia were also bastions of democratic liberalism and social democracy.

East Prussia became an exclave—cut off geographically from Germany by the loss of the Polish Corridor. It remained the heart of the old agrarian Junker elite, which included President von Hindenburg. The continued domination of the Junkers, combined with the loss of the Polish Corridor and its alienation from the democratic sentiments of the rest of Prussia, made it a hotbed of reactionary and anti-Polish agitation.

Bavaria was the second largest state and referred to itself as the Free State of Bavaria. The deposed Wittelsbach dynasty never renounced its claim to the throne, and many Bavarians were monarchists and separatists. It was also home to the deeply Catholic, separatist Bavarian People's Party (BVP) and the NSDAP, which was headquartered in the Bavarian capital of Munich.

Hanover was a former kingdom that had been dissolved and turned into a Prussian province after the Six Weeks War (1866) between Prussia and Austria, when the Hanoverian ruling family sided with the losing Austrians. Many Hanoverians demanded the restoration of the kingdom as a separate state, free from Prussia. This idea is promoted by the conservative German Hanoverian Party (DHP).

No other state carried significant influence on national politics, though local events often resonated throughout Germany. Smaller states often leaned much further to an extreme than the Reichstag did (Thuringia and Saxony to the right; Hamburg to the left).

PROLOGUE: A DIRGE FOR STRESEMANN

Last night, 6 October 1929, you decided it would be a good time to try to settle your nerves. The last few days have been hectic. As a member of the Reichstag, one rarely finds time for relaxation, even in the best of times. And these are not the best of times.

Berlin offers many distractions, with a nightlife every bit as vibrant as Paris's. As you leave the Reichstag building you turn down toward Potsdamer Platz. Though it's late, the square there still bustles with cafés full of the city's well-heeled. Too busy for your mood—the frantic pace of urban life is just too jarring on your nerves tonight. So no thought of visiting Kurfürstendamm, Berlin's internationally famous hub of nightlife, or visiting a cabaret. You decide instead to make your way to the large park of the Tiergarten for a beer. Its tree-lined avenues always calm you and remind you of Germany's past glories, with the numerous patriotic monuments to Prussian monarchs, overseen by the magnificent Victory Column celebrating Germany's victory over France in 1871. Statues of Goethe, Lessing, Fontane, Wagner, and Lortzing speak of Germany's unrivaled literary contributions. The Beethoven-Haydn-Mozart memorial does the same for music.

But for now, a walk is what you want after sitting in those interminable faction meetings. As you walk on, the Romanesque revival edifice of the Kaiser Wilhelm Memorial Church in the center of the Breitscheidplatz appears ahead of you, gloomy and forlorn—a structure built by one emperor to celebrate his grandfather, who had founded a Reich that no longer exists. You think back, has it really only been ten years since the end of the war? Only ten years since the Allies imposed the Dictate of Versailles on a helpless Germany? Only ten years since the new constitution was declared in Weimar, creating the current republic and abolishing the monarchy?

The wounds are still so fresh. The recent proposal in the Reichstag of the Young Plan to renegotiate war reparations has torn open these scars and unleashed a fearsome debate. The conservative nationalists and upstart National Socialists have declared the Young Plan an act of treason, a second stab in the back tantamount to the original betrayal of Germany in 1918. The communists denounce it as just another example of capitalistic imperialism. The same debates as in 1919.

So little has changed since the revolutionary days of 1918 and 1919. Every party has its own private army that it sends out into the streets to battle its rivals. One scandal after another has rocked every party. Even the military has been exposed for undermining the government and acting independently.

Meanwhile, the day-to-day work of the Reichstag grinds on as bill after bill exposes how little the different parties have in common. Every issue is on the table—bills to decriminalize sodomy and bills to make it a capital offense. Bills to outlaw abortion, to legalize it, and to make it a capital offense. The war novel *All Quiet on the Western Front* has sold 1.5 million copies since its publication in January, yet some in the Reichstag want to ban it. The military will not admit Jews, yet the Republic has granted them full citizenship. Germany is a democracy, and yet the political parties have armed paramilitaries that openly oppose the government. There is a limited budget, and yet the Marxists want more money for the uninsured, the liberals demand that social spending and taxes be cut, the nationalists insist on an increase in the naval budget, and the aristocratic conservatives require subsidies for their indebted agrarian estates.

You have tried to keep an open mind. Many consider you a *Vernunftrepublikaner*—one who can support the Republic as the only reasonable alternative to civil war or invasion. But you also see all of its flaws and wonder if, when all is said and done, the radical critics might not have a point.

Perhaps a totally new system is required.

Funeral

The distractions of the city and your thoughts of politics almost made you forget, for the moment at least, why you felt such a strong urge to walk and clear your head. Gustav Stresemann, your party colleague in the DVP, has died. He was the greatest of Germany's postwar statesmen, onetime chancellor and longtime foreign minister, a Nobel Peace Prize laureate, an architect of the policy of normalizing Germany's relationships with her former enemies and slowly wringing concessions in the onerous Versailles Treaty. He brought about, as much as anyone could (or should), a partial rapprochement with France. He gained access to the League of Nations, including membership on the all-important Security Council. He had even recently brought a further revision and reduction in war reparations to the Reichstag in the form of the Young Plan.

Under his leadership, the Republic seems to have finally caught its breath. The economy has been steadily returning to its robust prewar levels. Political violence has largely disappeared. The fanatical parties of the Left and Right are marginalized. Indeed, for the first time, a coalition government was able to serve out its entire four-year term before mandatory Reichstag elections were called in 1928, which again returned a strong proconstitution coalition.

At age fifty-one, though, Stresemann has died unexpectedly. Tomorrow—no, wait, you realize it is already well after midnight—today is his state funeral.

You pick up the early edition of the *Berliner Tagesblatt* from a kiosk. Nearby, the lean and hard-faced men lining up in the dark in the hope of a day's work make you a bit nervous. You realize your aimless rambling did not bring you to the respectable propriety of the Tiergarten. You stay in the light of the kiosk to read the paper. One of the men asks you for a cigarette. Startled at first, you offer him two. These men are Germans, after all.

Who knows—he could have fought at the front. You yourself were an officer in the reserves. Times are hard, especially for veterans.

Sensing a man of means, a street prostitute approaches and propositions you. Her looks are as lean and hard as the men's, her dress a gaudy proletarian imitation of what she must imagine the cabaret girls

wear. No point chastising her—there are so many at this hour of the night you would go hoarse lecturing them all on their low morals.

These women—the spread of venereal diseases, the rise in abortions, the growing number of street children without fathers. But you stop yourself before your blood pressure rises. You were trying to take your mind off all the problems. You simply look back down at your paper.

You do not have to look long for news about the funeral. The government has orchestrated what promises to be the largest state event in years. Even British newspapers have been paying tribute to Stresemann's career and describe him as "one of Europe's architects of peace."[3] The London *Times* has already eulogized him as a man who "[saw] in cooperation the only escape from chaos. . . . [who] did inestimable service to the German Republic; his work for Europe as a whole was almost as great."[4] But these tributes seem a bit optimistic, especially when you think of the morass in the Reichstag.

You have heard rumors that it was actually the Reichstag that killed him. No, not an assassination (hopefully those days have passed when death squads—some say with the support of the military—assassinated supporters of the Republic). Instead, you have heard that his participation in the excited and sometimes stormy faction meeting the other night, lasting for four hours, at which he urged waverers to support the Unemployment Insurance Bill, apparently was the final and fatal drain on his strength. He went straight home, dined moderately, and had a stroke. You sensed his frustration and exhaustion in one of your last conversations with him, when he said:

If the allies had obliged me just one single time, I would have brought the German people behind me, yes; even today, I could still get them to support me. However, they [the allies] gave me nothing and the minor concessions they made, always came too late. Thus, nothing else remains for us but brutal force. The future lies in the hands of the new generation. Moreover, they, the German youth, who we could have won for peace and reconstruction, we have lost. Herein lies my tragedy and their, the allies', crime.[5]

Now, with the growing rift in the ruling coalition about how to grapple with the economic crisis, you are unsure what will happen. Indeed, the divisions in the Reichstag seem unbridgeable.

When the Reichstag assembled yesterday, Stresemann's seat on the ministerial bench was draped in black and a wreath laid on it. White chrysanthemums adorned the place where he had sat as deputy. Yet even what appeared as an act of unifying respect for a German statesman of international renown soon revealed the deep rifts.

When the vice president opened the session, eulogizing Stresemann's work and declaring that his name should be written in letters of gold, the communists and extreme nationalists refused to stand—a deliberate act of disrespect. In fact, you have heard that Joseph Goebbels, one of the leaders of the NSDAP in Berlin, commented about Stresemann's death, "A stone has been removed from the road to German freedom."[6]

Procession

As day breaks, you eat in a café and prepare for Stresemann's funeral. It begins in the Reichstag building, where Stresemann's mortal remains were moved after lying in state in his official residence in the Foreign Ministry, with a police guard on duty day and night. As the coffin leaves the steps of the Reichstag, you cannot help but look up and read the monumental engraved words on the pediment: "For the German People." Ironic, you think—a parliament building originally dedicated to the German people by an authoritarian and deposed kaiser now housing a liberal democracy.

The venerable President von Hindenburg and members of the cabinet and the Reichstag are all attending the funeral, which will take a special route to enable the crowds to pay their tribute and even follow the procession all the way to the gates of the cemetery. The streets are full—an estimated two hundred thousand Germans and visiting dignitaries have turned out—and hung with the black-red-gold of the Republic. Never mind that many of the onlookers and dignitaries, the soldiers and officers, would rather march beneath the black-white-red of the Kaiserreich. The apparent support for the Republic is overwhelming. Perhaps, for all its trials, the Republic truly does have the faith of the nation?

The clear and crisp October skies do not match the somber mood and dress of the onlookers. Columns of soldiers slow step down the street. Muffled drums and sonorous church bells accompany the procession. Concrete pillars, placed at the sides of the roadway, emit dense black smoke to cast a pall. Statesmen in top hats walk in procession behind a black casket draped in the flag of the Republic, on a black carriage drawn by black horses. Mourners are held in order by lines of uniformed police.

After only one block, the cortege passes through the central arch of the Brandenburg Gate. Another irony! Isn't that gate supposed to be a triumphal arch dedicated to the military glory of the now deposed Hohenzollern dynasty? And wasn't the central arch reserved exclusively for use by the imperial family until 1918? And didn't the gate open up onto Unter den Linden, the renowned boulevard of linden trees, which formerly led directly to the city palace of the Prussian monarch?

Yet in November 1918, the communist leader Karl Liebknecht declared the German Socialist Republic from a balcony of that palace, ending more than four hundred years of royal occupation of the building. And now it is used as a museum. Your head spins thinking how rapidly everything you had grown up with disappeared seemingly overnight in those fateful days.

Heedless, the cortege plods on until it reaches the Foreign Ministry. There, in a dramatic moment, the carriage halts. Hats are doffed and two minutes of silence are observed beneath the window where Stresemann had worked.

The procession proceeds through the suburb of Kreuzberg. Even here, you have to ponder the rapid changes in Germany. Until 1921, Kreuzberg was not even part of Berlin. Your grandparents remember it as a rural retreat, with its idyllic hill on which was built the Prussian National Monument for the Liberation Wars against Napoleon. Now, though, it is one of Berlin's industrial boroughs, notorious for its working-class tenement housing. It has Berlin's highest population density and its most active Communist Party locals. You wonder if these ill-educated Kreuzberg workers have any idea what that old monument, now blocked behind the factories and tenements, stood for?

Isn't this, too, the part of Berlin where many immigrants, especially Jews from the East, have settled recently? In fact, the Jewish Mosse family and their local press empire are located here in the "press quarter." Jews controlling the German press from a communist district in the capital of the Reich? You spontaneously snort at the thought. It sounds like a plot from one of those histrionic speeches by that radical Austrian corporal, Hitler. And, you remind yourself, the night before, you had absentmindedly read a copy of the *Tagesblatt*—a left-liberal paper published by that same Mosse family. Nothing is straightforward anymore.

Monument

Finally, the procession reaches the Luisenstadtischer cemetery, where you and many other mourners will pass by the open grave.

You have heard that the German sculptor Hugo Lederer has been chosen to design the funerary monument. You ponder that for a moment. Is Lederer even a German?

He was born in Austria, not Germany. Well, not exactly. Technically he was born in Austria-Hungary, in the dual monarchy of the Habsburg Empire. But that nation and dynasty no longer exist. They disappeared in the anarchy of 1918—just like the Kaiserreich and the Hohenzollern dynasty. So you assume he is an Austrian—that ridiculous new statelet that

was forbidden by the Allies from joining Germany, even though its German population clearly voted for union in a referendum. Just another example of how Versailles is a victor's peace, another example of the selective application of Wilson's Fourteen Points, another betrayal of German self-determination.

And you remember that Lederer is actually from the city of Znaim—in what used to be Austrian Moravia. But now it is called by its Slavicized name Znojmo and it belongs to the artificial state of Czechoslovakia. How perverse—a state that did not even exist until created by the same politicians in Paris who decided to deny the local German population the right to self-determination! At the thought, your blood again begins to boil, despite the solemnity of the occasion. You may not be so single-mindedly radical as the National Conservatives or Hitlerites, but you are a German patriot after all!

And one cannot question Lederer's patriotism. What can he do about the fact that German Europe has been carved up like a butchered hog to feed the petty interests of other nations? In fact, Lederer, you recall, designed the largest of all the Bismarck towers during the Kaiserreich—the one in Hamburg. You have been to several of these Bismarck towers, with their powerful squat designs evoking the indomitable spirit of the Iron Chancellor. Every year, each of these towers—and there are hundreds—serves as a beacon when its brazier is lit to honor Bismarck and to commemorate his achievement in unifying Germany in 1871. It reminds us all of the need not only to restore Germany's historical borders but also to unite within it those Germans excluded by Versailles. At least on that point, all parties can agree. Except the Communists, of course.

Yes, Lederer seems to embody all of the contradictions of Germany since the war. A German without a Germany, denied self-determination, his homeland dismembered by the dictate of Versailles, but still a patriot. He designed monuments to the fallen German heroes of the war as well as the fallen statesmen of the Republic. An Austrian or a German? One who looks idealistically back to the heroes of the past, or one who dares to pragmatically confront the present?

Just like you, he seems not so sure where Germany or its future lies.

Not every German, you know, shares your passion for a pan-German solution, but something has to change. . . .

2

Historical Background

The World That Was: The Kaiserreich (Imperial Germany), 1871–1918

Before 1871, German-speaking Europe consisted of dozens—at times, hundreds—of sovereign entities. Most nominally came under the Holy Roman Empire of the German Nation until its dissolution in 1806, but that empire never included all of German-speaking Europe, never exerted a strong central identity, and always included non-Germans.

Consequently, the various German-speaking regions remained fiercely loyal to local identities. Divisions based on mutually unintelligible dialects, deep religious cleavages (Lutheran, Calvinist, Catholic, Jewish), differing regional traditions, and long-standing political-institutional distinctions between rival German states counteracted a common cultural bond. In short, a Prussian was no more a Bavarian than an American was an Englishman, and neither was politically German.

Nonetheless, by the eighteenth century, and accelerating during the Napoleonic Wars, a period of frequently violent political consolidation began. Two German states—Austria and Prussia—came to dominate the numerous lesser states. In a complicated struggle, Prussia emerged the dominant power.

In 1871, following victory in the Franco-Prussian War, German princes called on King Wilhelm of Prussia to take up the imperial crown and rule as **kaiser**. The resulting Kaiserreich unified twenty-seven smaller German states under the Hohenzollern Prussian monarchy but excluded Habsburg Austria (not to mention the German-speaking Swiss cantons). Royal families from the smaller states, such as the Wittelsbach of Bavaria, kept their crowns but swore fealty to the Hohenzollern emperors.

Kaiser (emperor) was the title of the Hohenzollern monarchs of Germany, 1871 to 1918, and also the title of the Habsburg monarchs of Austria (and Austria-Hungary), 1804 to 1867/1918.

The sudden creation of an entirely new political reality, unifying formerly sovereign entities with deep traditions, inevitably created tensions. With their deep particularism, especially in the Catholic Rhineland and Bavaria, many Germans resented being ruled from the Prussian capital, Berlin. As a compromise, the Kaiserreich left local matters largely in the hands of the constituent states.

However, to create national cohesion, the new state launched sustained campaigns to promote a strong national identity—an identity based on a jingoistic chauvinism that sought to rally Germans against enemies both external (France, United Kingdom, Russia) and internal (Jews, Catholics, socialists, Poles).

This nationalization effort, conducted through the schools, press, political and cultural organizations, and the military, met with considerable success, but not without alienating many Germans and producing an increasingly narrow and racialized view of German identity. Following broader trends in Europe and the Americas, most Germans came to integrate race consciousness into everyday life. The German race was defined loosely as including anyone who had a German-speaking ancestry that excluded Jews. This idea evolved into pan-Germanism—the idea that all Germans should be integrated into a single nation-state, particularly German speakers in neighboring countries such as Austria-Hungary, Russia, and France. As it fused with **Lebensraum** ideas, the notion inevitably led to militarily expansionistic racial ideas since such a state would require annexation of those neighboring territories where these German speakers lived and the simultaneous expulsion of non-Germans.

Lebensraum was the social Darwinist *völkisch* idea that Germany must expand territorially to be a healthy and vigorous *Volk*; this included displacing groups judged racially inferior.

Indeed, pan-Germanist thinkers, especially those organized in the Pan-German League, adopted openly ethnocentric and racist ideologies. Antisemitism became a regular feature of public discourse. The citizenship and even the humanity of Black Africans in Germany's colonies became a subject of public debate and efforts to exclude them and their children, especially mixed-race children. This racial prejudice also targeted the Slavic (mostly Polish and Czech) minorities in the East, leading to a policy of Germanization to eradicate non-German culture, language, and settlement. This process included removing non–ethnic German property owners (by forcing them to sell) and workers (by refusing to hire them) in ethnically mixed territories and replacing them with ethnic Germans in a movement called "inner colonization." These widespread ideas laid the basis for later genocide.

But the conservative monarchist Chancellor von Bismarck realized that nationalism alone would not hold together the new Kaiserreich. The rise of the **Social Democratic Party (SPD)** in the 1870s revealed that serious social and economic issues divided Germans along class lines. Urban workers, what Marxists called the **proletariat**, demanded better working and living conditions to alleviate their squalid circumstances.

The Marxist **Social Democratic Party (SPD)** had opposed the Kaiserreich but embraced the Republic and tried to reconcile liberal political models with Marxist ideas of class-oriented social justice.

The **proletariat**, especially in Marxist terminology, is the exploited working class under capitalism, those who do not own but rather work in the means of production.

To suppress the socialist movement, Bismarck employed a double-pronged approach. First, using repression, the so-called Anti-Socialist Laws outlawed trade unions, closed socialist newspapers, prohibited the display of socialist symbols, and otherwise harassed members of the SPD.

When repression failed, Bismarck launched the second prong—social welfare. He introduced old-age pensions, accident insurance, medical care, and unemployment insurance, all of which formed the basis of the modern European welfare state. He and German industrialists hoped that these paternalistic programs would bind workers to the state. Bismarck further won the support of both industry and skilled workers with his industrial **tariff** policies, which protected German industry and industrial jobs from competition, although they alienated liberals who wanted free trade. Despite these efforts, Bismarck's plan to stop the growth of the SPD failed, and by 1912 it had become the largest party in Germany—indeed, the largest socialist party in the world.

Tariffs are a form of regulation on foreign trade that taxes products to encourage or safeguard domestic production.

Additionally, Catholics, a one-third minority in the largely Protestant Kaiserreich, resisted efforts to subordinate their religious identity to **secular** nationalism, especially in education. Bismarck and most Protestants shared a deep suspicion that Catholics were actually more loyal to Rome than to Berlin. The result was the *Kulturkampf* (culture struggle) launched by Bismarck—an anti-Catholic campaign that only led to the hardening and organizing of Catholic opposition, especially in the form of the Catholic Centre Party. Bismarck eventually dropped the *Kulturkampf* as counterproductive, and Catholic elites were steadily incorporated into the national elite. Lutheran chauvinism, however, continued to alienate most Catholics.

Secular may refer to any attitude, activity, or thing that has no religious or spiritual basis; in Germany, the state was secular and had no state religion.

The Junker class alone retained unrivaled prestige. These Protestant aristocrats of eastern Prussia prided themselves on a deep sense of state service, most importantly in the military. In fact, the Imperial Army's active officer corps consisted almost exclusively of Junkers, and they infused everyday life with hypermilitarization and propagated the conviction that a state should resemble an army in its authoritarian and hierarchical structure. In short, the Junkers were no friends of democracy. Socially conservative, linked to a state-affirming Protestantism, and dedicated to the economic interests of large landholders, the Junkers dominated German life with their extraordinary status and access to power, creating a pervasive ethos of agrarian conservativism among the Kaiserreich's elite.

Despite Junker resistance, the transition from an agrarian to an industrial society accelerated, undermining the complicated fabric of a pre-industrial social order. The link between an increasingly outdated agrarian world and political power meant that the Kaiserreich escalated its protectionist policies, most notably grain tariffs, to protect the Junker estates from international competition. Consequently, Junkers saw no reason to modernize, while small farmers, who did not produce grain for the international market, saw no benefit. In increasingly sharp contrast to the Junker estates, smaller farms experienced disruptive economic liberalization as they became victims of outside market forces. In effect, the traditional village subsistence life all but disappeared, leaving small farmers vulnerable to impersonal market forces. While this created a viable class of middle-sized farms, the sociopolitical consequences fractured the countryside.

An ideological reaction to these challenges developed that fused Christianity and a romanticized idealization of the peasantry into a conservative, rural-centered worldview. This agrarian idealism touted the innate superiority of rural life as the source of true German virtue in express opposition to perceived urban decadence. It consciously pitted itself against urban values including secularism, atheistic proletarian Marxism, and liberal capitalism and its presumed agent, the Jewish moneylender.

The concept of *Blut und Boden* (blood and soil) linked racialized nationalism to this agrarian idealism. It celebrated the relationship of a *Volk* to its land and placed a high value on the virtues of rural living. This included a growing awareness of the need to secure food production for Germany's growing population. The goal was agrarian autarky (self-sufficiency in food) within the German racial community so that Germany could free itself from dependence on foreign imports and the global market. But this only increased anxieties about the demographics of Germany's eastern borderlands. Slavs, especially Poles, were increasing while Germans were decreasing as a percentage of the population. Few German farms in the East could exist without Polish seasonal labor as Germany's rural youth migrated to the cities or abroad. These changes threatened to Slavicize the German East, to urbanize German youth, and to undermine the German military by weakening national food security and decreasing the relative number of ethnic German army recruits. By playing on these fears, political agrarianism established itself as a major political force, linking an agrarian *völkisch* identity to a hostility to urban modernity (with a heavy dose of antisemitism).

Yet Germany was changing, as the growth of the SPD indicated. After 1850, Germany rapidly industrialized, with particular strengths in coal, iron, chemicals, and railways. By 1913, the Kaiserreich had grown from forty-one million to sixty-eight million people. Much of this growth was in the cities. The Kaiserreich augmented these changes with heavy investment in technology and science, gaining more Nobel Prizes in science than the United Kingdom, France, Russia, and the United States combined. In 1914 it was the most militarily powerful, industrialized, scientifically advanced, and educated nation on the continent of Europe, with the United Kingdom its only serious rival.

Not surprisingly, the middle classes, driving most of the industrial advances, clamored for political inclusion. They organized in various liberal parties. Yet, for all their vigor, their dominant ideology of liberalism failed to achieve many of its goals. The traditional elites only grudgingly accorded the liberal middle classes access to power and status—access that usually came at the price of acknowledging traditional authority. Consequently, protectionism applied to industry as well, despite the liberal belief in free markets; it cemented a pro-monarchy conservative-liberal alliance of "iron and rye." Despite a rich tradition of democratic and revolutionary activity, by the start of World War I the clear majority of liberals had linked their interests to the military, nation-state, and Junker class. And why not? Despite the internal tensions and compromises, the Kaiserreich had become a Great Power, boasting the world's strongest army, second-largest navy, and third-largest colonial empire.

Yet this confidence bordered on hubris. Nationalist rhetoric grew ever more histrionic, demanding new territories and colonies and openly looking for military adventures. After the removal of Bismarck in 1890, the young Kaiser Wilhelm II engaged in increasingly reckless foreign policies that left the Kaiserreich diplomatically isolated. When the great crisis of 1914 arrived, the German Empire had few allies.

In the World War (1914–18), Germany became the de facto head of the **Central Powers**. Despite initial successes, plans for a quick victory in the West failed, and the war on the western front stalemated against the forces of the British Empire and France. The Allied naval blockade led to the feared food shortages, and Germany had to repeatedly send troops to bolster its allies Austria-Hungary and the Ottoman Empire on other fronts. Nonetheless, Germany ultimately had great success on the eastern front against tsarist Russia, which collapsed in revolution under the strain. The new **Bolshevik** government in Russia ended involvement in the war, and Germany forced it to cede vast eastern territories in the Treaty of Brest-Litovsk in early 1918. However, the costs had been enormous, and few German reserves remained.

The **Central Powers** included Germany, the industrially less advanced Austria-Hungary, the internally divided Ottoman Empire, and the relatively small Kingdom of Bulgaria.

Bolshevik refers to anything relating to the ruling party of the Soviet Union or its policies, initially linked to Lenin and later Stalin.

Further, the German declaration of unrestricted submarine warfare in early 1917, intended to strangle the British, failed. That declaration—along with the Zimmermann Telegram—brought the United States into the war, and its reserves of money, food, armaments, and soldiers tipped the balance.

Meanwhile, Germans had become war weary. The death toll mounted. The injured returned home to every village. Food shortages, caused by the conscription of farm laborers and the Allied naval blockade, led to food strikes and riots and starvation. In response, the high command, under Field Marshall von Hindenburg and General Ludendorff since 1916, imposed a military dictatorship, enforcing rigid censorship and tightly regulating the economy (including price controls, production quotas, and rationing).

Facing a looming defeat, they gambled on one last offensive in spring 1918 before the Americans could arrive in force and Germany starved. This failed. In September 1918, Ludendorff appeared before the Reichstag and noted that if there were not an immediate cessation of hostilities, the German army could collapse. By October 1918, the German armies were in full retreat, the Austro-Hungarian Empire and the Ottoman Empire had fragmented, and the German people had lost faith in their political system. The Kaiserreich was on its last legs.

Birth of the Republic, 1918–1919
The November Revolution
In October 1918, as the front dissolved, the kaiser and his advisers agreed in desperation to introduce a British-style parliamentary system, but events quickly overtook this belated effort.

On 29 October, sailors in Kiel mutinied and elected workers' and soldiers' **councils** modeled after the soviets of the Russian Revolution of 1917.

The SPD put itself at the front of the movement, demanding that Kaiser Wilhelm II abdicate. When he refused, Chancellor Prince von Baden simply announced that he had done so and frantically attempted to establish a regency under another member of the House of Hohenzollerns. As those efforts unraveled, Philipp Scheidemann (SPD) proclaimed a German Republic at the Reichstag building on 9 November 1918, while the kaiser fled to the neutral Netherlands:

Workers and soldiers! The four war years were horrible, gruesome the sacrifices the people had to make in property and blood. The unfortunate war is over. The killing is over. The consequences of the war, need and suffering, will burden us for many years. The defeat we strove so hard to avoid, under all circumstances, has come upon us. Our suggestions regarding an understanding were mocked and ignored. The enemies of the working class, the real, inner enemies who are responsible for Germany's collapse, they have turned silent and invisible. They were the home warriors, which upheld their conquest demands until yesterday, as obstinate as they fought the struggle against any reform of the constitution and especially of the deplorable Prussian election system. These enemies of the people are finished forever. The Kaiser has abdicated. He and his friends have disappeared; the people have won over all of them, in every field. Prince Max von Baden has handed over the office of Reich chancellor to Representative Ebert. Our friend will form a new government consisting of workers of all socialist parties. This new government may not be interrupted in their work to preserve peace and to care for work and bread. Workers and soldiers, be aware of the historic importance of this day: exorbitant things have happened. Great and incalculable tasks are waiting for us. Everything for the people.

Everything by the people. Nothing may happen to the dishonor of the Labor Movement. Be united, faithful and conscientious. The old and rotten, the monarchy has collapsed. The new may live. Long live the German Republic.[1]

But preexisting cleavages in the socialist movement came immediately to the fore. Karl Liebknecht, co-leader with Rosa Luxemburg of the new communist **Spartacus League**, declared a more radical Free Socialist Republic that same day at the royal residence in Berlin, to inaugurate a Soviet-style revolution:

The day of the revolution has come. . . . Peace has been concluded in this moment. The old has gone. The rule of the Hohenzollerns, who have resided in this palace for centuries, is over. In this very hour we proclaim the Free Socialist Republic of Germany . . . where there are no more servants, where every honest worker will receive his honest pay. The rule of capitalism, which has turned Europe into a cemetery, is broken.[2]

The unexpected power vacuum and threat of Bolshevik-style revolution led a desperate von Baden to unilaterally transfer the chancellorship to Friedrich Ebert (leader of the SPD since 1913), who reluctantly accepted. Ebert had presciently preferred a more constitutional transfer, but in view of the mass support for radical reforms among the workers' councils, he hastily established a socialist coalition government called the Council of People's Deputies.

Although the Berlin Workers' and Soldiers' Council confirmed the new government, the Spartacus League opposed it.

Despite the new government's dubious constitutionality, its representatives immediately signed an armistice on 11 November 1918 to prevent the total collapse of the army and occupation of German soil, effectively ending military operations. It was an unconditional German capitulation. Meanwhile, Germany devolved into civil war. Ebert called on the army to put down a mutiny in Berlin in December. The ensuing street fighting left several dead and injured on both sides. Radical socialists, outraged by the perceived treachery of Ebert and the SPD, formed the **German Communist Party (KPD)**, openly allied with the Bolsheviks, and took up arms against the new government.

The **German Communist Party (KPD)** rejected the possibility of justice under capitalism and pursued a revolutionary vision of rebuilding society according to the Bolshevik model of the Soviet Union.

During this time, from November 1918 to January 1919, the Council of People's Deputies, under pressure from the nongovernmental workers' and soldiers' councils, issued numerous decrees advancing progressive social and political change. It introduced the eight-hour workday, labor reform, social welfare relief, national health insurance, and universal suffrage, and abolished undemocratic public institutions.

To ensure that his fledgling government maintained control, Ebert made an agreement with the army, led by Ludendorff's successor general Wilhelm Groener. The Ebert-Groener Pact stipulated that the government would not reform the army so long as the army swore to protect the state. Despite their opposition to the new government, the military realized that the army had collapsed; they knew full well what had happened in Russia and wanted to prevent a repeat. For the military, the pact ensured that the

traditional officer class retained control. For the fledgling government, it guaranteed victory over the Far Left. As an additional bonus, it assuaged concerns among the middle classes about how radical the revolution might be. Radical socialists, however, considered it a betrayal. The Far Right opposed it since it validated social-democratic and liberal power.

Regardless, the pact proved decisive. In January the Spartacus League began an insurrection in Berlin, the Spartacist Uprising. The army, allied with right-wing paramilitary *Freikorps* units, brutally suppressed the uprisings, culminating in the summary executions of Rosa Luxemburg and Karl Liebknecht. The SPD coalition had survived. But the SPD alliance with the military and *Freikorps* led to a lasting bitterness between the SPD and KPD. Luxemburg and Liebknecht became martyrs for the Left—killed on the orders of the SPD—and future cooperation became difficult at best.

The *Freikorps* consisted primarily of demobilized soldiers led by former officers and paid by conservative groups (including the army) to fight in the border skirmishes and to attack the Left. They were outside the control of the government but retained close contact with the military, even after they were officially disbanded in 1920.

In this volatile climate, elections held on 19 January 1919 created a provisional National Assembly, dominated by moderate parties. Charged with writing a democratic constitution, delegates removed themselves from Berlin, which was wracked by street fighting, and convened in the small city of Weimar, giving the future Republic its unofficial name.

Elsewhere, fighting continued. In Munich, radicals declared a Soviet republic, but once again, *Freikorps* units and remnants of the army intervened. The fall of the Munich Soviet Republic resulted in the growth of far-right death squads and a wider movement in Bavaria, including the **NSDAP**. In the eastern provinces, monarchist forces fought the Republic as well as Polish nationalists determined to expand their own nation at Germany's expense.

The **NSDAP**, or National Socialist German Workers' Party, better known as the Nazi Party, were fascists led by Adolf Hitler.

Burden from the War

The human costs of the war were so staggering that they had dramatic social, economic, and cultural consequences just as consequential as the political fallout. The scale of death and maiming was unprecedented and shocking to contemporaries. Approximately two million German soldiers had died—roughly 15 percent of the thirteen million who had served; or, to think in terms of military-age men, approximately 13 percent of all men born between 1880 and 1890 were killed. But the casualty figures for the wounded and prisoners of war added another seven million. In short, about 55 percent of Germans who served were either killed, wounded, or captured. Civilian losses added approximately 750,000 from malnutrition and another 150,000 from war-related disease, especially the Spanish Influenza.[3] Witnessing the deaths by artillery, machine guns, and gas in a climate of constant, nerve-wracking fear and hunger at the front also led to the mental collapse of many surviving soldiers. Though the phenomenon of post-traumatic stress disorder was not recognized as such, the trauma millions of veterans experienced was apparent after the war. Indeed, the works of Erich Maria Remarque and contemporaries described this hell and its consequences in vivid detail.

In and of itself, the demographic consequence threatened the Republic. Women entered the urban workforce, with their employment in factories with ten or more workers increasing by 52 percent. Many women became accustomed to their new control over disposable income and liberation from the home. Yet returning veterans expected their jobs back and an immediate return to prewar male-dominated gender norms. Competition for jobs only added to the gender conflicts of the 1920s, feeding a misogynistic climate. Indeed, many young women had deferred marriage and family during the war, only to find that there was not only an absolute deficit of men but also a limited pool of men who were not physically or psychologically damaged. Disabled veterans, war widows, and war orphans needed and demanded state assistance to survive. Here, too, the numbers were staggering: 2.7 million disabled veterans, 1,192,000 war orphans, and 533,000 widows.

Almost all of these people would otherwise have been in their prime productive years. Instead, they had become a substantial financial burden for a generation.

The resulting social consequences constantly tore at the fabric of the Republic. There was a consensus that war victims were the responsibility of the state, but determining, institutionalizing, and financing the nature of that responsibility proved overwhelming. Politicians disagreed on every point. Who should manage the war-related welfare system—the Reich, the states, or private entities? How much compensation was appropriate for each claim? Should a petitioner's economic status play any role? There were even debates on the long-term psychiatric consequences of shell shock (PTSD), though no provisions were offered. The Reich Pension Court, established to process claims, was soon overwhelmed. The failure to adequately provide for war victims (veterans, widows, and orphans) led to acrimonious recriminations, but every effort to create a unified movement foundered on the political factionalism of the Republic. As in every other aspect of the Republic, war victims organized in their political silos, creating separate socialist, communist, and nationalist organizations frequently working at cross-purposes.

German culture inevitably bent to the horror of mass death and the climate of bitterness—a climate exacerbated by the sense of defeat (a defeat for which the population had been wholly unprepared, based on blindly optimistic wartime propaganda) and the moral onus of guilt laid on Germany by the Allies. The dark themes of German Expressionism, typified by the graphic, war-obsessed works of painters such as Otto Dix and movies such as *The Cabinet of Dr. Caligari*, set the new tone. The political divisions in Germany meant that the Republic failed to create a unifying and healing culture of national mourning and remembrance. Instead, such efforts were again either localized or politicized.[4] The dedication of the Tannenberg National Memorial in 1927—an event meant to honor unknown soldiers—exemplified how political factions co-opted even national monuments. Reich president von Hindenburg deliberately appeared in his imperial uniform rather than that of the Republic. Members of the national conservative *Stahlhelm* paramilitary lined the road for ten kilometers—also wearing uniforms of the Kaiserreich. In his speech, von Hindenburg used the occasion to defend the absolute sanctity of the **Reichswehr**, scandalizing world opinion by denying any German responsibility for the war:

[Germany entered the war as] the means of self-assertion against a world full of enemies. Pure in heart we set off to the defense of the fatherland and with clean hands the German army carried the sword. Germany is prepared to prove this before impartial judges at any time.[5]

The **Reichswehr** (defense of the realm) was the official name of the armed forces of Germany from 1921 to 1935.

Rather than providing a moment of national mourning and the creation of a new national ritual, the event only further divided Germans, stoking revanchist sentiments among conservatives and alienation among liberals and Marxists.

In the meantime, Germany faced an economic catastrophe. World demand for exports dropped after the war. The loss of raw materials and foodstuffs from occupied territories and colonies disrupted supply chains. The financial system and currency were in shambles due in large part to the profligate issue of war bonds. Inflation eroded savings, and war bonds, in which many patriotic Germans had invested their life savings, were valueless. The centralized war economy created serious distortions in distribution, production, and compensation that were not quickly repaired. The United Kingdom also continued its blockade well into 1919 to ensure that Germany signed the peace treaty. And the labor market suffered as veterans were no longer emotionally or physically fit for the workplace.

The Treaty of Versailles

In these conditions, with no ability to resist militarily, the German peace delegation was powerless to revise the Allies' demands in the Treaty of Versailles in the spring of 1919 (see Supplemental Documents: Treaty of Versailles). The treaty demanded German disarmament, substantial territorial concessions, and reparations. It also insisted that Germany accept full responsibility for the war in Article 231, the so-called War Guilt Clause. Almost every German perceived this as the deepest insult because it placed a moral onus on Germans and implied that their sacrifices not only had been in vain but also had been immoral. To reinforce the accusation of criminality, an additional article charged Kaiser Wilhelm II with "supreme offense[s] against international morality and the sanctity of treaties," demanding that "the Government of the Netherlands surrender to them of the ex-Emperor in order that he may be put on trial." Other articles noted the right of the Allies to set up military tribunals for people believed to have committed war crimes.

The War Guilt Clause had been included largely as a formal justification for reparations—payments for war-related damages. Reparations were a regular part of such treaties. In fact, Germany had included them in its treaties with Austria in 1866, France in 1871, and, most recently, in a final arrangement with Soviet Russia in August 1918. So it was not surprising that the Treaty of Versailles included reparations. Indeed, the reparations bill was determined only in 1921 and was based on Germany's capacity to pay, not on Allied claims. In the interim, Germany was required to pay only for Allied occupation costs. All things considered, the burden was designed not to be debilitating, yet some voices even outside of Germany warned that reparations would undermine not only the new Republic but also long-term international relations (see Supplemental Documents: John Maynard Keynes).

Given the cultural identity of the Kaiserreich, with its Prussian military prestige, the demilitarization clauses of the treaty were particularly shocking. Versailles comprehensively restricted the German armed forces. The provisions were intended to eliminate offensive capability but also to encourage international disarmament. While international disarmament failed to happen, Germany had little choice but to disarm itself, leading to persistent complaints that the real goal of Versailles was to leave Germany permanently open to invasion and extortion by France. The treaty required demobilization to no more than one hundred thousand men, the abolition of conscription, the dissolution of the general staff, the limitation of military schools for officer training, and complete demilitarization of the Rhineland, including demolition of border fortifications. Arms trade, stockpiles, and manufacture of a variety of weapons were prohibited, including chemical weapons, armored cars, and tanks. The German navy was reduced to a meager coastal defense force, and its air force was entirely disbanded.

Violating Germans' broad sense of national identity to include all German speakers, Versailles then imposed significant territorial and population losses. All combined, Germany surrendered twenty-five thousand square miles and seven million people in Europe. The surrender of Western Prussia, Posen, and Upper Silesia to the new state of Poland alone left almost a million German speakers inside Poland. Though Versailles regulated and guaranteed their rights, they, like German speakers in all the other annexed territories, were denied self-determination and subject to the annexing nations' legal right to "liquidate" German property. In addition, while the Kaiserreich had held the third-largest colonial empire (after the United Kingdom and France), it was forced to surrender all of its overseas colonies.

When the full severity of the treaty and the exclusion of German representatives as negotiating partners became apparent, the National Assembly's initial reaction was to appeal to the Allies' sense of fairness based on international precedents. Foreign Minister Brockdorff-Rantzau wrote an eloquent but futile "Protest" to French premier Clemenceau (see Supplemental Documents: German Delegates' Protest). He accepted German defeat and the inevitable concessions but balked at the unrestrained nature of Allied revanchism:

> We were aghast when we read . . . the demands made upon us, the victorious violence of our enemies. The more deeply we penetrate into the spirit of this treaty, the more convinced we become of the impossibility of carrying it out. The exactions of this treaty are more than the German people can bear.[6]

Germany's first democratically elected chancellor, Philipp Scheidemann (SPD), resigned rather than sign the treaty. In a passionate speech before the National Assembly, he called the treaty a "murderous plan" and exclaimed, "Which hand, trying to put us in chains like these, would not wither? The treaty is unacceptable."[7]

But Germany had no choice—a state of civil war existed, the military had collapsed, and people were starving. When President Ebert asked von Hindenburg if the army were capable of any meaningful resistance, he responded by having his chief of staff, General Groener, cable that the military position was untenable. Only after receiving this assessment did the National Assembly ratify the treaty. But every German political party denounced the treaty as a **Diktat**.

A **Diktat** is a dictated and punitive peace that the winners force upon losers.

In reaction to the treaty, the Republic immediately split into two fundamental camps. On the one hand, the socialists, the Centre Party, and the liberals agreed that the only way to move forward from irretrievable defeat was to play for time and gradually erode Versailles with concessions. They pragmatically adopted ***Erfüllungspolitik*** (policy of fulfillment) and used every opportunity to try to persuade the victors to diminish, amend, and eventually nullify the treaty.

Erfüllungspolitik was the pragmatic approach to the Treaty of Versailles; its proponents hoped that a moderate policy of engaging the Allies would encourage them to revise the treaty.

On the other hand, the **DNVP**, the NSDAP, and most of the Reichswehr denounced any compliance with Versailles as treason and labeled those willing to submit as the "November criminals." They advanced a confrontational ***Katastrophenpolitik*** (policy of catastrophe) and used every opportunity to encourage noncompliance and resistance. This policy resulted in the disasters of the early 1920s, including the French occupation of the Ruhr, crippling hyperinflation, numerous uprisings, street battles, and assassinations. Right-wing terrorists murdered hundreds of moderate leaders associated with *Erfüllungspolitik*.

The **DNVP**, or German National People's Party, called for a revolutionary social reorganization along authoritarian and *völkisch* lines. It initially appealed to monarchists seeking to restore the Kaiserreich, but became increasingly inspired by Italian-style fascism.

Katastrophenpolitik, in contrast to *Erfüllungspolitik*, sought to improve Germany's position by openly defying Versailles, resulting in crises that would so wreck Germany that the victors would have to renegotiate the treaty.

Despite the divisions, almost every German agreed that Germany had been falsely blamed for the war. Indeed, no German government accepted the Treaty

of Versailles as legitimate. Government officials openly rejected Germany's post-Versailles borders. In 1925, Foreign Minister Stresemann declared that the reincorporation of territories lost to Poland was his major task. A Reichswehr memorandum of 1926 declared the intention to reincorporate this territory as its first priority, to be followed by the return of the Saar territory, the annexation of Austria, and remilitarization of the Rhineland. Far from resolving issues, the war and treaty had only exacerbated them.

The Weimar Constitution

Although the National Assembly had to deal with numerous pressing issues, its primary task was the creation of a new constitution. The liberal politician Hugo Preuss (**DDP**) gave the first draft a decidedly democratic liberal framework (see Supplemental Documents: Weimar Constitution). Although disagreements arose over issues such as the national flag, religious education, and the rights of the states, these were resolved by August 1919. The constitution passed overwhelmingly (262 to 75), but many deputies abstained, and members from conservative parties (DNVP and DVP) and the left wing of the SPD opposed it, revealing the fault lines that would plague the Republic. As the Republic's first president, Ebert signed the new constitution into law on 11 August 1919.

The **DDP**, or German Democratic Party, sought to balance the political rights of all, but made sacred private property and capitalist enterprise, thus ensuring the persistence of class differences.

The constitution established a democratic parliamentary republic with a legislature elected under proportional representation. With important exceptions, the states governed their respective territories as they saw fit, creating a degree of federalism that respected the tradition of particularism, though national law superseded local law in the event of a conflict. Adjudication of conflicts was the jurisdiction of the Supreme Court.

As a whole, the constitution enshrined the values of liberal democracy. It was arguably the most progressive constitution in the world at the time. In the first elections, held on 6 June 1920, pro-Republic parties obtained a solid 80 percent of the vote, with the socialist parties achieving 45 percent. Led by Scheidemann, they created and led the first cabinet in the Weimar Coalition (SPD, **Centre Party**, and DDP).

The **Centre Party** adhered to broad-based Catholic corporatism. Corporatism is a political ideology that advocates the organization of society by associations of groups such as farmers, workers, or scientists on the basis of their common interests.

Despite this solid base of support, several factors led to unexpected problems.

The allocation of presidential powers was deeply problematic. The government structure deliberately mixed presidential and parliamentary systems, with the president acting as a replacement kaiser and assuming some of the powers of a monarch. In particular, the president could dismiss the chancellor, even if the chancellor retained the confidence of the Reichstag. Furthermore, the president could appoint a chancellor who lacked the support of the Reichstag. In addition, Article 48, the so-called *Notverordnung* (emergency decree) provision, gave the president broad powers to suspend civil liberties.

The proportional electoral system allowed a wide diversity of views. However, the lack of minimum thresholds to win representation facilitated the rise of splinter parties, many of which represented the extreme ends of the political spectrum. It was possible to win a seat in the chamber with as little as 0.4 percent of the vote. This made it difficult for any party to establish and maintain a workable parliamentary majority.

Even without these real or perceived problems, the constitution existed under extremely disadvantageous social, political, and economic conditions. The historian Richard J. Evans concluded:

All in all, Weimar's constitution was no worse than the constitutions of most other countries in the 1920s, and a good deal more democratic than many. Its more problematical provisions might not have mattered so much had the circumstances been different. But the fatal lack of legitimacy from which the Republic suffered magnified the constitution's faults many times over.[8]

Views on the November Revolution

Given the contentious nature of the birth of the Republic, Germans ultimately interpreted every action by the Reichstag through the lens of the November Revolution and military defeat. From the start, they were sharply divided over the cause of Germany's defeat, responsibility for the Treaty of Versailles, and the legitimacy of the constitution. No fundamental or even trivial question could be asked without in some way framing it in relationship to these issues, but there was no consensus even on what the November Revolution meant.

Ernst Troeltsch, a Protestant theologian and philosopher, rather calmly remarked on how the majority of Berlin citizens perceived 10 November 1918, the day after the proclamation of the Republic:

On Sunday morning after a frightful night the morning newspapers gave a clear picture: the Kaiser in Holland, the revolution victorious in most urban centers, the royals in the states abdicating. No man dead for Kaiser and Empire! The continuation of duties ensured and no run on the banks! Trams and subways ran as usual which is a pledge that basic needs are cared for. On all faces it could be read: Wages will continue to be paid.[9]

Rosa Luxemburg, a founder of the KPD assassinated by right-wing paramilitaries during the revolution of January 1919, understood the events of November in a radically different light:

The abolition of the rule of capital, the realization of a socialist social order—this, and nothing less, is the historical theme of the present revolution. It is a formidable undertaking, and one that will not be accomplished in the blink of an eye just by the issuing of a few decrees from above. Only through the conscious action of the working masses in city and country can it be brought to life, only through the people's highest intellectual maturity and inexhaustible idealism can it be brought safely through all storms and find its way to port.[10]

Theodor Wolff, a liberal publicist, optimistically wrote on that day in the *Berliner Tagesblatt* (Berlin Daily):

Like a sudden storm, the biggest of all revolutions has toppled the imperial regime including everything that belonged to it. It can be called the greatest of all revolutions because never has a more firmly built fortress been taken in this manner at the first attempt. Only one week ago, there was still a military and civil administration so deeply rooted that it seemed to have secured its dominion beyond the change of times. Only yesterday morning, at least in Berlin, all this still existed. Yesterday afternoon it was all gone.[11]

Paul Baecker, a conservative journalist, in stark contrast to Wolff, penned an early version of the stab-in-the-back narrative in the *Deutsche Tageszeitung* (German Daily Newspaper):

The work fought for by our fathers with their precious blood—dismissed by betrayal in the ranks of our own people! Germany, yesterday still undefeated, left to the mercy of our enemies by men carrying the German name, by felony out of our own ranks broken down in guilt and shame. The German Socialists knew that peace was at hand anyway and that it was only about holding out against the enemy for a few days or weeks in order to wrest bearable conditions from them. In this situation they raised the white flag. This is a sin that can never be forgiven and never will be forgiven. This is treason not only against the monar-chy and the army but also against the German people themselves who will have to bear the consequences in centuries of decline and of misery.[12]

Kurt Tucholsky, the Republic's most famous left-leaning publicist, proposed that neither Wolff nor Baecker were correct and accused the SPD leaders Ebert and Noske of betrayal—not of the monarchy but of the revolution, regarding it not as a revolution but a coup d'état:

The German Revolution of 1918 took place in a hall. The things taking place were not a revolution. There was no spiritual preparation, no leaders ready in the dark; no revolutionary goals. The mother of this revolution was the soldiers' longing to be home for Christmas. And weariness, disgust and weariness. The possibilities that nevertheless were lying in the streets were betrayed by Ebert and his like. Fritz Ebert, whom you cannot elevate to a personality by calling him Friedrich, opposed the establishment of a republic only until he found there was a chairman's post to be had; comrade Scheidemann è tutti quanti all were would-be senior civil servants. The following possibilities were left out: shattering federal states, division of landed property, revolutionary socialization of industry, reform of administrative and judiciary personnel. A republican constitution in which every sentence rescinds the next one, a revolution talking about well acquired rights of the old regime can be only laughed at. The German Revolution is yet to take place.[13]

Walter Rathenau, the liberal democratic foreign minister assassinated in 1922, called the revolution a "disappointment," a "present by chance," a "product of desperation," a "revolution by mistake." It did not deserve the name revolution because it did "not abolish the actual mistakes" but "degenerated into a degrading clash of interests":

A chain was not broken by the swelling of spirit and will, but a lock merely rusted through. The chain fell off and the freed stood amazed, helpless, embarrassed, and needed to arm against their will. The ones sensing their advantage were the quickest.[14]

Erich Ludendorff, the authoritarian general, completely invalidated the revolution as anti-German and insinuated a link between the revolution and defeat, alluding to the guilt of the home front:

Germany, lacking any firm hand, bereft of all will, robbed of her princes, collapsed like a house of cards. All that we had lived for, all that we had bled four long years to maintain, was gone. . . . The new rulers and their camp-followers abandoned all resistance, and without any authority signed our unconditional capitulation to a merciless enemy. . . . The authorities at home, who had not fought against the enemy, could not hurry fast enough to pardon deserters and other military criminals, including among these themselves and their nearest friends. They and the soldiers' councils worked with zeal, determination, and purpose to destroy everything military. This was the gratitude of the newly formed homeland to the German soldiers who had bled and died for it in millions. The destruction of German power, achieved by these Germans, was the most tragic crime the world has witnessed. A tidal wave had broken over Germany, not by the force of nature, but through the weakness of the Government represented by the chancellor and the crippling of a leaderless people. By the Revolution the Germans have made themselves pariahs among the nations, incapable of winning allies, helots in the service of foreigners and foreign capital, and deprived of all self-respect. In twenty years' time, the German people will curse the parties who now boast of having made the Revolution.[15]

Oswald Spengler, the idiosyncratic conservative, anticipated an inevitable and bloody counterrevolution to correct the disaster of November:

I witnessed the repellent scenes that occurred on November 7, 1918, in Munich, sometimes in close proximity, and I nearly choked from disgust. And then the way in which Kaiser Wilhelm was sent packing, the way that every louse took it upon himself to hurl excrement at the man, the man who worked selflessly and self-sacrificingly for thirty years on behalf of Greater Germany. I know very well that the mob in other countries is dastardly beyond all measure, but does it match ours in its beastliness? . . . I see that the German Revolution is taking the typical course; slow dismantling of the existing order, overthrow, wild radicalism, reversion. What gives us hope today is the certainty that the monarchy will emerge strengthened from this crisis; . . . like France in 1793, we will have to live through this misfortune to the very end; we need a good castigation, the likes of which will make the four years of war seem harmless in comparison, until the time has come for the small group that was called to leadership in 1813 and in 1870 alike: the Prussian nobles and the Prussian civil servants, the thousands of our technicians, apprentices, craftsmen, workers with Prussian instincts; until, above all, the terror also generates such indignation and despair that a dictatorship, something Napoleonic, is generally perceived as the salvation. But then blood must flow, the more the better.[16]

Adolf Hitler, leader of the NSDAP, racialized these national conservative views:

It remained for the Jews, with their unqualified capacity for falsehood, and their fighting comrades, the Marxists, to . . . place responsibility for the loss of the world war on the shoulders of Ludendorff. . . . If we review all the causes which contributed to bring about the downfall of the German people we shall find that the most profound and decisive cause must be attributed to the lack of insight into the racial problem and especially in the failure to recognize the Jewish danger. . . . We were overthrown by that force which had prepared those defeats by systematically operating for several decades to destroy those political instincts and that moral stamina which alone enable a people to struggle for its existence and therewith secure the right to exist. . . . While the flower of the nation's manhood was dying at the front, there was time enough at home at least to exterminate this vermin. But, instead of doing so, His Majesty the Kaiser held out his hand to these hoary criminals . . . and so the viper could begin his work again. This time, however, more carefully than before, but still more destructively. While honest people dreamt of reconciliation these perjured criminals were making preparations for a revolution.[17]

The "Stab-in-the-Back" Conspiracy Theory

The views of extremist conservative thinkers gave birth to one of the most destabilizing anti-Republican narratives—the stab-in-the-back conspiracy theory. Anti-Republicans argued that, at the time of the armistice on 11 November 1918, no Allied force had set foot on Germa6n soil; the western front was still almost 1,400 kilometers from Berlin; and Russia had been defeated, and France almost defeated in the Spring Offensive. In short, the kaiser's armies had not been defeated in the field. How, then, if the military were winning, could Germany have lost the war?

The conspiracy theory asserted that the army had in fact not lost the war on the battlefield but was instead betrayed by civilians on the home front. Marxists launched strikes in the arms industry at a decisive moment of the offensive, leaving soldiers with an inadequate supply of materiel. Democrats fomented the crisis to abolish the monarchy. Pacifists and internationalists undermined morale. These were the November criminals who delivered the deadly blow to the military, betrayed the monarchy, and then signed the *Diktat* of Versailles. In this view, the entire Republic was the product of traitors—a swamp of corruption, degeneracy, and national humiliation.

Of course, it was not the objective truth or falsity of the claim that mattered, but what Germans believed. The stab-in-the-back conspiracy theory offered a clear and simple answer to Germany's defeat, targeted an enemy at home, and provided a path to national regeneration. Indeed, the expression "stab in the back" evoked Richard Wagner's 1876 opera *Götterdämmerung* (Twilight of the Gods), in which the deceitful Hagen murdered his honest rival Siegfried with a spear in his back.

Supporters of the Republic pointed out that when the Spring Offensive of 1918 inevitably failed, the writing was on the wall. The United States had resupplied the Allies, and its fresh armies were ready for combat. By the summer, German forces were in retreat. German troops stationed in Russia were deemed unfit for transfer to the western theater due to their radicalization and threat of mutiny. The rapid collapse of the other Central Powers in late 1918 exacerbated Germany's deteriorating strategic position. As the German military faced outright collapse, its commanders repeatedly informed the government that they could no longer resist an invasion of German soil, and a negotiated settlement had to be found immediately to prevent complete defeat. Meanwhile, the home front was a military dictatorship. The press was highly censored; the economy was directed entirely for the war effort; all peace initiatives were thwarted; and any opposition was ruthlessly suppressed. In short, the military was in total command. Instead of taking responsibility for the looming collapse, the high command arranged for a rapid transfer of power to a civilian government. Only to avoid taking the blame for the imminent defeat did the shift to civilian control occur. Since the kaiser had been forced to abdicate and the military relinquished executive power, the new civilian government sued for peace; its signatory, Matthias Erzberger (Centre), was later assassinated for this alleged treason.

Almost immediately following the signing of the treaty, the military and conservatives sought to shift blame for defeat away from themselves. In autumn 1919 Ludendorff was dining with the head of the British military mission in Berlin, General Malcolm, who asked him why he thought Germany lost the war. Ludendorff replied with a list of excuses, including that the home front had failed the army:

Malcolm asked: "Do you mean, General, that you were stabbed in the back?" Ludendorff's eyes lit up and he leapt upon the phrase like a dog on a bone. "Stabbed in the back?" he repeated. "Yes, that's it, exactly, we were stabbed in the back."[18]

Against all evidence, Ludendorff informed the general staff that this was to be the official military version and convinced von Hindenburg, who testified before an inquiry committee in November 1919 that the German army had been on the verge of winning the war in 1918:

History will render the final judgment on that about which I may give no further details here. At the time we still hoped that the will to victory would dominate everything else. When we assumed our post we made a series of proposals to the Reich leadership which aimed at combining all forces at the nation's disposal for a quick and favorable conclusion to the war; at the same time, they demonstrated to the government its enormous tasks. What finally became of our proposals, once again partially because of the influence of the parties, is known. I wanted forceful and cheerful cooperation and instead encountered failure and weakness.

The concern as to whether the homeland would remain resolute until the war was won, from this moment on, never left us. We often raised a warning voice to the Reich government. At this time, the secret intentional mutilation of the fleet and the army began as a continuation of similar occurrences in peace time. The effects of these endeavors were not concealed from the supreme army command during the last year of the war. The obedient troops who remained immune to revolutionary attrition suffered greatly from the behavior, in violation of duty, of their revolutionary comrades; they had to carry the battle the whole time.

The intentions of the command could no longer be executed. Our repeated proposals for strict discipline and strict legislation were not adopted. Thus did our operations necessarily miscarry; the collapse was inevitable; the revolution only provided the keystone.

An English general said with justice: "The German army was stabbed in the back." No guilt applies to the good core of the army. Its achievements are just as admirable as those of the officer corps. Where the guilt lies has clearly been demonstrated. If it needed more proof, then it would be found in the quoted statement of the English general and in the boundless astonishment of our enemies at their victory.[19]

The story resonated in part because it tapped into widespread antisemitism. In 1919 Alfred Roth published *The Jew in the Army*. He claimed that most Jews involved in the war were profiteers and spies, and he blamed Jewish officers for fostering a defeatist mentality. In fact, in October 1916 the army had ordered a "Jewish census" of troops, with the express intent to prove that Jews were cowards, war profiteers, and anti-German. Instead, the census showed the opposite: Jews were overrepresented in the army and in fighting positions at the front. The military consequently suppressed the results of the census, which allowed right-wing publishers, dominated by Alfred Hugenberg (DNVP), to push the spurious connection between Jews and communism and defeatism.

Years of Crisis, Reform, and Resurgence, 1919–1929
Confronting Political Violence
Given the context, the birth of the Republic failed to unify Germans. Instead, an extreme nationalist movement emerged that repeatedly blamed the Republic for leading to defeat, revolution, and humiliation. Meanwhile, the radical Left accused the ruling coalition of having betrayed the workers' movement and being a mere prop for the militarists and capitalists. Both agreed that the Republic must be de-

stroyed, and they launched numerous uprisings while simultaneously attacking each other.

Yet the government, assured of the support of the military through the Ebert-Groener Pact, dealt severely and successfully with the occasional outbreaks of violence even as the army and its *Freikorps* allies committed hundreds of acts of gratuitous violence against workers and leftists.

This further alienated the KPD, which saw the Republic's action as additional evidence that the SPD had betrayed the ideals of the revolution. The success of the *Freikorps* at destroying the Bavarian Soviet Republic only encouraged the antidemocratic Right to use violence to seize power.

In addition, the military itself initially operated an extralegal covert wing, the so-called Black Reichswehr. It funneled money, arms, uniforms, and leadership to various paramilitaries operating in Germany and in the numerous border wars after the war. These units were occasionally thinly disguised as labor battalions, and its members worked fluidly with paramilitaries aligned with the NSDAfP and DNVP and others. They engaged in acts of sabotage against the French occupation and carried out assassinations.

Consequently, right-wing death squads acted with impunity—shielded by the military and repeatedly absolved of wrongdoing by the courts. Assassinations of alleged November criminals became common. Hundreds of political assassinations occurred— almost all committed by right-wing activists. The judiciary, comprised almost exclusively of conservative holdovers from the Kaiserreich, issued sentences that revealed extraordinary leniency toward right-wing assassins and a corresponding severity against the few leftists who engaged in political violence (see table 1).[20]

In this climate, on 13 March 1920, twelve thousand *Freikorps* soldiers occupied Berlin and installed Wolfgang Kapp (a right-wing journalist) as chancellor. The national government fled to Stuttgart and called for a general strike against the putsch. The strike meant that no official pronouncements could be published, and, with the civil service out on strike,

the **Kapp Putsch** collapsed after only four days, on 17 March.

A **putsch** is the German version of a coup d'état— a violent attempt to overthrow a government by replacing its leaders.

Inspired by the general strike, a workers' uprising began in the Ruhr region when fifty thousand people formed the Red Army and took control of the province. The workers, who were campaigning for an extension of the plans to nationalize major industries, supported the national government, but the SPD leaders in the government did not want to lend support to the left wing of the SPD or KPD, which favored the establishment of a socialist regime. As a result, the regular army and the *Freikorps* ended the uprising on their own authority— without receiving any formal authorization from the government, but with clear consent from the right wing of the SPD leadership. The repression of an uprising of socialist supporters by the *Freikorps* on the instructions of SPD ministers repeated the pattern of the Ebert-Groener Pact and became a further source of conflict within the socialist-communist movements, contributing to the weakening and fracturing of the largest bloc that supported the young Republic.

Despite such instances of left-wing political violence, terrorism and insurrections remained largely the purview of the Right after 1919. One example of the link of right-wing terror to political events came with the Treaty of Rapallo. In 1922, the Reichswehr and civilian leaders, in an attempt to subvert the military restrictions of Versailles, signed the Treaty of Rapallo with the Soviet Union, which allowed Germany to train military personnel in the USSR in exchange for military technology. While the Reichswehr leadership supported the treaty, it forced Germany to publicly renounce territorial claims against the USSR. As a result, two extremist junior army officers assassinated foreign minister Walther Rathenau (DDP). He was also targeted because he was part of

TABLE 1 Judicial sentencing for assassinations

	Assassinations by the Right		Assassinations by the Left	
	Total	**Average**	**Total**	**Average**
Assassinations	354		22	
Unpunished	326	92%	4	18%
Executions	0	0%	10	46%
Life sentences	1	0.2%	3	14%
Prison terms	90 years	3 months	250 years	11.4 years

the delegation that signed the Versailles Treaty. In addition, he was a Jew.

The assassins were members of the right-wing terrorist group Organization Consul, which had carried out numerous assassinations. They believed Rathenau's death would bring down the government by prompting the radical Left to take revolutionary action. They hoped to use this as an opportunity to establish an authoritarian regime or a military dictatorship with the aid of the Reichswehr.

The terrorists' aims were not achieved, however, and civil war did not come. Instead, millions of Germans gathered on the streets to express their grief and to demonstrate against counterrevolutionary terrorism. When the news of Rathenau's death became known in the Reichstag, the session fell into turmoil. Karl Helfferich (DNVP) in particular became the target of criticism because he had just recently made a vitriolic speech against Rathenau.

The assassination finally energized Republican authorities to act decisively to stabilize the Republic, and the Reichstag passed the Law for the Protection of the Republic, which increased the penalties for attacks on Republican institutions and officials, established a special court to handle anticonstitutional actions, and laid down regulations for the strict control of associations, meetings, and printed matter (see Supplemental Documents: Law for the Protection of the Republic). Only the DNVP, the Bavarian People's Party, the Communists, and some members of the liberal **DVP** voted against it. Bavarian repre-

sentatives considered the law a gross overreach by Berlin, and the KPD feared that it would inevitably be used against them (as it was). But conservatives opposed the express political intent of the law to stop the Right. Indeed, during the official memorial service for Rathenau, Chancellor Wirth (X) had admitted as much when he called out,

> There stands the enemy who drips his poison in the wounds of the nation. There stands the enemy; and there can be no doubt about it: this enemy stands on the right.[21]

The **DVP** was a right-wing liberal party that was strongly nationalistic but otherwise prioritized the interests of big industrialists, with a degree of ambivalence toward the Republic.

The shift toward ending political violence was not immediately effective, however. In 1923, the small, local NSDAP under Adolf Hitler in Munich launched the Beer Hall Putsch (aka the Munich Putsch). On 8 November 1923, in a pact with Ludendorff, the NSDAP took over a meeting of Prime Minister von Kahr of Bavaria at a beer hall. Ludendorff and Hitler declared that the Berlin government was deposed and that they were taking control of Munich. Bavarian authorities, however, thwarted the three thousand insurrectionists. Hitler was arrested and sentenced to five years in prison for high treason. The sentence, though, was the minimum allowable under law. The same conservative judges, who routinely sentenced striking workers and communists to death or to life in prison for lesser offenses, again proved highly sympathetic to right-wing terrorists even though four police officers had been killed. Hitler served less than eight months in a comfortable cell, receiving a daily stream of visitors before his early release in 1924. While in jail, Hitler dictated *Mein Kampf* (My Struggle), which laid out his ideas. During this time, Hitler also decided to focus on legal methods of gaining power.

Yet, overall, the reactions to Rathenau's assassination strengthened the Republic. For as long as the Republic existed, the date 24 June remained a day of public commemorations. In public memory, Rathenau's death increasingly was seen as a martyr-like sacrifice for democracy.

Stabilizing the Economy

The year 1923 was a year of hyperinflation as well as uprisings. Without stabilizing the economy, there was little hope of ending the violence. In the early postwar years, with the economy in shambles, inflation was already growing at an alarming rate, but the government simply printed more banknotes to pay the bills. As a result, the value of the **German mark** decreased tenfold between December 1918 and April 1920. Yet in 1923, the government engaged in a high-risk attempt to convince the Allies to renegotiate reparations, launching a conscious policy of *Katastrophenpolitik* to simultaneously defy obligations under Versailles and deliberately sabotage the economy to convince the Allies of the treaty's unfairness. The consequences were, as intended, catastrophic.

The **German mark** left the gold standard in 1914 due to wartime inflation. This so-called paper mark continued to lose value, and hyperinflation in 1923 necessitated a new so-called rentenmark, set at a rate of one trillion to one. In 1924, the currency was again revalued and the reichsmark (RM) was introduced and remained until 1948.

A new cabinet that excluded the SPD (the largest party) claimed it could no longer make reparations payments, and it defaulted by refusing to ship any more coal across the border. In response, French and Belgian troops occupied the industrial heartland of the Ruhr area inside Germany to compel the coal shipments. This occupation outraged the German public. The government called for strikes and encouraged passive resistance, which lasted eight months. To keep up the strikes, the state paid striking workers. Yet, as tax revenues collapsed, and lacking any reserves, all the Republic could do was print more money, fueling hyperinflation. As inflation eroded currency value, workers demanded raises to keep up with inflation, while many businesses profited by simply paying off their debts with worthless currency.

The value of the mark collapsed. In 1919, a loaf of bread cost one mark; by 1923, the same loaf of bread cost one hundred billion marks. The state and economy were in free fall. The Allies would not renegotiate under pressure. Under these conditions, Stresemann created a new grand coalition that brought the SPD back. The coalition ended resistance, agreed to resume reparations, and introduced a new currency. As reparation payments resumed, the subsequent Locarno Treaties returned the Ruhr to Germany, but fears of hyperinflation lingered.

Katastrophenpolitik had failed abysmally.

Subsequent governments pointed to this abject failure to justify *Erfüllungspolitik*. Economic stability, they argued, led to political stability, which in turn would ultimately erode Versailles. But it was a long-term approach, and it required both patience and favorable economic conditions.

Social Reform

Despite the instability, the provisional governments carried out a wide range of progressive social reforms during and after the revolutionary period. In 1919, legislation provided for a maximum forty-eight-hour workweek, restrictions on night work, a half-holiday on Saturday, and a break of thirty-six hours of continuous rest during the week. Health insurance was extended to wives and daughters without independent incomes, as well as to those only partially capable of gainful employment, employed in private cooperatives, or employed in public cooperatives. Progressive tax reforms increased taxes on capital and on the highest income brackets from 4 to 60 percent. The government met the demand of the veterans' associations that all aid for the disabled and their dependents be administered by the central government. The government also agreed to continue the nationwide network of state and district welfare bureaus that had been set up during the war to coordinate social services for war widows and orphans.

The National Youth Welfare Act of 1922 obliged all municipalities and states to set up offices for child protection and codified the right to education. New laws regulated rents and increased protections for tenants. Health insurance coverage was extended to new categories, including seamen, people employed in the educational and social welfare sectors, and all primary dependents.

Unemployment benefits were increased. Following the economic problems of 1923, a regular program of assistance consolidated unemployment relief, although in June 1920 the maximum amount that a family of four could receive in Berlin was 90 marks, well below the minimum cost of subsistence of 304 marks. In 1924, the government introduced a modern public relief program, followed in 1925 by a reform of the accident insurance program that allowed work-related diseases to become insurable risks. In 1927 a national unemployment insurance program was introduced. Affordable state-funded housing construction was also greatly accelerated, with over two million new homes constructed from 1924 and a further 195,000 modernized.

But problems lurked under the surface. By 1929, unemployment had crept up to 10 percent, and unemployed workers were expected to survive on state support of 849 RM per year. Even for the employed, real wages reached the level of the prewar era only in 1928. The average monthly pay was between 100 and 250 RM, with an expectation for the majority of workers that they work more than forty-eight hours per week. By no German standard were these wages above the poverty level. Indeed, as a reflection of chronic poverty, doctors estimated that 30 percent of youth were malnourished.

Golden Era, 1924–1929

For all the turmoil, after the crisis year of 1923, Germany recovered—indeed, it thrived by many estimates. Stresemann, who served as foreign minister from 1923 to 1929, embodied to the world a renewed Germany, steadily reclaiming its position in world affairs. His tenure marked a period of relative stability for the Republic, known as the Golden Twenties. Prominent features of this period were a growing economy and a consequent decrease in civil unrest; political assassination and insurrection all but disappeared. Restoring civil stability and stabilizing the currency promoted confidence in the German economy and helped the recovery so ardently needed for the German nation to keep up with reparation repayments, while at the same time feeding and supplying the nation.

In one way, even the hyperinflation had helped. Following the Ruhr Crisis of 1923, the Allied Reparations Commission asked the U.S. expert Charles Dawes to find a quick solution to reparations. Within months, the Dawes Commission developed the Dawes Plan (1924) that allowed U.S. banks to lend money to German banks, with German assets as collateral, to help pay reparations. The German railways, the National Bank, and many industries were mortgaged as securities for the currency and the loans. Once in place, the economy rebounded and the Republic continued with the payment of reparations with the influx of American capital. Shortly after, the French and Germans agreed that the borders between their countries would not be changed by force, but left open the prospect of negotiated changes. Other foreign policy achievements included the evacuation of the Ruhr and improved relations between the Soviet Union and Germany.

In 1926, Germany was admitted to the League of Nations as a permanent member. Meanwhile, trade increased and unemployment fell. Indeed, for the first time, a government remained in power for its full term (1924–28).

In this context, the 1920s saw a remarkable cultural renaissance.

German artists, especially in cosmopolitan Berlin, looked to contemporary progressive cultural movements such as impressionism, expressionism, and cubism coming from Paris as well as radical artistic innovations emanating from the Soviet Union. They often condemned the excesses of capitalism and demanded revolutionary cultural changes. German literature, cinema, theater, and music entered a period of great creativity as innovative street theater brought plays to the public, and the cabaret scene and jazz became wildly popular. Many new buildings followed the straight-lined, geometrical style being popularized in the United States. Examples of the new architecture included the Bauhaus Building, the Grosses Schauspielhaus, and the Einstein Tower.

But not everyone was happy with the cultural changes taking place. Conservatives and reactionaries feared that Germans were betraying traditional values by adopting popular styles from abroad, particularly those popularized by Hollywood and the New York fashion scene. For instance, the euphoria surrounding the African American dancer Josephine Baker in the metropolis of Berlin, where she was declared an "erotic goddess" and greatly admired, led to condemnations of Americanization, with explicit negative references to the degeneracy of negrification and Jewish influences. Not surprisingly, many artists such as George Grosz regularly faced lawsuits and fines for defaming the military and for blasphemy. The new modes also stirred up patriarchal resentments. Many feared that modern young women were being either liberated or masculinized, or both, by wearing makeup, cutting their hair short, smoking, and breaking with traditional mores.

Foreign Relations

Reparations: The Dawes Plan and the Young Plan

The Reichstag considered the Dawes Plan a temporary measure and expected a future revision. In 1928, Foreign Minister Stresemann called for this final plan. The ensuing Young Plan of 1929 proposed additional payment reductions and early evacuation of the Rhineland by France in 1930, five years ahead of schedule (see Supplemental Documents: Hjalmar Schacht). Almost all observers, including the Allies and German cabinet, saw the Young Plan as yet another dramatic foreign policy success of *Erfüllungspolitik*.

Yet the Far Right was desperate to find an issue to recover the support it had lost in the 1928 elections. Political violence was counterproductive; the economy was growing; the government had scored numerous foreign policy successes; and the SPD-led coalition was contentious but stable. The Right turned to lingering resentment over the Treaty of Versailles. In response to the Young Plan, the DNVP, in coalition with ultranationalist groups, actively encouraged a return to the *Katastrophenpolitik* of 1923 by openly defying the requirements of the Versailles Treaty. They sponsored the so-called Law against the Enslavement of the German People, or Freedom Law (see Supplemental Documents: Law against the Enslavement of the German people). The bill not only renounced Versailles but also made it a criminal offense for any official to cooperate with the treaty. The small NSDAP was especially vocal in its support.

The law would mean that the government was committing a criminal action if it recognized any portion of the Versailles Treaty—including making reparation payments, negotiating any aspect of the treaty, or acknowledging international borders set by the treaty. Negotiating or supporting the Young Plan, for example, would have violated the Freedom Law. The French and Belgians threatened that passing such a law would result in international intervention —including military force—to bring Germany into compliance. The cabinet of Hermann Müller (SPD) made clear that they would not support the law or violate the treaty, and would instead continue with their *Erfüllungspolitik*, including ratification of the Young Plan:

> The Government of the Reich, in agreement with the immense majority of the German people, knows that improvement in the external situation cannot be imposed by a German law. It can only be attained by negotiations with the associates of Germany.[22]

Pushed by the Right, seeking to find a wedge issue after their electoral defeat in 1928, the Freedom Law and the Young Plan became the central intertwined political issues of late 1929.

Poland and the Eastern Border

Complicating matters, the cabinet was simultaneously seeking to resolve a number of issues with Poland. The creation of the Second Republic of Poland by the Treaty of Versailles infuriated nationalists. Poland annexed significant German territories, including the Polish Corridor, a region that separated East Prussia from the rest of Germany. Poles successfully argued that access to the Baltic Sea via the port of Danzig was essential for the otherwise landlocked Poland. For Germans, this territorial redrawing reduced the size of Germany, created an isolated and militarily indefensible exclave (East Prussia), abandoned hundreds of thousands of German nationals in a foreign and hostile state, and severed a centuries-old claim to land in the East considered historically German. Yet the American diplomat David Hunter Miller dismissively concluded, "The Corridor and Danzig should be ceded to Poland. . . . In the case of Poland they are vital interests; in the case of Germany, aside from Prussian sentiment, they are quite secondary."[23]

Already facing an agrarian depopulation crisis, especially acute in the East, since the nineteenth century, Germans regarded these border changes as deliberately calculated to economically, militarily, and racially weaken Germany. Polish and German nationalists immediately attempted to change the facts on the ground, starting with a series of small-scale but bloody border wars after 1918. Without a standing army, Germany relied on right-wing paramilitaries, which remained a problem even after the wars ended. Yet, Poland prevailed against these militias and annexed the promised province, resulting in a mass exodus of German speakers (encouraged by the Polish state).

The refugees put constant pressure on the successive cabinets of the Republic to address the Polish Question. Indeed, although Stresemann's foreign policy made conciliatory gestures toward the West, his attitude toward Poland remained hostile. Not a single German party accepted the Polish annexations. No German cabinet offered any guarantees about Germany's eastern frontiers.

Lacking an army, the cabinet developed a plan to wreck Poland's economy and gain political concessions via a trade war. Even the free-trade, liberal DDP-leaning newspaper the *Frankfurter Zeitung* (Frankfurt Newspaper) wrote in 1924, "Poland must be mortally wounded after the trade war. With her blood her strength will flow away as well, and finally her independence."[24] The economic consequences for Germany were minimal since only 3 to 4 percent of German trade was with Poland. Poland, on the other hand, suffered tremendously, since it had little choice but to trade with Germany. The trade war exacerbated the situation in Poland to such an extent that it helped lead to a coup in 1926 that placed the general Józef Pilsudski in charge of what was, in effect, a dictatorship.

In retaliation, ethnic Germans faced escalating pressure from the local Polish population and officials. Germans traveling between East Prussia and the rest of Germany were regularly harassed by Polish nationalists. In May 1925 a train passing through the corridor on its way to East Prussia crashed due to apparent sabotage on the line: the spikes had been removed from the tracks for a short distance and the fishplates unbolted. Twenty-five people, including twelve women and two children, were killed; some thirty others were injured.

The Polish government retaliated by other means as well. Per Versailles, Poland could force ethnic Germans to choose between Polish or German citizenship. Poland was also authorized to liquidate the property of German nationals (see Supplemental Documents: Treaty of Versailles—Poland). Thus, Germans in Poland either had to accept Polish citizenship or face losing their land. Consequently, in 1925 Poland began land reform, ostensibly to improve agricultural efficiency. The first annual list of properties to be reformed included 10,800 hectares from thirty-two German landowners and only 950 hectares from seven Poles. In fact, the Polish governor of Pomorze stressed, "The part of Pomorze through which the so-called corridor runs must be cleansed of larger German holdings."[25] Thousands of complaints were issued to the International Court of the League of Nations about violations of German minority rights—to no avail. The result was a steady exodus of Germans and the rapid Polonization of West Prussia. By some accounts, Germans had made up 40 percent of the population in the Polish Corridor in 1910; by 1921, that number had already been cut in half to 18.8 percent. By 1923, as many as eight hundred thousand ethnic Germans had left. Though the reasons for the exodus were complicated, for most Germans the cause was clear—Poland's anti-German policy of forced assimilation.

By 1929, however, Polish economic hardship and German inability to staunch the population losses led both sides to commit to a peaceful settlement, though both sides pointed out that any attempt to permanently revise borders would mean war. To end the crisis, the German government began negotiating a treaty that would resolve these matters, the so-called Liquidation Treaty (see Supplemental Documents: German-Polish Agreement), and conceptually linked this treaty to certain provisions in the Young Plan—a linkage that made sense financially but only inflamed tensions politically.

Military Affairs
The Reichswehr and Armored Cruisers

The Treaty of Versailles and the revolution did not destroy most of Germany's traditional institutions, with the notable exception of the monarchy. The civil service, the schools and universities, the judiciary, and, most importantly, the military remained in the hands of the same men who ran them in the Kaiserreich. Most retained their conservative, authoritarian preferences.

After the dissolution of the imperial army in 1918, Germany's military forces consisted of the irregular *Freikorps* and a few regular units. The *Freikorps* were formally disbanded in 1920, though they continued to exist in underground groups, and on 1 January 1921 a new Reichswehr was created. One unintended advantage of the limitations of Versailles was that the Reichswehr could afford to pick the best recruits for service. However, with inefficient armor and no air support, the Reichswehr had limited combat abilities (see Supplemental Documents: Treaty of Versailles—Military Restrictions).

However, for all its professionalism, the Reichswehr was, based on the Ebert-Groener Pact, a "state within a state," autonomous from the government and free from civilian oversight (see Supplemental Documents: Philipp Scheidemann). There were rumors that the Reichswehr attempted to skirt the treaty in various ways—via secret budgets, money laundering, even training in the Soviet Union. That the Reichswehr was subverting international law was not a surprise. Although technically in the service of the Republic, the army was predominantly officered by conservative reactionaries who were sympathetic to right-wing organizations, including terrorists. Hans von Seect, the head of the Reichswehr, declared that the army was not loyal to the Republic and would defend it only if it were in the military's interests. During the Kapp Putsch in 1920, for example, the army refused to fire on the right-wing putschists. However, as right wing as the army was, it was hostile to the NSDAP, which it viewed as mostly thugs. Indeed, the Reichswehr considered the party's **Sturmabteilung (SA)** its main opponent. Regular officers saw the SA, which demanded the creation of a "people's army," as a threat to their existence. The army did not refrain from firing on the SA when it suppressed the NSDAP's unsuccessful Beer Hall Putsch in 1923.

The **Sturmabteilung (SA)** (assault unit) was the NSDAP paramilitary, also known as stormtroopers or Brown-shirts. The primarily young men were notorious for their street brawls.

The Reichswehr's officers were also utterly devoted to von Hindenburg, who, as Reich president, was the formal head of the Reichswehr and consistently defended its absolute sanctity. Yet it was general Kurt von Schleicher, as head of the Defense Ministry's Office of Ministerial Affairs that looked after the Reichswehr's political interests, who made day-to-day decisions. It was unimaginable that the Reichswehr would act without, first, the consent of von Hindenburg, and, second, the coordination of von Schleicher. How they would act under a different president and defense minister, though, was unpredictable.

One of the debates confronting the Reichswehr involved the navy. The military proposed building three new *Deutschland*-class armored cruisers, derisively referred to as "pocket battleships" by the English press. Political opposition to the new ships was significant. The Reichswehr therefore decided to delay ordering the first ship until after the Reichstag elections in 1928, hoping for a conservative majority. The question over whether to build the new ships was a major issue in elections, particularly with the SPD, which campaigned with the slogan "Food for children, not armored cruisers."

After the SPD victory in those elections, the issue posed a dilemma for the new SPD-led cabinet (see Supplemental Documents: Otto Wels). Liberal parties, which were an integral part of the ruling coalition, made it clear they would bring down the government if it failed to fund the new ships. This position was supported by a majority in the Reichstag, so the SPD leadership reluctantly went along. In October 1928, the KPD attempted to derail construction by calling a popular **referendum** against construction, but it failed.

A **referendum** is a vote by the electorate on a single political question. It is a form of direct democracy.

The issue provoked an international response as well. When the Allies learned the particulars of the design, they attempted to prevent Germany from building the ships as a violation of Versailles. The Reichswehr offered to halt construction on the first ship in exchange for admittance to the Washington Treaty, which regulated naval size. This agreement would have effectively abrogated the clauses in Versailles that limited Germany's naval power. The United Kingdom and the United States favored making concessions to Germany, but France refused. Since the ships seemingly did not violate the technical terms of the treaty, the Allies could not prevent Germany from building them after a negotiated settlement proved unattainable. Yet, to continue building the ships, the Reichstag had to pass an annual naval funding bill, meaning that the divisive issue of guns or butter would resurface every year.

Paramilitary Violence

By 1929, the violent days of the early Republic had faded. Assassinations of leading politicians had ceased. No uprising had occurred since 1923. The Black Reichswehr and *Freikorps* had disbanded. The Reichswehr and Republic had achieved a modus vivendi. But threats lurked just below the surface. Street fights, especially between the rival **paramilitaries** of the NSDAP and KPD, often resulted in riots and death. Low-level state officials faced real threats of terror attacks. And most of the large parties continued to maintain paramilitary organizations of such size that they collectively dwarfed the Reichswehr.

A **paramilitary** organization is a semimilitarized force whose organizational structure, tactics, training, and subculture are similar to those of a professional military, but it is not formally part of a country's armed forces.

Well-organized paramilitaries were legal (provided they did not actively oppose the Republic), and members could wear uniforms and train openly. All were affiliated with a political direction, but they were not legally identified with a party. While this distinction had little real meaning, it did mean that political parties could not be held accountable for their paramilitaries' often unruly, frequently violent, occasionally murderous actions. For example, the Red Front was banned, but not the KPD. The fact that these paramilitaries waged street fights meant that many people believed they should be banned—if not all of them, then at least those that engaged in clearly documented violence. Unless specified otherwise, the bans were for one year but could be renewed.

The government, using the 1922 Law for the Protection of the Republic, made some attempts to ban either the NSDAP or the SA. This happened in 1923 after the Munich Putsch, but it only increased that party's popularity and the ban was soon lifted. Most agreed that a ban on a party violated the essence of constitutional democracy. The Supreme Court indicated that a party ban would be constitutional only in the context of a direct threat (an actual insurrection by a party).

Upon Hitler's release from prison in 1924, he convinced the Bavarian authorities to lift the ban on the NSDAP and reformed the party under his undisputed leadership. The new party was no longer a paramilitary organization, and it officially disavowed any intention of taking power by force. The party and the SA were kept separate and the legal aspect of the NSDAP's work was emphasized. In a sign of this change, the NSDAP admitted women. In all public statements, the official stance of the NSDAP was the new Legality Strategy—a shift away from attempting to seize power through violence and towards electoralism. However, the street actions by the SA and

incriminating evidence found in a police raid on a Nazi lawyer's office made many wonder if the NSDAP was sincere. Indeed, the NSDAP was repeatedly hauled into court to address the violence of the SA. In these courtroom exchanges, state's attorneys attempted to get Hitler to incriminate the NSDAP as supporting violence against the Republic, which would allow the state to use the Law for the Protection of the Republic to ban the NSDAP. Hitler generally deftly parried each attempt without disavowing the party's revolutionary goals, and conservative judges revealed their political sympathies for anti-Republican nationalists (see Supplemental Documents: Transcript from the Ulm Reichswehr Trial).

In May 1929, the SPD interior minister used the Law for the Protection of the Republic against the Left and banned the Red Front, the KPD's paramilitary. This action was precipitated by the involvement of the Red Front in protests after the government of Berlin, which was controlled by an SPD-led coalition, banned celebrations of International Workers' Day (1 May). Police, led by the SPD chief of police, shot and killed more than thirty demonstrators. Not only was the Red Front banned, but all its assets were confiscated by the government. Furthermore, all attempts at creating successor organizations were banned. Even the SPD agreed with the Right that the greater threat came from the KPD, not the NSDAP.

Sexuality and Eugenics
The Eugenics Movement and Sterilization
Germany's hypermilitarized context had inevitable ideational corollaries. Social Darwinism, for example, had entered the German scientific community at the end of the nineteenth century and become a central tenet for many political parties. Proponents contended that modern society had interrupted the natural struggle for existence by preserving the weak—at the national, social, or even individual level. They feared that in Germany, "defective" persons were reproducing faster than healthy ones. The widely respected natural scientist Ernst Haeckel had written that humans were not always morally obligated to prolong life, and he proposed the establish-

ment of a commission to determine which of the chronically ill should be put to death by poisoning (euthanasia). In 1915, psychiatry professor Alfred Hoche described the end of atomistic individualism and the transformation of the nation into a higher organism, the *Volk*. This quasi-mystical image portrayed society as an organism with its own health and identified human beings as functional or dysfunctional parts of a larger whole.

These ideas were generally called eugenics or race hygiene, and they increasingly informed population policy, public health education, and government-funded research. Proponents of eugenics argued that modern medicine and costly welfare programs interfered with natural selection by keeping the "unfit" alive to reproduce and multiply. Instead, natural selection should be allowed to eliminate the weak. They further contended that members of the "fit," educated classes were marrying later and using birth control methods to limit family size. The result was an overall biological "degeneration" of the population—more unfit, fewer fit. As a solution, they proposed "positive" government policies such as tax credits to foster large, "valuable" families, and "negative" policies, mainly the sterilization of genetic "inferiors" but also euthanasia, to limit the number of unproductive members of society.

Eugenics advocates included physicians, public health officials, and academics in the biomedical fields, on the political left and right. Serving on government committees and conducting research on heredity, experts warned that if the nation did not produce more fit children, it was headed for extinction. A growing segment, linking eugenics to race, championed "Nordics" as a "eugenically advantageous" race and discussed "race mixing" as a source of biological degeneration.

German supporters of eugenics were part of an international phenomenon. The English scientist Francis Galton had coined the term "eugenics," meaning "good birth," in 1883. German biologist August Weissmann's 1892 theory of "immutable germ plasm" fostered growing international support for eugenics, as did the rediscovery in 1900 of Aus-

trian botanist Gregor Mendel's theory that the biological makeup of organisms was determined by certain "factors" that were later identified with genes. The term "gene" was first used by a Danish scientist in 1909.

The United States was at the forefront of eugenics: Connecticut banned anyone "epileptic, imbecile or feeble-minded" from marrying in 1896; Indiana passed a eugenic sterilization law in 1907; in 1927 the U.S. Supreme Court ruled in *Buck v. Bell* that it was legal to forcibly sterilize intellectually disabled patients. Perhaps most notoriously, in 1932 the U.S. Public Health Service partnered with the Tuskegee Institute (University) in a study titled "The Effects of Untreated Syphilis in the Negro Male." The medical officials deliberately lied to and withheld treatment from approximately six hundred black sharecroppers in Alabama—a clear case of race-based eugenics linking the medical profession, university research, and the state. The study continued until 1972.

Since 1900, reform-minded advocates of eugenics worldwide had offered biological solutions to social problems common to societies experiencing urbanization and industrialization. After classifying individuals into labeled groups using the scientific methods of the day (observation, family genealogies, physical measurements, and intelligence tests), they ranked the groupings from "superior" to "inferior." The political, social, and economic turmoil since the war had radicalized many German professionals and created popular support for the idea of the *Volk* as a higher good than the individual. Eugenicists criticized new and costly welfare programs as wasting national resources on the most unproductive members of society.

The war had further increased eugenicists' concerns about the loss of valuable genetic stock, based on the idea that Germans with the "best" genes volunteered for war, showed heroism during the fighting, and were consequently killed or injured at a higher rate, while those with the "worst" genes did not fight and continued to propagate. Along these lines, even the SPD's newspaper, *Vorwärts*, often wrote favorably of eugenics and estimated the war dead at 1,728,246 soldiers and 24,112 sailors—all supposedly of the best genetic stock.

Considering the growing belief that the *Volk* was more important than individual rights and needs, eugenicists argued that the state had the authority to do whatever necessary to help the *Volk*. In 1920, two leading eugenicists, Karl Binding and Alfred Hoche, published the influential treatise *Permitting the Destruction of Life Unworthy of Living* (see Supplemental Documents: Karl Binding and Alfred Hoche, *Permitting the Destruction of Life*):

> If one imagines a battlefield strewn with thousands of dead young men . . . and if, at the same time, one juxtaposes that image with our mental asylums, with their care for their living inmates—one is deeply shaken by the shocking discordance between the sacrifice of the finest examples of humanity on the largest scale, on the one hand, and by the greatest care that is devoted to lives that are not only absolutely worthless, but even of negative value, on the other hand.[26]

Their solution to the economic burden of institutionalized patients was their elimination. The Hippocratic Oath was a vestige of "ancient times." Instead, a "higher civil morality" had to consider the health of the state and abandon the unconditional preservation of valueless lives.

In 1921, the German Society for Race Hygiene advocated a eugenics program that favored voluntary sterilization, which became the most common proposal for preventing unproductive "inferiors" from reproducing and for saving on costs of special care and education.

Voluntary sterilization was already customary in the Free State of Saxony in the 1920s. In 1923, Gustav Boeters, a medical officer in Zwickau, revealed that he and other surgeons had been sterilizing the intellectually disabled without their consent. Seeking legal sanction for such practices, he publicized a proposed model law in a number of newspapers and offered it to the government of Saxony for consideration. The so-called Lex Zwickau was not adopted, but the medical profession continued to discuss the matter throughout the 1920s (see Supplemental Documents: Lex Zwickau, Proposed Eugenics Law).

The Women's Movements, International Women's Day, and Mother's Day

If eugenicists frequently discussed "negative eugenics" (preventing the unfit from reproducing), they also emphasized "positive eugenics" (encouraging the fit to reproduce). Here, they focused on motherhood and found an even wider base of support grounded in fears of moral degeneracy, changing gender norms, and even national demographic decline. These concerns were even integrated into Article 119 of the constitution, which called for the "preservation and increase of the nation . . . [and] the purity, health, and social welfare of the family" and stated that "families of many children shall have the right to compensatory public assistance." These issues once again fit into a broader context of women's rapidly changing position in German society since the late nineteenth century.

Men dominated Germany's unification process after 1871 and gave priority to the fatherland theme and related male issues such as military prowess and patriarchy. Nevertheless, formal organizations for promoting women's rights grew in number before the war. Women of all political views began to network and participated in the growth of international organizations. These organizations reflected the broader political fragmentation in Germany. Separate organizational streams with differing ideological goals emerged between liberal feminism, socialism (and later communism), conservative Christianity, and *völkisch* movements—divisions that continued in the Republic.

Middle-class liberals promoted political emancipation and claimed leadership over the suffrage and broader feminist movement, but were far from radical, promoting maternal clichés and **bourgeois** responsibilities. But they worked diligently toward equality with men in such areas as education, financial opportunities, and political life.

> **Bourgeois** values are the materialistic values and conventional attitudes of the middle class, the bourgeoisie. In Marxist terminology, this is the ruling class under capitalism—the wealthy capitalists who own the means of production, especially industry.

Working-class women traditionally were not welcome in the liberal feminist movement. Instead, socialists organized proletarian women separately. Their goals were more radical: they demanded free access to contraception and abortion and reform of divorce laws, and asserted that "Your body belongs to you." Marxists especially demanded rights and protections for female workers and their children. Yet, in a clear reflection of bourgeois domesticity, they also supported a "family wage" that would ensure that the (male) worker earned enough to provide for his family so that his wife could stay at home.

Still other women's groups were organized around religious faiths and integrated patriarchal views. According to these movements, women should maintain their traditional, indeed divinely created roles as wives and mothers within monogamous marriage. Women were regarded as the basis of morality and had to be protected and honored—but within patriarchal contexts.

Conservative women generally adhered to established faith communities, and they also actively engaged with the various secular national conservative and even *völkisch* movements. For example, the women-dominated German National Association of Commercial Employees remained vocally antifeminist and antisocialist, as well as *völkisch*, antisemitic, and pan-German. Indeed, one branch of this movement interpreted women in the context of the nation-state and militarism as part of the *völkisch* Right, for whom women were the biological basis of the future. They had to bear as many sons and daughters as possible for the future—the sons for the military, the daughters to raise the next generation of sons. Drawing on eugenicist ideas, völkisch thinkers argued that Germany's rapidly declining birth rate meant that Germany was being "outbred" by its rivals—especially the Slavs. As a corollary, this movement increasingly emphasized selective breeding to ensure that children were congenitally fit and racially pure.

In reality, little opportunity existed for women of these different milieus to work together. Yet, by the end of the Kaiserreich, many German women and men were demanding female suffrage. In the wake of the November Revolution of 1918, they succeeded when Article 109 of the constitution stated, "Men and women have the same fundamental civil rights and duties." Consequently, the majority of the electorate became female, in part because so many men died in the war or were so physically or psychologically wounded that they were unlikely to vote. In 1919, the first year women could vote in Germany, they secured 10 percent of the seats in the Reichstag.

Although the devastating consequences of the war provided the immediate context, the shift in women's roles had been underway for decades. While the proportion of working women remained about the same as before the war, women began to take new kinds of jobs previously dominated by men. They occupied more jobs that were socially visible, such as tram conductors and department store clerks, as well as (in smaller numbers) factory workers, lawyers, and doctors. While many of these positions returned to men in the postwar decade, women also moved into professions where they became firmly established, especially teaching, social work, and secretarial work. More than eleven million women were employed in Germany in 1918 at the war's end, accounting for 36 percent of the workforce.

As women gained more power in both society and government, some exercised freedoms unimaginable before the war. Everyone discussed the emergence of a New Woman and a new family (see Supplemental Documents: Paula von Reznicek). The psychologist Alice Rühle-Gerstel commented:

> Women began to cut an entirely new figure. A new economic figure who went out into public economic life as an independent worker or wage-

earner entering the free market that had up until then been open only for men. A new political figure who appeared in the parties and parliaments, at demonstrations and gatherings. A new physical figure who not only cut her hair and shortened her skirts but began to emancipate herself altogether from the physical limitations of being female. Finally, a new intellectual-psychological figure who fought her way out of the fog of sentimental ideologies and strove toward a clear, objective knowledge of the world and the self.[27]

Yet these New Women were a small minority with a presence limited to the large cities. The countryside remained wed to traditional views. Most Germans regarded the New Woman as the embodiment of moral decadence and a threat to social stability (see Supplemental Documents: "Enough Now").

Hopes for economic gains and a stronger voice in politics went unfulfilled. War veterans reclaimed their jobs and their expectations to be the family breadwinners, with the almost universal backing of all parties and business leaders. The slogan *Kinder, Küche, Kirche* (Children, Kitchen, Church) was promoted as the proper path for German women, which would reestablish the stability and prosperity destroyed by the war. Indeed, even Article 119 of the constitution referred to motherhood as under the "protection and public assistance of the state."

The mainstream goal became not to achieve full equality or emancipation but to make motherhood more attractive. Motherhood was upgraded from a responsibility to a calling through home economics courses, homemaker helper programs, and social work projects. In this way, politicians of the Center and the Right endeavored to make traditional roles attractive to a new generation by underwriting the father's authority and the mother's responsibility within the family.

Most German women continued to hold traditional views, criticizing younger women who adopted the liberated urban life. The better-off classes already largely confined women to the domestic sphere. The Catholic and Protestant milieus agreed with this

vision. With economic uncertainty, an increasing number of women turned toward conservative parties. These male-dominated parties welcomed them, but they were generally relegated to "women's issues" such as welfare and education. The NSDAP was unique in that it refused to allow women to serve in its Reichstag faction, though it encouraged them to join its various auxiliaries. Joseph Goebbels (NSDAP) declared,

> The National Socialist movement is the only party that keeps women out of daily politics . . . not because we see something less valuable in women, but because we see something of different value in them and their mission. . . . Things that belong to a man must remain his. To which belong politics and defense.[28]

Indeed, in a backlash against the New Woman, the percentage of women in the Reichstag actually dropped to under 7 percent in 1928.

In an important political cultural manifestation of these gender debates, three competing holidays emerged in Germany—a Communist International Women's Day, a Socialist International Women's Day, and a Mother's Day divided between liberal, Christian, conservative, and eugenically oriented *völkisch* fascist movements.

In 1910, the German socialist Clara Zetkin proposed an International Women's Day at the Second International Socialist Women's Conference in Copenhagen. The idea came from the United States, where women of the American Socialist Party decided in 1908 to initiate a special national day for women's suffrage. The first International Women's Day was then celebrated on 19 March 1911 in Germany, as well as Denmark, Austria-Hungary, and Switzerland. The date highlighted the revolutionary character of the observance because 18 March was the day of remembrance for the March Revolution of 1848; in addition, the Paris Commune had begun in March 1871. Speakers made these connections explicit. With the declaration of the Republic in November 1918, however, it seemed that Women's Day might cease to exist after the provisional government proclaimed full suffrage for men and women, thus fulfilling the pre-war demands of International Women's Day.

But the Russian and German Revolutions had deepened cleavages in the socialist camp. In 1921, the KPD introduced 8 March as an international day of remembrance for women who had launched the Russian Revolution. Zetkin became a member of the KPD and took Women's Day with her. The KPD's Women's Day motto was: "Against Reactionary Social Policies! Against Fascism! For Protection of Labor! For International Understanding! For the Solidarity of the International Proletariat!" It served as a platform for demands for shorter working hours without wage reductions, for lower food prices, for regular school meals, and for legal abortion.

The SPD had to start from scratch, but it refused in 1919 and again in 1920 to reinstate its own Women's Day, fearing it would be too radical. Not until 1923 did they reintroduce their International Women's Day, but it had no set date and was not implemented until 1926. From then on, there were two competing International Women's Days.

Conservative women launched a vigorous defense of older gender roles, but just as the Marxists split, so, too, did the non-Marxists. Liberals, Christians, and *völksich* conservatives presented differing views that had in common only a rejection of Marxism. Yet they found tenuous agreement on the idea of a Mother's Day to rival International Women's Day.

Mother's Day was a relatively new idea, again largely based on a U.S. model. The National Association of Florists began advertising a Mother's Day in its shop windows in 1923, from a seemingly apolitical perspective—the ostensible goal was to sell more flowers—and beginning that year some smaller towns initiated official Mother's Day celebrations. A few years later, a national movement emerged to request that the Reichstag institute a national holiday.

Starting in 1926, the florists engaged the Cooperative for Racial Recovery to run its national campaign. The choice was not a coincidence since the head of the Association, Dr. Rudolf Knauer, had linked the proposed holiday to "the inner conflict of our *Volk* and the loosening of the family"—code words for conservative Christian morality as well as eugenics.[29] Indeed, the Cooperative had a clear agenda. It promoted *völkisch* eugenics to counteract the decline in German population growth by promoting larger families, in part through a glorification of motherhood. In 1927, it advertised that a "woman's proper role" was "at the side of her husband as a priestess at her oven and mother to a horde of children." Its leader, Hans Harmsen, led the Evangelical Special Conference for Eugenics. Its goal was to increase the rate of childbirth among congenitally healthy "racial" Germans while simultaneously freeing the nation from "destructive genetic material." This meant prioritizing the number of children in the "genetically valuable and socially productive classes" in order to offset the fecundity of the "inept, inferior population groups." Women, therefore, were to be educated to follow their "natural occupation" as mothers.[30] Consequently, abortion, contraception, sexual liberation, and divorce were to be abolished, while euthanasia was promoted.

The Protestant Salvation Army popularized the idea, and the churches embraced it as reinforcing a woman's Christian duty as mother and wife. Nationalist conservatives linked it to militarism, especially honoring mothers of fallen soldiers for their sacrifices in the World War and promoting motherhood to ensure that women bore enough future soldiers. Even liberals, who presented a domestic ideal of woman as a stay-at-home mother who maintained the presentational propriety of the family home, could support Mother's Day (though many liberals also accepted notions of formal political equality and many liberal middle-class women were New Women).

Race and Culture

Given the deep divisions on other identity issues, it was little wonder that the Republic found no consensus on matters of race and culture. In fact, debates on race and culture became tied to questions of citizenship, of who was really German.

Legally, German citizenship was based on the principle of jus sanguinis, where citizenship was determined or acquired by the nationality of one's parents. On 22 July 1913, the Nationality Law of the German Empire and States established that "a German is one who possesses citizenship in a state or immediate citizenship in the realm." However, it did not add any further clarification. Thus the Kaiserreich had no restrictive *völkisch* conceptualization of race in this legal definition. During the Republic, however, the praxis of naturalization of a growing number of foreigners increasingly addressed the matter. Offices were established that issued German Diaspora Certificates to authenticate the German ancestry of noncitizens. Guidelines were surreptitiously issued that established the distinction between "German descent" and "foreign descent," whereby those of German descent were privileged. These secret guidelines also included a further attribute of "culturally alien," which singled out Jews, former colonial subjects, and political leftists to exclude them from naturalization.[31] In effect, a racial, cultural, and political litmus test existed in fact if not in law.

The "Jewish Question"

Though various Germans questioned the citizenship rights of Slavs (especially Poles), Africans, foreign-born aliens, and those judged eugenically unfit, the most heated debate focused on Jews. Jews had exercised full rights as citizens since the creation of the Kaiserreich, and Article 135 of the constitution ended all religious-based restrictions. The general process of assimilation and acculturation, well under way in the nineteenth century, accelerated under the Republic. The success of Jewish Germans spoke for itself. Out of nine German Nobel Prize winners, five, including Albert Einstein, were Jews.

But cultural biases ran deep. Christian churches had long promoted hostility toward Jews, and German culture, like most of Western culture, simply updated medieval anti-Jewish tropes to fit the modern era. The most significant change in anti-Jewish attitudes was its fusion with a racialized social Dar-

winism after 1880 to create antisemitism—the belief that Jews were a racially distinct and destructive group rather than a religious or cultural group. The growth of antisemitism, especially among the nationalist and *völkisch* parties, challenged the status of Jews, which had been improving since the French Revolution. Since earlier bigotry had targeted Jews as religiously or culturally different, conversion or assimilation could end their discrimination. But antisemites regarded Jews as a separate race who could never be German. Indeed, the Kaiserreich had even seen the rise of antisemitism as a political platform in a number of parties, some built primarily around the issue.

Further, antisemites promoted conspiracy theories that Jews were behind every possible scheme to enslave Germany: they had created democracy to destroy traditional authority; Marxism to destroy capitalism; civil liberty to allow them to infiltrate society; and international finance to manipulate the nations of the world into the World War. All of this was ostensibly part of a global plot to enslave Germany and the world, a plot allegedly exposed in *The Protocols of the Elders of Zion*, a wildly successful book fabricated by the Russian secret police under the last tsar to scapegoat Jews. All of this fit well with the stab-in-the-back conspiracy theory.

Politicians in every party except the Marxists and DDP (and even in those parties, on occasion) regularly resorted to anti-Jewish and increasingly antisemitic rhetoric—some, such as the Centre, subtly, others, such as the NSDAP and DNVP, blatantly. The Reichswehr had an unofficial policy of not admitting Jews, even though Jews had served Germany loyally in the war. Ultimately, an almost casual prejudice against Jews permeated society—Jews were simply regarded as different, not fully German, regardless whether by religion, culture, or race.

The resulting conflict over Jews' Germanness was fought not just in public propaganda but also in the courts, where Jews successfully prosecuted antisemites using antidefamation laws (see Supplemental Documents: German Penal Code §166). For example, Joseph Goebbels (NSDAP) was twice sentenced for religious-based attacks on the vice president of the Berlin police force, Bernhard Weiss (a Jew and DDP member). NSDAP publicist, scandalmonger, and conspiracy theorist Julius Streicher was repeatedly taken to court for religious libel and incitement to violence for his antisemitic harangues and cartoons in *Der Stürmer* (The Attacker).[32] The penal code, however, specified defamation based only on insults to one's beliefs. It did not have a clause that specifically criminalized defamation based on one's race, which opened up a legal defense whereby antisemites could claim that they were not attacking Judaism as a religion or Jewish cultural practices but Jews as a race.

Anti-Jewish bigotry thus took many forms. Some Germans such as the NSDAP were avowed antisemites. They saw Jews as a fundamentally different and destructive race. Other were hostile to Jews for cultural or religious reasons. But many defended Jews as full citizens and true Germans.

Marxists and liberal democrats argued that Jews were citizens with equal rights (see Supplemental Documents: August Bebel, "Antisemitism," and Leo Baeck, *Essence*). Not all of them liked Jews—many were bigoted—but as an ideological point they did not reject Jews, deny their humanity, or support any restrictions on their civil liberties. They generally regarded antisemitism as an antidemocratic or anti-Marxist ideology. Quite simply, Jews were Germans first.

Catholics and Protestants saw their differences with Jews as grounded in religion (see Supplemental Documents: Good Friday Prayer and Martin Luther, *The Jews*). They were bigoted against Jews— especially in their denunciations of Jews as "Christ killers"—but they generally accepted that if a Jew converted to Christianity, they were saved and no longer a Jew. Thus Jews were not biologically distinct and were equally capable of receiving salvation. Theirs was a religious anti-Judaism that did not necessarily preclude full civil liberties for Jews.

Most conservatives disliked Jews as having a separate culture (see Supplemental Documents: Heinrich von Treitschke). They believed that Jewish values

inherently opposed German ideals such as nationalism and Christianity. These conservatives' views could be extreme, especially when linked to Martin Luther's vehement, violence-laced denunciation of Jews and Judaism, which came close to racial antisemitism. But most accepted that if a Jew embraced German culture and espoused nationalism (if they assimilated), they could plausibly be loyal Germans. Theirs was a type of socially acceptable, even casual racism that they considered so self-evident that they did not even think of themselves as racist.

But this environment had been steadily radicalized by *völkisch* movements that espoused the idea that Jews were a not just a separate religion or culture, but a biologically distinct and destructive race. Since their allegedly deleterious traits were supposedly hereditary, only a genetic solution would solve the Jewish Question. Therefore, they could not be assimilated and had to be completely isolated from Germany. This was a racial antisemitism that increasingly came to see Jews as the reason for all of Germany's suffering. In this view, purging Germany of Jews became an act of national salvation.

For all the talk, though, Jews comprised less than 1 percent of the population—only 564,000 Jewish Germans out of a total population of sixty million. Although many organized in Jewish cultural and religious organizations, they were patriotic, thoroughly assimilated, largely secular, and thought of themselves almost exclusively as Germans.

Censorship and All Quiet on the Western Front

Article 118 of the constitution was explicit: "Censorship is forbidden." However, the Republic faced regular skirmishes over calls for censorship and charges of blasphemy. Most famously, the international best seller *All Quiet on the Western Front* by Erich Maria Remarque incited a sustained press war that ended in physical violence. Published in 1929, it sold 1.5 million copies in Germany alone. A highly anticipated film version that included the new technology of sound was being made in the United States, to be released in Germany in 1930, but demands for its censorship were made even before its release (see Supplemental Documents: Request to Ban *All Quiet*).

All Quiet on the Western Front did more than present a gritty image of the World War from a veteran's perspective—it yet again forced a confrontation with the meaning of the war and the Republic that emerged from it (see Supplemental Documents: Carl Zuckmayer, Review of *All Quiet*). That subject inevitably polarized German opinion. The SPD and pacifist liberals read it as an antiwar novel and an indictment of imperial militarism; for them, it legitimized the revolution and the Republic. The KPD denounced it as liberal petit bourgeois sentimentalism and pacifism that stood in the way of real change. Most conservatives read it as an insult to the German military and nation; others condemned it for its negative portrayal of doctors, clergy, and teachers. Yet some conservatives found in Remarque's common soldiers a reflection of their own experiences at the front and read *All Quiet* as a call for a romanticized renewal of Germany based on soldierly comradeship. Indeed, some conservatives such as Ernst Jünger wrote war novels almost identical to Remarque's (e.g., *In a Storm of Steel*). On the extreme Right, however, the NSDAP labeled Remarque a traitor, accusing him of being both a Marxist and a Jew (he was neither) who should be shot. They actively disrupted distribution of the book.

In short, Germans read *All Quiet* through their preexisting political filters. Culture, as with every other aspect of Weimar, was always interpreted politically. Not surprising, then, that many called for the book's suppression.

Industrial Relations
Unemployment Insurance, Deflation, and Austerity

Regardless of the numerous pressures, the Republic took proactive steps to look after its more vulnerable citizens. After all, the primary force behind the revolution had been workers and those most vulnerable to the consequences of the war. They remained mobilized in trade unions, cultural associations, and political parties, especially the SPD and KPD, which combined polled from 33 to 45 percent nationally. Democracy required mass support, and mass support depended on satisfying this urban constituency.

The law of 16 July 1927 enlarged an already highly developed system of social insurance with compulsory unemployment insurance (see Supplemental Documents: Law on Job Placement). All insured workers were legally entitled to relief if they were able and willing to work and were unemployed through no fault of their own. Insurance contributions were made equally by the employer and the worker.

At the time the law was passed in 1927, it had the support of both a right-wing coalition government and the SPD. The Republic was in a prosperous economic phase. The unemployed rate was fairly low. Politicians calculated that the economic boom since 1924 would continue, and the scheme would be financially viable. But already in 1928 there were signs of recession, and in the winter of 1928–29 the number of unemployed rose to nearly three million. The state had a dire liquidity problem due to falling tax revenues and skyrocketing unemployment insurance payments. Since the level of relief was fixed by law and the reserves were insufficient, the government had to help out with loans.

Even before the new burdens of unemployment insurance, the government had been spending more than it received in taxes and had run deficits since 1925. And although exports had risen 40 percent since 1925, Germany spent more on imports than it earned from exports, meaning that the state was losing money every year due to the trade imbalance. In line with contemporary economic theory, liberals and most conservatives supported deflation as the correct response to an economic crisis. The goal was to prevent a return to the devastating hyperinflation of 1923, which had been caused when the state simply printed more money to cover expenses, even though less money was coming in. Instead of that approach, which was universally considered a disaster, the state proposed **austerity**—drastically cutting state expenditures, most importantly on social services and the new unemployment benefits. But austerity would also mean no spending on other additional budget items, including armored cruisers, farmers' relief, and public work projects.

Austerity is characterized by policies that aim to reduce government budget deficits through spending cuts, tax increases, or a combination of both.

Economists fully expected that the policy of deflation would temporarily worsen the economic situation before it began to improve, but there was no acceptable alternative. Deflation would lower the price of goods and services, thus increasing the German economy's competitiveness and then restoring its creditworthiness. Theoretically, all of this would result in more jobs, more state income, and the renewed ability of the state to borrow to fund social spending. Even the Allied reparations agent, Parker Gilbert, supported the deflationary approach. Ironically, many argued that this policy would have the added benefit of showing the Allies that Germany simply could not pay the reparations, forcing them to further reduce the payments.

Nationalization and Aryanization

Some argued that the state needed to do more than facilitate capitalism; they wanted it to guarantee national prosperity, good social relations, affordable living standards, and employment. The Socialization Law of 1919 promised just that (see Supplemental Documents: Socialization Law). Nationalization—having the state take over an industry—had strong roots going back to the Kaiserreich, with the state running the post office and railways. In addition, private firms organized as cartels with government encouragement to increase international competitiveness. During the war, the demands of "total war" led the state to play an even more decisive economic role. The War Ministry regulated essential raw materials, enforced agreements between workers and owners, converted consumer industries to war production, rationed industries and consumers, priori-

tized use of rail freight, set prices, and even closed theaters to save energy.

While other countries also engaged in the nationalization of industry, the Soviet Union went much farther. It eliminated private ownership in all large industries. For many, nationalization was therefore associated with Bolshevism. For others, it was simply an essential part of modernity where the state took on the responsibility for safeguarding the economic security of its people (as required by the constitution) and military viability in an era of industrial warfare. Many therefore called for nationalization, especially of the banks, to provide economic stability.

As with many issues, antisemitism bled into the nationalization question. Conservatives routinely accused Jews of running the banks and using them to oppress Germany. Some even claimed that the war was initiated by Jewish bankers who then profited from it. They denounced Jews as "internationalists" who operated out of New York and ran a world conspiracy based on their control of finance capital. These same Jews, they claimed, ran the Versailles arrangement and profited from the reparations. Further, rural Germans widely accused Jews of being the cause of their misery by exploiting them through their control of rural lending. The Jews, they argued, were the ones charging usurious rates, withholding credit, and foreclosing on their farms. Many demanded Aryanization of banks rather than nationalization. Banks would remain private, but Jews would be replaced by **Aryans**.

Aryan is a *völkisch* term for the "Germanic peoples" who were allegedly the racially purest original people who constituted a *Herrenvolk* (master race).

Agricultural Affairs
Bailing out the Junker Elite

Under the Republic, the large landowners demanded state protection, including high tariffs. These agrarian tariffs from the Kaiserreich really only applied to grain, which was mostly produced on large estates, and thus the tariffs benefited only the Junkers. In fact, tariffs led to substantial price increases on imported food and agricultural products, increasing the cost of living for urban workers. Liberals argued that tariffs also violated free trade, undermined long-term prosperity and efficiency, and decreased industrial profits since businesses had to raise wages to keep up with workers' higher costs of living.

But for the Junkers, the question of indebted large estates was existential. Due to the postwar collapse in grain prices, a failure to modernize, and the cutting off of East Prussia from Germany, the Junker estates were not profitable and had been retained only with massive private loans. Now, these estates were drowning in debt and beginning to default on their loans. Prussia and East Prussia established regional programs to ease credit. A federal law proposed a series of measures collectively known as *Osthilfe* (Eastern Aid) to provide further support by subsidizing rail freight costs, lowering local taxes, and, most importantly, allowing credit at extremely favorable terms. None of these measures helped smaller farmers and they only further distorted the agrarian economy, forced open to the world market by the treaty.

Junkers found an ideological means to rally mass support for this one-sided advantaging of their self-interests by linking grain tariffs to anti-Versailles patriotism, militarism, and antisemitism. The war had exposed the dangers of Germany's low agrarian productivity when the country failed to feed its population during the British blockade. The resulting starvation was one of the main reasons for the collapse of the home front. Nationalists now argued that grain tariffs were essential to autarky, which itself was the key to national survival. High tariffs would force Germans to rely on German production by making agrarian imports too expensive, thus stimulating domestic production. Germany would be freed from the international market, which was controlled, they frequently argued, by Jewish bankers. The trick would be to make German agriculture more productive to keep food prices down—either through more intensive methods or through acquisition of new farmland.

The Small Farmer's Plight

In reality, small farmers were largely incapable of modernizing and becoming competitive. Hyperinflation had destroyed their capital reserves, and tight credit prevented them from borrowing to purchase modern equipment and imported fertilizers and feed. Much of the credit was in the hands of U.S. banks as short-term loans with relatively high interest rates. Paying off this debt was undermined by inexpensive agricultural imports and rising taxes. In addition, the global economic recession, punctuated by the New York stock market crash in 1929, led to a national decline in demand for agrarian products as German city dwellers tightened their belts, which led to further drops in food prices.

The inevitable consequence was an increasing number of bankruptcies in the small towns that depended on agricultural trade, as well as a steadily rising number of farm **foreclosures**. Neither the government nor the associations representing agricultural interests were able to provide effective relief. The political result was a radicalization of the rural population and a splintering of agricultural special interest groups.

Foreclosure is a legal process in which a lender attempts to recover the balance of a loan from a borrower who has stopped making payments to the lender, by forcing the sale of the asset used as the collateral for the loan.

What did small farmers want, specifically? Some—any—form of relief for small farmers. Many looked for debt relief, including state loans or forgiveness of debt for small farmers facing foreclosure. Unfortunately, the government was already unable to balance its books. Furthermore, liberals viewed debt relief as a form of agrarian communism—a violation of free market principles.

Even more controversially, many demanded land reform. This meant redistributing indebted or unproductive lands of large estates to smaller famers and allowing some form of subsidized settlement in the

East. As early as 1919 the National Assembly passed a Settlement Law intended to do just that. It walked a political tightrope: appease the Left by confiscating and redistributing land from Junker estates; appease farmers by opening more land; and appease *völkisch* conservatives by moving urban youth to Germanize the rural East (see Supplemental Documents: Reich Settlement Law). The constitution clearly granted the right of public domain to the Reichstag, particularly in regard to land (see Supplemental Documents: Weimar Constitution—Economic Life). Taking such action, however, pitted vested interests against each other. Proponents saw it as putting idle and indebted land to productive use, employing Germans, lowering food prices, creating more equality, and securing the racial survival of the nation through food autarky. Opponents, however, saw this type of land reform as a violation of private property. In addition, the indebted large estates targeted by land reform belonged to people such as President von Hindenburg and the Junker elite, who had no intention of allowing their land to be appropriated.

Unable to implement meaningful reform and facing economic uncertainty, small farmers were susceptible to radical solutions. They already harbored distrust toward the Republic. The parliamentary culture of the Reichstag had little to do with the corporatist practices of rural life. But also the association of the Republic with urban Germany—especially Berlin, with its bewildering modern culture—remained alien to life in the countryside. Sexual liberation, cultural influences from Africa and America, coalition cabinets and parliamentary procedures—none of these made much sense. Moreover, many farmers, struggling with large debts and difficult banks, were receptive to the antisemitic propaganda about Jewish bankers. The stereotype of the *Kuhjude* (cow Jew), who made small loans at usurious rates and then took the family cow when the farmer defaulted, was already ingrained in the rural imagination—it offered a simple answer to a complex issue.

As a result, the *Blut und Boden* thinking of prewar romantic agrarianism continued to thrive and radi-calize. As one prominent example, the Artaman League sent urban adolescents to the countryside to work, in part to promote the physical and spiritual benefits of rural life but also in hopes of transforming them into *Wehrbauern* (soldier peasants) to fight off a feared Slavic population boom in the East (see Supplemental Documents: Fritz Hoffmann, "The Artamans"). These ideas formed an important bridge between urban conservatives and rural populations, allowing opposition to both the liberal middle class and the Junkers and presenting farm life as superior to the moral swamp of the city with its secularism and Marxism. This vague ideology, linked as it was to *völkisch* nationalism and hostility to the Republic, only pushed farmers to extremes as the agrarian crisis deepened.

Indeed, finding no support for their demands among their traditional leaders in the Junker class, small farmers launched local riots, protests, and even terrorist attacks beginning in 1928. Though localized, this Rural People's Movement engendered sympathy from the millions of Germans living in the small towns. Most of these efforts were too localized to have any national influence. To overcome these divisions, and recognizing the mobilizing potential of the movement, in February 1929 a coalition of agrarian leaders formed the Green Front to bring together the various agricultural special interest groups. They hoped that a united organization, one that might grow into a single national party, would finally allow farmers to have a powerful voice.

The conservative small farmers of the **CNBP** rejected modern culture and countered with a pronounced nostalgia for a life tied to the pre-industrial countryside.

The Green Front leader, Martin Schiele, defected from the Junker-dominated DNVP to lead the **National Christian Farmers League (CNBP)**. Schiele attempted to persuade future governments that only a cabinet that excluded socialists, addressed the needs of smaller farmers, made accommodations to large farmers, implemented austerity, and made cabinet members independent of their parties would have his support. In effect, while expressing rural needs, he also aimed at undermining the parliamentary system dominated by the SPD.

Where Does the Republic Find Itself Now?

Now, in 1929, the revolutionary wave that overthrew the Kaiserreich has long since crested. Despite strains, the economy has recovered. Germany stands poised to reassert its rightful place as the leading nation of the European continent.

Internationally, Germany is slowly but surely reintegrating into world politics through a series of small but significant concessions. Germany, France, Belgium, the United Kingdom, and Italy signed the Treaty of Locarno in 1925, which recognized Germany's borders with France and Belgium and effectively normalized diplomatic relations in the West. In 1926 the League of Nations subsequently admitted Germany. The Dawes Plan lowered reparations in 1924; the final amount is no longer linked to Allied demands but Germany's ability to pay. The Young Plan, if passed, will lower payments yet again.

Economically, the introduction of a new currency and other economic reforms have led to improvements. Industrial production has regained prewar levels. Trade is strong, driven by Germany's continued dominance in engineering, chemicals, optics, and steel. Reparations, though insulting, have proven no real burden to the economy. True, agriculture lags behind, but farm efficiency is increasing. Global economic depression has heightened tensions between workers and owners, but once the economy gets back on track, the rising tide should lift all boats.

Intellectually, Germany leads the world in the sciences. German recipients dominate the Nobel prizes, especially in physics. Chemistry, likewise, relies on German professors and researchers at the great chemical concerns such as BASF and Bayer. Carl Benz rivals Henry Ford as the inventor of the automobile, and German engineering innovation is the envy of the world. The German university system, especially its graduate seminar model, is institutionalizing itself internationally. Little wonder that, on average, ten thousand U.S. students travel to Germany every year to attend its prestigious universities.

Culturally, writers such as Thomas Mann, Hermann Hesse, and Bertolt Brecht have unrivaled international stature. German historians have redefined the academic discipline. Oswald Spengler has found international fame with his *The Decline of the West* and its portrayal of the inevitable decay of Western civilization. In philosophy, Martin Heidegger, Max Scheler, and the Frankfurt School influence intellectuals around the world. The visual and performing arts, including such new forms as cinematography, are not just innovative but commercially successful internationally.

Socially, Berlin rivals Paris and New York as a center of nightlife. A libertine sensibility dominates the image of the capital, with its lascivious cabarets, African American jazz music, and open gay scene. Indeed, Germany has become the center of the entirely new field of sexology. Women have full legal equality, and laws on abortion and homosexuality have been liberalized.

Politically, even though the presidential election of 1925 brought the monarchist von Hindenburg to office, many liberals and socialists voted for him out of a sense of national loyalty. Indeed, von Hindenburg has shown himself willing to tolerate the Republic and lend his unsurpassed credibility to the state, despite his regularly expressed sympathies for the DNVP and hostility to the Versailles system. Political violence seems a thing of the past. Radical parties such as the NSDAP and the KPD find few supporters. The last coup attempt, in 1923 by Adolf Hitler's regionally marginal NSDAP, has laughingly been labeled the Beer Hall Putsch, more theater than threat.

Reichstag Election of 1928

The Reichstag election of 1928 has validated this new sense of confidence and stability. The SPD remains the largest party after winning 153 of the 491 seats—almost a third of the votes in an election contested by over forty parties (see fig. 4).

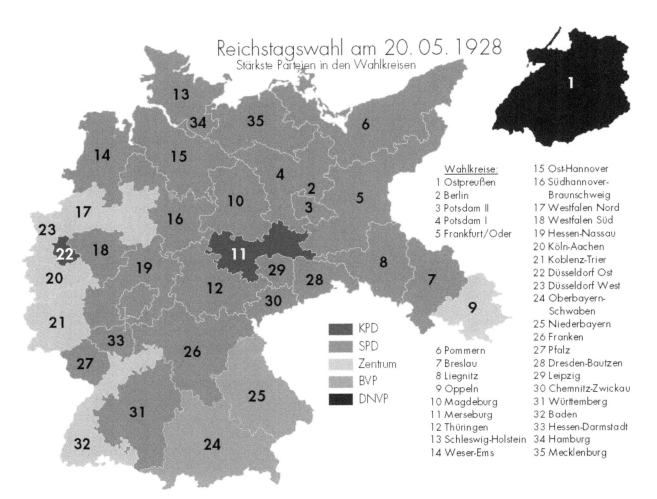

FIGURE 4 1928 election results by district, shaded according to the party with largest share of the vote.

Alex Kireev, "Weimar Germany. Legislative Election 1928," Electoral Geography 2.0, 2007, https://www.electoralgeography .com/new/en/countries/g/germany/weimar-germany-legislative-election-1928.html.

Voter turnout was 75.6 percent, providing the pro-Republic coalition led by the SPD with a solid mandate. Indeed, the only other party to gain significantly was the KPD. True, the two main Marxist parties may loathe each other, but their combined electoral victories (totaling 42 percent of Reichstag mandates) represent a significant turn away from the right-wing policies of the early 1920s. Radical right-wing parties have been marginalized; the NSDAP won only twelve seats, and the DNVP lost thirty seats. Prussia, by far the largest state in Germany, is an even stronger SPD stronghold ruled by an SPD-led coalition.

Figure 5 reveals that the center-left victory is none-theless tenuous. The conservative nationalist parties (DNVP, DVP, BVP, and other smaller right-wing parties) remain powerful (the NSDAP is represented separately by black). No majority center-right coalition is possible with just the conservative nationalist parties, but neither is a center-left without defections from the conservative nationalist block. The ruling Grand Coalition in 1928 consequently includes both the DVP and the Centre Party's conservative Bavarian offshoot, the **Bavarian People's Party (BVP)**. The coalition has suffered from internal divisions, but a general sense of compromise and confidence has pervaded under the firm but compromising hand of

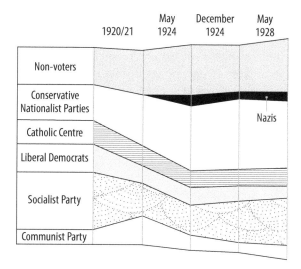

FIGURE 5 Composition of the Reichstag, 1920–1928.

Adapted from Friedrich Arnold Krummacher and Albert Wucher, eds., *Die Weimarer Republik: Ihre Geschichte in Texte, Bilder, und Dokumente, 1918–1933* (Munich: Kurt Desch, 1965), 141.

Stresemann. Most in the government hope his recent death will not mean the end of the coalition.

The **Bavarian People's Party (BVP)** was a Bavarian offshoot of the Centre Party that leaned farther to the right and supported a strong degree of regional autonomy—at times, even independence for Bavaria.

Continuity with the Kaiserreich

Despite the abdication of the kaiser, the November Revolution, and the creation of a new constitution, the Republic must also cope with a great number of continuities from the Kaiserreich. Neither the agrarian nor the industrial economy has undergone a deep restructuring, despite a series of reforms that supposedly protect workers and peasants. The Reichstag largely continues the same parliamentary party alliances as before. The position of the Reich president is consciously viewed as a substitute for the kaiser. And the old elite insist on the maintenance of their social and cultural distinctions—for example, keeping the nobiliary particles "von" or "zu" in their family names even though hereditary nobility has been abolished.

Further, all of the leading politicians grew up under and were shaped by the Kaiserreich and its aristocratic, authoritarian militarism. In the ten years since the collapse of the Kaiserreich, there has been surprisingly little change in personnel in any of the key institutions. The same people continue to dominate the schools and universities, the Reichswehr, and the judiciary. Almost all of the civil servants served in those institutions before the revolution.

Individuals who had been at the top of the socioeconomic ladder under the Kaiserreich remain ensconced and unwilling to share that status. Bourgeois employers persist in their implacable hostility to unions. Aristocrats look down on the bourgeoisie. Protestants doubt the loyalty of Catholics. The military opposes any reform of its officer corps. Antisemitism thrives in all but the Marxist and left-liberal parties. Junkers demand and receive special preference for their estates, even as smaller farms struggle. In fact, much of one's attitudes toward the Republic depends on whether one was a winner or a loser in the Kaiserreich; the old elites resent the changes and express a corresponding hostility to the Republic. They look nostalgically to the past.

On the other hand, newly empowered groups—workers, women, Jews, socialists, bourgeoisie—place their hopes in the Republic. In short, the Republic is based as much on continuity with an authoritarian past as on hopes for a democratic future.

Late 1929

And now we find ourselves in the autumn of 1929. President von Hindenburg began the year with the traditional New Year's message, a custom dating back to the kaiser. His tone expressed the sullen resentment of many, especially regarding the Treaty of Versailles:

The entire German people greets today the beginning of the new year with deep bitterness, because a great part of our land is denied the freedom to which we have just claim—just in God's eyes and in man's eyes. We have long hoped for its attainment. And we still want to hope, despite harsh disappointment, that in the new year the German people will be given back its full right of self-determination.[33]

Since then, new crises have wracked the Republic. The stock market crash on Wall Street has produced a global shock wave. Foreign creditors have begun withdrawing loans, threatening insolvency in German companies, national default on reparation payments, and soaring unemployment. In late 1928, Stresemann warned, "The economic position is only flourishing on the surface. Germany is in fact dancing on a volcano. If the short-term credits are called in, a large section of our economy would collapse."[34]

The Grand Coalition partners have been attempting to agree on the best way to deal with the growing economic crisis, which is exacerbating differences on matters from foreign policy to cultural policy. The anti-Republic parties of the Left and Right (the KPD, NSDAP, and the DNVP) seem to be gaining strength. Stresemann's death at this critical moment accentuates the sense of parliamentary crisis.

Are the Golden Twenties over? Will Germany return to the political chaos and economic insecurity of the early 1920s? Does the NSDAP plan to seize power like the fascists did in Italy under Mussolini? Is the KPD planning another communist revolution? Will the Reichswehr continue to support the constitution? Will France, Poland, or the Soviet Union take advantage of this deepening crisis?

3
The Game

The game unfolds across three years from late 1929 to the end of 1932; a game session is equivalent to roughly half a year.

MAJOR ITEMS FOR DEBATE

The debates fall into several broad categories, each subordinated to a cabinet member's portfolio (see table 2). All "mandatory items" must occur on the agenda at the start of the corresponding session and cannot be avoided. All "discretionary items" must be fought for to be placed on the agenda. Victory conditions are tied to the mandatory and discretionary items (see "Agenda").

If you read the game materials, you should be well prepared:

- The "Historical Background" provides the broad context for the issues.
- The "Core Texts" introduce the main ideological frameworks.
- The "Supplemental Documents" provide specifics to each issue.
- Faction-specific readings (provided by the GM) give a party perspective on each issue.
- Your role sheet details your particular stance and goal.
- The role sheet and bibliography suggest extra readings to round out your views.

Foreign Relations (Foreign Ministry)
Foreign policy debates revolve around how Germany should relate to the Versailles system.

The Freedom Law: The Freedom Law would make any cooperation with Versailles a treasonable offense. Can Germany risk offending the world community in the name of German honor?

The Young Plan: The Young Plan would modify reparation payments and awaits Reichstag ratification. Would passing the Young Plan make reparations manageable or only kick the can down the road and simultaneously grant legitimacy to reparation payments?

The Liquidation Treaty with Poland: The treaty resolves trade issues and limits the transfer of German property in Poland to Poles. Is this simply validating the annexation of German territory?

Military Affairs (Defense Ministry)

Within the restrictions of Versailles, the Reichstag must grapple with the role of the largely autonomous Reichswehr, national security, and nongovernmental paramilitaries.

Naval bill: The military demands full funding of three armored cruisers. Can an increased military budget be justified when social spending is being cut and would it risk the ire of the Allies?

Paramilitaries: Political street violence is escalating. Should the Reichstag or president ban paramilitaries? A permanent ban would be a constitutional change and require a two-thirds majority.

2nd and 3rd naval bills: Since the naval funding bill is an annual expenditure, it must come up in two later sessions as a discretionary item to continue funding; otherwise, funding stops.

Sexuality and Eugenics (Justice Ministry)

Modernization has challenged every notion of gender, sexual norms, reproduction, and national health, eliciting visceral responses.

Mother's Day versus International Women's Day: Competing visions of womanhood mean competing visions of a woman-centered national holiday. Can the Reichstag agree on what it means to be a German woman?

Eugenics: The proposed Lex Zwickau advocates sterilization for various categories of people deemed "unproductive." Is this a great advance for national health or a descent into immorality?

Race and Culture (Interior Ministry)

Germans disagree on who is rightfully German and thus entitled to citizenship with some proposing restrictions based on politics, religion, or even race. Others argue that the only way to unify Germany is to unify culture through censorship.

Antisemitism and the "Jewish Question": No legislation restricting the rights of Jews has ever been proposed, but the strength of *völksich* nationalism makes it a constant national issue. Should the Reichstag take a clear stance?

Censorship and *All Quiet on the Western Front*: Everyone is talking about the book and movie. Should the Reichstag intervene to limit or possibly expand freedom of expression in this and future cases?

Industrial Relations (Economics Ministry)

In the growing economic crisis, scarce resources must be rationed against competing demands from the unemployed, agrarian constituents, big business, and the military.

Austerity: The budget is limited but unemployment is skyrocketing. Should unemployment insurance benefits to workers be cut to balance the looming deficit?

Nationalization of the banks: Many blame international banks for the economic crisis. Should the state step in and nationalize private property in the national interest? Should this include Aryanization of the banks by removing Jews from ownership?

Agricultural Affairs (Food Ministry)

The agrarian crisis has fractured the countryside, and calls for state intervention mount as rural foreclosures lead to violence and the specter of urban hunger.

Grain tariffs: The powerful Junker class insists upon high tariffs to protect their estates from international competition, even if this raises food costs, drains state coffers, and does nothing for small farmers. Should the state placate this important constituency at this high cost?

Small farmers' relief: Debt forgiveness or subsidized loans would protect small farmers from foreclosure, and land reform would confiscate and redistribute unproductive land. Would this only further distort the agrarian economy and violate property rights as a form of agro-Bolshevism?

TABLE 2 Major items for debate

| Theme | Ministry | ITEMS | | |
		Mandatory	Session	Discretionary
Foreign relations	Foreign	Freedom Law	1	Liquidation Treaty
		Young Plan	2	
Military affairs	Defense	1st naval bill	1	Paramilitaries
				2nd and 3rd naval bills
Sexuality and eugenics	Justice*	Mother's Day	5	Eugenic sterilization***
Race and culture	Interior	Antisemitism***	4	*All Quiet . . .*
Industrial relations	Economic	Austerity	2	Nationalization
Agricultural affairs	Food**	Grain tariffs	3	Small farmers' relief

*Inquiry committees also come under the purview of the justice minister.

**In games where the BVP (Bavarian People's Party) is not in play, the Food Ministry comes under the Economics Ministry.

***In games where antisemitism is eliminated, eugenic sterilization replaces it as a mandatory item. In such a case, it comes under the purview of the interior minister (rather than justice).

RULES AND PROCEDURES

Victory Objectives and Conditions

Your role sheet provides two sets of victory objectives (Factional—your party goals; and Personal—your individual goals). You should play to win the game in the same sense that politicians seek to get their agenda passed. Achieving your victory objectives may seem impossible, but the game situation is highly fluid, even unstable. Anything is possible with alliances, negotiations, success at the polls, dogged determination, successful propaganda, changing circumstances, and plain luck. Compromises are often necessary, but so is holding to principle. Sometimes simply staying in the game is a victory in itself.

Stability Index

The Stability Index abstractly represents the sense of crisis. The Index also reflects the degree to which forces that support the Republic versus those opposed are dominating events. Various events and actions cause the Index to rise or fall. The GM will provide regular updates. There are three categories for the Index:

- HIGH = > 50
- NEUTRAL = −50 to +50
- LOW = < −50

The Index begins at +50, reflecting the successes of the Republic since 1924.

The Index has ramifications for the following:

- Reichstag elections (high favors pro-Republicans, low favors anti-Republicans)
- Presidential election (high favors pro-Republicans, low favors anti-Republicans)
- Chances for an insurrection's success
- Your character's victory conditions

Formal Structures of the Republic

The constitution states, "The German Commonwealth is a Republic. Political authority is derived from the People." However, the actual power hierarchy is a complicated semipresidential system in which power is divided between the president, cabinet, and Reichstag, as expressed in the flowchart of the Republic's basic power arrangement (fig. 6). Solid arrows indicate direct authority, dashed lines indirect.

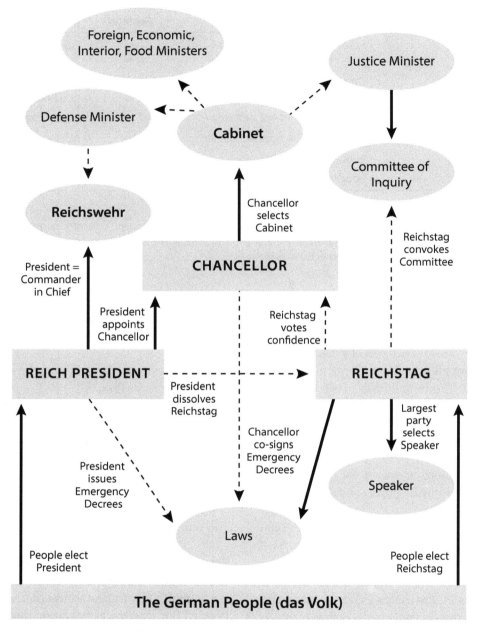

FIGURE 6 Flowchart of Republican institutions.

Image created by Robert Goodrich.

The German people (*das Volk*)
- Elect the president every seven years
- Elect the Reichstag at least every four years

The Reichstag
- Makes laws, grants amnesties, convenes inquiry committees
- Votes confidence in the chancellor, cabinet, individual ministers, or Speaker
- Selects the Speaker (chosen by the largest party)

The Speaker
- Controls debate and the agenda

The Reich president
- Issues emergency decrees
- Appoints the chancellor and approves the cabinet
- Dissolves the Reichstag and calls for elections
- Serves as commander in chief of the Reichswehr

The chancellor
- Selects the cabinet
- Countersigns emergency decrees

The cabinet (aka "the government")
- Deliberates on all matters and proposes legislation
- Ministers control portfolios and present relevant ministerial reports
- Defense minister communicates with the Reichswehr
- Justice minister oversees inquiry committees

The Reichswehr (the military)
- Answers to the president
- Acts autonomously from the Reichstag
- Coordinates with the Reichstag through the defense minister

The Supreme Court (embodied by the GM)
- Determines constitutionality of decisions and actions

Reich President (Head of State)

Paul von Hindenburg has been the Reich president since 1925. His popularity is immense, in part because of his reputation as the greatest German general of the war. Even many socialists and National Socialists find him appealing as a symbol of German pride.

The president does not directly shape legislation or exercise executive authority; these are left to the Reichstag and chancellor, respectively. However, the president does have a considerable amount of power, including

Appointing the chancellor as head of government and approving the cabinet (Article 53).

Granting amnesty or pardon to anyone for any reason (Article 49).

Calling for new elections to the Reichstag at any time after the beginning of the second session (Article 25).

Issuing emergency decrees. These must be countersigned by the chancellor. The president may take emergency measures without the prior consent of the Reichstag. This power includes the promulgation of emergency decrees that amount to martial law and the temporary suspension of constitutional rights. The president, in cooperation with the chancellor, may, in effect, rule without the Reichstag, but the Reichstag may nullify emergency decrees (Articles 48 and 50).

Presidential Government—The 25/48/53 Formula

There is the constitutional possibility of a constitutional but antidemocratic "presidential government" based on the so-called 25/48/53 formula, which refers to the three articles of the constitution that could make a presidential government possible. Article 53 allows the Reich president to appoint the chancellor. Article 48 allows the Reich president to sign into law emergency bills without the consent of the Reichstag; the chancellor must simply countersign them. Article 25 allows the president to dissolve the Reichstag if it overturns an emergency decree. In effect, the president could appoint a chancellor regardless of whether or not they control a majority in the Reichstag, as a minority government, and rule through emergency decrees without the Reichstag (see fig. 7).

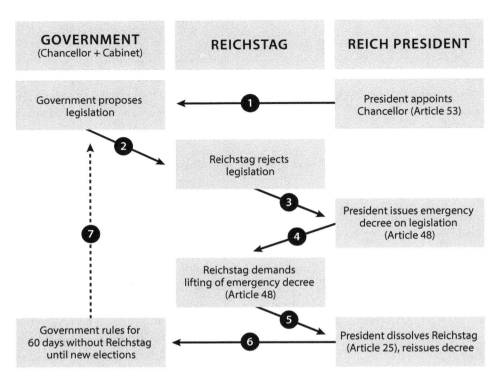

FIGURE 7 Flowchart of a presidential government

Image created by Robert Goodrich.

Presidential Election

The president is elected separately from the Reichstag and directly by all German citizens to a seven-year term. A regular presidential election must be held in April 1932 (the penultimate game session) unless a presidential recall has occurred. A presidential candidate must be a German citizen and may not be a member of the Reichstag. If a member of the Reichstag is elected, that member must resign from the Reichstag, but their party does not lose any votes.

NB: There is no constitutional mechanism to delay the scheduled presidential election except for a recall (see "Presidential Recall").

A presidential election will run as follows:

ROUND 1

Every player develops an election poster for their ideal candidate (even if that candidate does not run).

- Campaign materials are produced PRIOR to the election (usually due in session 5 for elections in session 6).
- Posters may be hung in class or otherwise distributed.
- The GM (or class, at GM's discretion) ranks the posters prior to the election.

Candidates are announced and a secret vote is taken.

- Players designate their current votes (splitting, abstaining, or all for one candidate). Since it is a secret ballot, there is no party discipline.
- The GM makes adjustments based on ranking of posters and the Stability Index before announcing results.
- The winner requires a simple majority of votes cast.

- If no one wins an absolute majority, a second round is required.

ROUND 2

Any party with a candidate in the first round may choose to drop out or run a substitute candidate (but no new party or independent may put forward a candidate). It is possible for a candidate to run as unaffiliated, with the consent of one of the parties that ran a candidate in the first round but now withdraws their candidate and gives permission for the new candidate to run in their stead, even without using the party's affiliation.

This second round occurs after a brief recess to allow caucusing, and it follows the same procedure as the first round.

- The winner does not require a majority but a plurality (highest number of votes).
- In the event of a tie, the presiding president will cast one vote. The new president immediately takes office.

Upon election, the president must make the following presidential oath in front of the Reichstag, according to Article 42 of the constitution:

I swear to devote my energy to the welfare of the German people, to increase its prosperity, to prevent damage, to uphold the Reich constitution and its laws, to consciously honor my duties, and to exercise justice to every individual.

Presidential Recall

A presidential recall has three steps.

1. Reichstag vote. Two-thirds of the Reichstag must vote for a recall. If the vote is unsuccessful, nothing happens; the regular presidential election will occur as scheduled in the penultimate session. If successful, the president may not exercise their powers, which devolve onto the chancellor, until a referendum is resolved.

2. Referendum. The GM supervises a referendum by secret ballot, following the rules for a presidential election but with only one round and a simple "yes" or "no" for the current president. The question reads: "Shall the current Reich president remain in office?" This referendum must pass by a simple majority.

If the referendum results in a majority "yes," the president is considered reelected for a new seven-year term; the regularly scheduled presidential elections do not occur. The Reichstag is automatically dissolved and a Reichstag election is held.

3. Presidential election. If the referendum results in a majority "no," an immediate new presidential election must occur, following all rules for a regular presidential election. Referendum posters may be reused for the presidential election.

The Camarilla

The Camarilla are the unofficial advisers around the Reich president. Von Schleicher runs the political wing of the Reichswehr and is currently the defense minister. Otto Meissner is the state secretary to the Office of the Reich President, a career bureaucrat who served loyally under the former president, the socialist Friedrich Ebert. There may be other members. Though they wield tremendous personal influence, they have no formal constitutional role in their capacity as members of the Camarilla. The Camarilla and president sit together, apart from the parties.

The Government (the Chancellor and the Cabinet)

The Chancellor

As the head of the government, the chancellor directs the work of the cabinet. Hermann Müller (SPD) is currently the chancellor of the Grand Coalition forged by Stresemann (DVP).

Although the chancellor is the head of the government, many powers of the office exist only in relationship to the president, and the Reichstag holds the chancellor accountable with its ability to motion no confidence. The chancellor does, however, have certain prerogatives, including:

- Selecting cabinet members
- Meeting with the president at any time
- Choosing to present the cabinet's position to the Reichstag on any matter
- Countersigning presidential decrees, thus exercising an effective veto power on such decrees (Articles 48 and 50)
- Fulfilling presidential functions should the president be unavailable (Article 51) or subject to a successful recall vote by the Reichstag (Article 43)

The Cabinet

The government includes the entire cabinet, comprised of the six ministry positions (portfolios) and the chancellor; there is no requirement that all of these positions be filled, and one person may fill multiple positions (see table 3). The cabinet decides government policy by majority vote.

The cabinet's primary role is to reach consensus and move legislation through the Reichstag by securing a majority in advance of any vote.

Protocol dictates that the minister with the relevant portfolio presents the government's position on any matter (unless the chancellor chooses to do so).

Members of the cabinet are expected to publicly support the cabinet's decisions, or at least refrain from public criticism—a position that may put them at odds with their party.

A minister may resign at any time, or be voted out by a Reichstag vote of no confidence against the individual, or be kicked out by the chancellor. These will not necessarily bring down the government. The chancellor may replace the vacant seat as they please.

The government collapses if one of the following happens:

- The ruling coalition loses a Reichstag majority for any reason: a party leaves the coalition; a party splits and reduces its numbers; an election changes the balance of power.
- The chancellor or the full cabinet lose a vote of no confidence in the Reichstag.

TABLE 3 Cabinet members

Chancellor	Herman Müller (SPD)*
Interior minister	Carl Severing (SPD)*
Foreign minister	Theodor Heuss (DDP)
Justice minister	Heinrich Brüning (Centre)
Defense minister	Kurt von Schleicher
Economic minister	Eduard Dingeldey (DVP)**
Food minister	Erich Emminger (BVP)**

*If there are fewer than three SPD players, Müller serves as chancellor, interior minister, and Speaker.

**If Emminger is not in play, Dingeldey heads the food and economic portfolios.

When the government collapses, the president may:

- Call on someone (including the current chancellor) to form a new government
- Call for new elections and afterward call for someone (including the current chancellor) to form a new government
- Do nothing and allow a minority government

When forming a new government, the Reichstag works on a European parliamentary model.

If a party has a majority (50 percent + 1 of votes in the Reichstag), the president usually but not necessarily calls on its leader to form a majority government.

If there is no majority party, the president usually but not necessarily calls on the leader of the largest party to form a majority coalition government with other parties (the current coalition under Müller is such a government). If that party leader is able to form a majority coalition, they create a new government with a division of cabinet positions as the coalition partners agree, usually with the leader of the largest party as chancellor. There is no limit to how many parties can be involved in a coalition. If the party leader chosen by the president to form a government cannot create a cabinet acceptable to the president, the president may ask another character to attempt to form a government.

The president may call on someone, including a person not in the Reichstag, to create a minority government. Lacking a majority, such a government has three legal options:

- A majority of the Reichstag may choose to "tolerate" the government (by abstaining, voting for its policies, and blocking any votes of no confidence), thus allowing the minority government to continue without necessitating a call for new elections.
- It can rule by presidential decree (see "Presidential Government—The 25/48/53 Formula").
- It can request that the president call for new elections.

Ministerial Reports and Questions for the Minister

Throughout the game, at the end of each session the GM will provide players with ministerial reports on important events requiring immediate action.

The cabinet must develop an official government position before the next session. At the beginning of the next session, the responsible minister (as indicated by the report) presents the government's position and proposals.

The presenting minister must remain at the podium after the report for "questions for the minister." During this time, the minister must answer all questions from the floor. The questioners do not approach the podium but must stand at their places and be recognized by the Speaker before asking. Questions must be in the form of a question (no speeches allowed—the Speaker will cut off any comments not in the form of a question and that person loses their right to raise a question). After all questions, the minister may return to their place and normal debate ensues.

Failure to make a report affects the Stability Index.

The Reichstag

The Reichstag is the German legislature. It operates according to parliamentary principles that differ from those in the United States, so make sure that you understand them. Every player (except those in the Camarilla) is a member of the Reichstag and sits with their party.

Speaker of the Reichstag

The Speaker is the presiding officer of the Reichstag, currently Paul Löbe (SPD). The largest party in the Reichstag selects the Speaker immediately after every Reichstag election. Except in small games, the Speaker may not be in the cabinet.

The Speaker controls the agenda and enforces the podium rule, which determines who can speak, in what order, and for how long. The Speaker calls sessions to order and announces the mandatory topic for discussion. The Speaker may take motions from the floor. The Speaker may recognize or ignore motions, adjust the agenda, table votes, and otherwise exercise authority over the proceedings of the Reichstag. The Speaker may ignore requests to speak entirely, including from the chancellor or other members of the cabinet (but must always allow players to present on their topics). At the end of each session, the Speaker selects the discretionary agenda topics.

If the Reichstag becomes unruly, the Speaker may call on the president to use whatever means necessary to restore order as long as it does not violate the constitutional immunity of the members of the Reichstag. The Speaker may select a secretary to help keep order; this role may be filled by the GM.

Voting in the Reichstag

Mandates (seats in the Reichstag, each with a vote) per party are based on the results of the 1928 Reichstag election. Each player controls an equal share of their party mandates (and thus votes). If there is a remainder after dividing equally, extra mandates go to the party leader (player #1). The mandate distribution for Indeterminates depends on the number of Indeterminate players (the GM will provide these numbers—see table 4).

If new elections occur, the total number of mandates and their distribution may change. Historical outcomes, the Stability Index, and your party's propaganda success determine these numbers.

TABLE 4 Reichstag mandates

Party	Mandates
SPD	153
DNVP	76*
X	61
KPD	54
NSDAP	12
Indeterminates	135*
Total	491

*If RLB (Agrarian League) is in play.
DNVP = 73; Indeterminates = 138.

Decorum

There is no protocol for behavior in the Reichstag. Heckling, interjecting, and voicing loud support may occur. The Speaker attempts to maintain order through the vigorous ringing of a bell to call the house to order, but members often ignore the Speaker. Members can enter or leave the meeting as they desire. Mass walkouts may occur.

Players must verbally identify themselves by name, party affiliation, and ministry portfolio (if applicable) when speaking.

When a member of the cabinet addresses the Reichstag to present the government's views, members of the Reichstag have the right to ask questions (see "Ministerial Reports and Questions for the Minister").

Varieties of Legislation

The members of the cabinet handle the day-to-day operations of the government, but they must secure the approval of the Reichstag whenever they take dramatic action.

Only **one-fifth** of the Reichstag is required to:

Convene an **inquiry committee** headed by the justice minister. A committee investigates any activity as directed—scandals and assassinations are good reasons. Before the start of the next session after a committee is convened, the jus-

tice minister informs the cabinet privately about the committee's findings. The cabinet then authorizes a report to the Reichstag, usually given by the justice minister (Article 34).

A **majority vote** (50 percent + 1 of votes; abstentions do not count) is required to:

Pass legislation, including the budget
Ratify treaties or declare war
Pardon criminals. The Reichstag regularly passes a Christmas amnesty paroling lesser political prisoners (Article 49).
Revoke emergency decrees issued by the president (Article 48)
Vote no confidence. A successful vote forces the resignation of the chancellor, a minister, entire cabinet, or the Speaker. If directed against the chancellor or the entire cabinet, the president may call a new election or ask someone else to be chancellor, probably with a new cabinet. In theory, the president could also reappoint the exact same chancellor and cabinet (Article 54).

A **two-thirds majority** is required to:

Amend the constitution (Article 76)
Pass Enabling Acts. Used frequently in the early days of the Republic, these grant the cabinet emergency powers, usually limited for a specific crisis.
Recall the president (see "Presidential Elections")

Motions of no confidence may come at any time (except during debate on a mandatory agenda item) for any reason from any Reichstag member. Indeed, if the government has just lost a vote, the logical step for the opposition parties is to make an immediate motion of no confidence. They must be voted on immediately and cannot be blocked for any reason. Any number of motions of no confidence may be made per session, but only if made against different persons.

Voting in the Reichstag

Quorum: No quorum is required unless the Reichstag is amending the constitution, which requires two-thirds of members to be present (Article 76).

Debate: Once the Speaker has opened a topic for debate, that debate cannot be interrupted until all required speeches are given. After the speeches, the Speaker may call for a vote.

Calling for a vote: Any Reichstag member may call for a vote. However, only the Speaker may place a vote on the agenda. If the Speaker refuses (see "Tabling"), the Reichstag may force a vote on an item by overriding the Speaker with a simple majority.

Voting: Once a vote begins, it must be taken immediately—no further debate is allowed, and it may not be interrupted or stopped for any reason.

Tabling: The Speaker may table a vote after all debate and not allow the motion to be voted on. The Reichstag may override the decision to table by majority vote and then move to an immediate vote on the previously tabled issue. Exception: the Speaker may not table a motion of no confidence.

Order of voting: The sponsoring party votes first; the Speaker then calls on parties to vote in any order.

Block voting: Parties usually vote by block (the party leader announces all party votes at once). However, party members may break with party discipline and refuse to allow block voting for their party.

Voting options: The party or individual may vote, abstain, or pass. If passing, the Speaker must call on every other party/individual before calling on the passing party/individual again. A party/individual may only pass once. If the party/individual abstains, the Speaker has the right to demand the reasons for the abstention.

Proxy voting: If absent, players are assumed to vote by proxy. In parties with more than one player, the leader of the party automatically controls those votes unless proxy instructions have been given to the GM. The instructions may be broad ("I authorize X to cast my votes on all matters as X sees fit") or narrow ("I authorize X to vote yes/no on this particular matter only").

Tallying: The GM or appointed secretary keeps a tally and announces results.

Ties: In the event of a tie, the president may cast a deciding vote; otherwise, a tie is a defeat.

Agenda

Every session except the last has at least one mandatory agenda item. Mandatory items cannot be altered for any reason (except by the GM). They must be resolved as the first agenda items of the session, in the order given, before any other action may be taken. Resolution requires full discussion though not necessarily a vote (see "Basic Outline of the Game" for the agenda sequence).

In the last five minutes of a session, the Speaker must determine two discretionary agenda items (A and B) for the next session. If time allows, these items will be debated in the next session in the order set by the Speaker after the mandatory items have been resolved.

To select the discretionary items, the Speaker should meet with the cabinet and solicit input from Reichstag members. Although the Speaker sets the discretionary agenda, the Reichstag may overrule by majority vote and set alternate discretionary agenda items. In either event, once the discretionary items have been approved, they may not be altered in the next session. However, after resolution of all approved agenda items for a session, new items may be added by the Speaker.

If a discretionary item is not resolved, it does not automatically roll over to the next session. It must again be approved for an additional session or it is dropped from the agenda.

Political Parties

PARTY DISCIPLINE

All parties operate with party discipline. If a party calls for party discipline (determined by majority vote of party members), all members must vote as a block, with the party leader casting the vote. Failure to abide by party discipline can lead to disciplinary action by the party. If party discipline is not invoked, members may vote as they see fit.

Members may always criticize their party privately, secretly, anonymously, and within party meetings. Parties forbid public criticism such as circulating critical articles, voting against the decision after party discipline has been invoked, conducting negotiations without the authorization of the party, speaking in the Reichstag against their party or fellow members, and so on.

The game does not forbid public criticism. However, there should be consequences. It is up to the party to determine how to discipline members. The options may include: expulsion from the party, removal from party posts, a reprimand, or reduction in party rank. A majority vote of all party members is required to discipline a member.

Only the GM may remove a member of the Reichstag from the legislature altogether.

In the event of a tie in an internal party vote, the party leader decides.

COALITIONS, ALLIANCES, MERGERS, NEW FORMATIONS, AND BANS

Coalitions are agreements between parties to form a government together. No single party has ever had an absolute majority of the Reichstag, so coalitions are the norm to achieve a working majority.

Potential coalitions are

- Weimar Coalition, aka *Volksblock* (SPD, DDP, X): left-center, pro-Republic coalition that formed at the start of the Republic; under various chancellors, 1919 to 1922
- Hindenburg Front, aka *Reichsblock* (Centre, BVP, DVP, DNVP): right-center, national-conservative block excluding Marxists and the NSDAP; elected von Hindenburg in 1925
- Bourgeois Block, aka *Bürgerblock* (DDP, X, BVP, DVP): nationalist-liberal moderate coalition excluding Marxists and *völkisch* parties; in power 1925 to 1928
- Grand Coalition (SPD, DDP, X, BVP, DVP): moderate pro-Republic coalition currently in power since 1928

- Populist Front, aka *Völkische Front* (NSDAP, DNVP, DVP): proposed far-right block that excludes moderates and Marxists

Alliances are formal agreements to vote together. These are not the same as mergers, since each party remains distinct, and they are not coalitions since they are not meant to form a government. Two alliances regularly discussed include

- United Front (KPD, SPD): a Marxist front to fight the extreme Right
- National Block (DNVP, DVP, and other right-of-center parties): a conservative front to fight both the Marxists and the NSDAP

Mergers occur when two or more parties agree to dissolve their parties and create a new united party. Such a merger means that future elections occur under the name of the new party. There is no guarantee that all mandates of the merging parties will go along, however. The GM will determine how successful the merger was. If the merger ceases to be useful, players can unmerge. Again, the GM will determine how successful the de-merger was.

Parties may disappear by voluntarily dissolving themselves, merging, being banned, or not receiving any mandates in a Reichstag election.

Banning a party is an extraordinary step. It requires a two-thirds vote since it alters the constitutional right to association (Article 124). If banned, a party may reform under another name.

Reichstag Elections

Scheduled elections: If no Reichstag election is called prior to the penultimate game session, one must occur in that session (the four-year term would end in early 1932). If the regularly scheduled presidential election also occurs in that session (i.e., it has not been preempted by a successful recall referendum), the Reichstag elections would occur after the GM announces the new president.

Calling elections: The president may call for early Reichstag elections at any time and for any reason after the start of the second session (Article 25). No more than one election may occur per session.

Influencing elections: Elections are unpredictable and the electorate volatile. Players may influence election by

- Campaigning successfully; as assessed in the quality of writing and speaking, the GM may adjust results
- Moving the Stability Index: the GM may adjust results so that a higher Index favors pro-Republican parties, and a lower Index favors anti-Republican parties

Election results: After the GM announces the results of elections, the following happens:

- The largest party selects the Speaker.
- The president calls on someone (usually but not necessarily the leader of largest party) to form a new government as the new chancellor; that person need not be a member of the Reichstag.
- The proposed chancellor consults with other parties, assembles a coalition, and proposes a cabinet to the president. If the president disapproves, they may ask for the same proposed chancellor to create a government more to their liking, or ask someone else to form a government to their liking.
- If the president approves the government, the new chancellor presents the members of the cabinet and the goals of the new government to the Reichstag.
- The new Speaker announces the agenda.
- The eldest Reichstag member (Zetkin, KPD) addresses the Reichstag as the first agenda item (if Zetkin is not in play, this step is ignored).

Extraparliamentary Forces

Assassination

Assassination by right-wing death squads was common in the early 1920s. But since 1924, assassination of leading politicians has all but ceased. Nonetheless, the threat still exists, and threats, often delivered in not-so-veiled homilies in the Reichstag, right-wing broadsheets, or in anonymous letters, should be taken seriously.

Foreign Intervention

Foreign powers may choose to intervene. The French intervened in the early 1920s and still occupy the Rhineland. The Comintern (the Moscow agency that coordinates international communism) has supported a variety of communist revolutions around the world. The Vatican regularly issues proclamations in support of Catholics. The United Kingdom has no desire to see the Versailles system unravel. Italy seeks to extend its influence into Austria and the Balkans. Poland and Czechoslovakia have significant tensions on their new borders with Germany. Anyone may appeal to any foreign power for assistance (military, diplomatic, financial, or otherwise) by writing to the GM in their role as the relevant foreign counterpart. You will need to research who this counterpart might be.

Green Front

The Green Front is a nonparty block of often competing agrarian interests that was formed in 1929 with the hope of creating a single united organization that will ideally grow into a unified national agrarian party to strengthen farmers' voices. Its members include the CNBP, RLB, DBP, X, and NSDAP.

Paramilitaries

Several parties have affiliated but autonomous para-militaries with military-like training. These are (usually) legal and often intervene directly in political affairs. They may engage in street fighting and insurrections, and include

- BVP = Homeland Defense (*Heimatschutz*); only in Bavaria
- CNBP = Rural People's Movement (*Landvolkewegung*); a terrorist protest movement
- DNVP = Steel Helmet (*Stahlhelm*); the largest paramilitary by far, but respectable
- KPD = Red Front (*Rotfrontkämpferbund*); currently banned
- NSDAP = Storm troopers aka Brownshirts (*Sturmabteilung*, or SA); openly militant, thuggish
- SPD/X/DDP = Banner of the Realm (*Reichsbanner*); a joint paramilitary, respectable

Reichswehr

Since Versailles restricts the Reichswehr to one hundred thousand men, it has limited combat abilities. However, it is a handpicked elite led by conservative officers with monarchist loyalties who defend its autonomy from Reichstag control. It appears to be utterly devoted to von Hindenburg, but von Schleicher makes day-to-day decisions.

Character Death and Respawning

German politicians sometimes were assassinated, died unexpectedly, or lost all relevance. What happens if your character dies or your party is eliminated? Do you automatically lose? Not to worry! You simply respawn, but as another character. The GM will inform you of your new character. Your victory objectives become those of your new character.

BASIC OUTLINE OF THE GAME

Our game begins in late 1929, just after the U.S. stock market crash and as the German Reichstag begins deliberation on the Freedom Law and Naval Bill. You are part of the Reichstag, belonging to one of the various political parties. Beginning with the Young Plan, you must debate a variety of matters ranging from foreign affairs to cultural matters, all informed by primary sources.

Each session covers roughly six months of historical time, and you will have to confront unfolding events that directly impact Germany while also dealing with domestic elections and unrest. You face a series of events where you, not the dead hand of history, decide what will happen. Thus, within the parameters of the historical reality of the Republic, you must consider all of the options actually available and confront the consequences of your choices.

Importantly, every decision made by you has an impact on the Stability Index, a measure of how volatile the German electorate has become: the greater the instability, the greater the radicalization of the German electorate. Thus you must decide how best to maneuver politically in the Reichstag, all the while considering the impact on the next election.

If the Reichstag cannot resolve its internal disputes based on majority rule, the game allows for a variety of tactics: dissolution of the Reichstag, emergency decrees, street violence, martial law, assassination, and mass insurrections.

Typical Game Session Cycle

1. Start of class
   a. GM announces/posts updates
      i. Stability Index
      ii. Party mandates
      iii. Speaker and cabinet
   b. Speaker announces/posts agenda
2. Reichstag actions
   a. Agenda items
      i. Discussion of mandatory agenda items
         1. Cabinet presents its stance
            a. Questions for the minister
         2. Speeches and debate
         3. Caucus, vote, or table
      ii. Discussion of discretionary items
   b. Interruptions
      i. Only after full debate of agenda item being discussed
      ii. Votes of no confidence, street violence, emergency decrees, dissolution of parliament, caucuses, etc.
3. End of class
   a. Speaker sets new discretionary items
4. After class
   a. GM provides ministerial reports and updates
   b. Cabinet meets outside of class to determine stance on ministerial reports
   c. Players meet outside of class to plot strategy

Mandatory Agenda Items

Session 1: Freedom Law; Naval Bill #1
Session 2: Young Plan; Austerity
Session 3: Grain Tariffs
Session 4: Antisemitism (if not used, then Eugenic Sterilization)
Session 5: Mother's Day
Session 6: Presidential Election
Session 7: (no mandatory item)

Initial Reichstag Agenda

Session 1

1. Freedom Law by Hugenberg (DNVP); rebuttal by interior minister
2. Naval Bill #1 by Defense Minister von Schleicher
3. If time permits, proceed with items from Session 2.

Session 2

1. Young Plan by Chancellor Müller (SPD)
2. Austerity by Economic Minister Dingeldey (DVP)
3. Discretionary Item A as determined by Speaker at end of Session 1
4. Discretionary Item B as determined by Speaker at end of Session 1

Debriefing

After the game, the GM debriefs players, providing historical closure to determine the fate of German democracy and individual players. The debriefing also helps players to exit from the game, provides an opportunity for reflection, and gives the GM a chance to set the record straight by telling the players what really happened.

ASSIGNMENTS

Every player should engage the class through oral participation (speaking in the Reichstag sessions and caucusing), writing (your papers), and visual creativity (the campaign poster).

Oral Participation

Depending on class size, the GM will inform you how often and at what length you must speak before the Reichstag to receive full credit. In smaller classes, you should expect to speak on a daily basis; in larger classes perhaps only once per week. In part, your speeches will be directly related to your papers, but not necessarily so. You may need to speak on a topic before your paper on that topic is due.

Some characters are required to speak on set matters. Hugenberg (DNVP) speaks on the Freedom Law. Clara Zetkin delivers the "First Address" after any Reichstag election. Cabinet members present the government's views, often triggered by GM updates.

You must also actively engage members of your party and other members of the Reichstag during caucus sessions (in-class breaks from formal Reichstag debates). During a caucus, you should approach other players to convince them of your agenda. You can reiterate your position, cut deals, horse-trade, threaten, and cajole. This is a good time to consult with the GM if you need clarification. Caucuses also allow you to prepare and use whatever powers you may have. Thus active use of caucuses is essential to ensure your success.

Papers

Depending on the GM's need, you will write two papers (3–5 pages) or three papers (2–4 pages). Your role sheet defines your topics. The GM will provide length and citation expectations. In general, though, you must draw on the "Core Texts" and factional readings.

Visual Creativity (Election Poster)

You must produce an election poster for the presidential election for your preferred candidate (listed in your role sheet) prior to the start of the election (usually the penultimate session, unless preempted by a successful presidential recall referendum). You are not obligated to vote for this candidate.

The poster should be on a half poster board (14″ × 22″) unless otherwise specified by the GM. It may be designed in any style related to the aesthetics of the era; you may imitate models or be more creative. Your poster may be in either German or English. It must clearly convey either the party or the candidate. You should look at historical examples of electoral posters as models. These are readily available on the internet—just make sure your models are from BEFORE 1933. A Google image search of "Weimar Republic election posters" will provide plenty. Please remember the ban on Nazi and antisemitic discourse.

GAME POINTS (WINNING)

You can win as an individual or as a faction, or as both. Your role sheet provides specifics. Points are awarded based on the status quo at the end of the game. Use the victory points score card to track your progress (see table 5).

TABLE 5 Victory points score card

Factional	POINTS	Discretionary Items	STATUS
Factional Absolute Victory		**Foreign Relations**	
Factional Absolute Defeat		Liquidation Treaty	
Stability Index Goal (10 points)			
Presidential Election (10 points)			
Indeterminates/Splinters who join faction*		**Military Affairs**	
Type of Government (20 points)		Paramilitaries	
Mandatory Agenda Items (5 points each)		Naval Bills (#2, #3)	
#1—Freedom Law			
#2—Naval Bills			
#3—Young Plan		**Eugenics and Sexuality**	
#4—Austerity		Eugenic Sterilization	
#5—Grain Tariffs			
#6—Antisemitism			
#7—Mother's Day		**Race and Culture**	
TOTAL		*All Quiet*—censorship	

Personal	POINTS		
Personal Absolute Victory			
Personal Absolute Defeat		**Industrial Relations**	
Best Paper (3 @ 10 points each)		Nationalization	
Best Poster (10 points)			
Best Speech (10 points each per session)			
Stability Index Goal (10 points)		**Agricultural Affairs**	
President or Chancellor (15 points)		Small Farmers' Relief	
Cabinet Minister (5 points)			
Money (1 point per million RM—optional rule)			
Discretionary Goals (5 points each)		**Other**	
TOTAL			

*Points for Indeterminate and Splinters are as follows:

   9–15 players = 6 points each (18 points max)
   16–21 players = 3 points each (18 points max)
   23+ players = 2 points each (24 points max)
 For the Camarilla = 5 points each regardless of class size (20 points max)

4

Roles and Factions

No single model captures the political spectrum of the Republic, especially because it shifted over time. However, figure 8 uses a traditional "left-right" political spectrum and places the political parties (within the large arrow), paramilitaries (above, with arrows to affiliated parties), and special interest groups (in ALL CAPS) in their approximate relationship to each other. Since both extremes were anti-Republic, a horseshoe effect brought the extreme ends closer together so that tactical alliances between the NSDAP and KPD against the Republic were possible. On the far right, many groups straddled the pro- and anti-Republic line, indicating their indeterminacy on that point. But keep in mind that every party consisted of a spectrum, with a left and right wing as well as a moderate middle trying to hold the wings together.

THE MAIN PARTIES/FACTIONS

Camarilla (Authoritarian / Monarchist / Militarist / Reactionary)

The circle of men immediately around President von Hindenburg (the so-called Camarilla) is highly influential. These fellow Junkers share the president's basic experiences and worldviews—military service, authoritarian social order, Protestant conservativism. They served in the war and are unrepentant monarchists. Above all, they promote the interests of an autonomous military, free of civilian control. Naturally, in accord with the president's public statements, they hold Germany faultless for the war and seek an end to Versailles. Some observers suggest that they subvert the rule of law. Others suspect that they manipulate the aged von Hindenburg, who seems to many to be drifting into senility. If true, then the presidency may be in the hands of forces hostile to the Republic. However, their workings are so secretive that only a handful of leading politicians have any meaningful insight into their goals. The Camarilla includes:

President von Hindenburg. He personifies the conservative nationalist interests of the Junkers. He is the single most popular man in Germany. A hero of

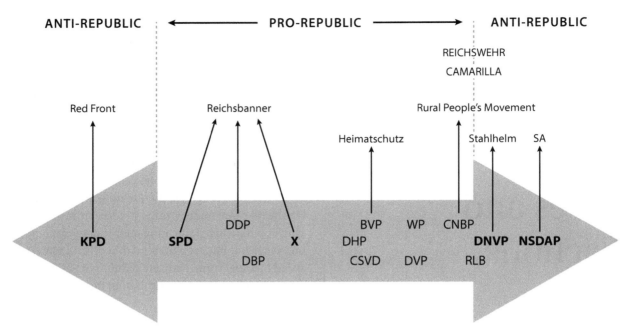

ANTI-REPUBLIC ← **PRO-REPUBLIC** → **ANTI-REPUBLIC**

REICHSWEHR

CAMARILLA

Red Front

Reichsbanner

Rural People's Movement

Heimatschutz

Stahlhelm   SA

DDP

BVP   WP   CNBP

KPD   **SPD**   **X**   DHP   DNVP   **NSDAP**

DBP   CSVD   DVP   RLB

FIGURE 8 Political parties, paramilitaries, and special interest groups.

Image created by Robert Goodrich.

the war for most, even for some of his opponents, few doubt his integrity. He stands as a bastion of the old regime at the top of the new. His goals are correspondingly unclear to many. He is rumored to desire a restoration of the monarchy, or perhaps a military dictatorship.

General von Schleicher. As head of the Office of Ministerial Affairs, he officially deals with all matters relating to joint concerns of the army and navy. He is tasked with liaising between the military, other departments, and politicians—a sort of political fixer. He has interpreted his mandate broadly, allowing the Reichswehr to engage directly in politics, but no one knows where von Schleicher stands, apart from his unwavering support for the Reichswehr.

Otto Meissner. He has served as head of the Office of the Reich President since 1920, serving with equal loyalty and skill under presidents Ebert (SPD) and von Hindenburg. His opinions and goals are unknown, and he has never joined any political

organization. He appears to embody the spirit of German bureaucracy—diligent, formal, and obscure. Does he have influence over the president, or is he just a civil servant?

Centre Party (Christian Democratic / Political Catholicism / Corporatist)

The Centre Party (*Zentrumspartei*, X) belongs to the Christian democracy movement that emerged in the early nineteenth century. Its central concern has been the preservation of Catholic rights, a position that has made it open to many liberal ideas. At the same time, it closely allies with the conservative Catholic elite. Loyal to the pope in church matters, the Centre is independent of the Holy See on secular matters. Its conservative wing longs for a return to the moral and social harmony of the preindustrial world. Its labor wing, organized in the Christian trade unions, attempts to transcend its Catholic character and create a modern Christian middle party that accepts industrial modernity. Generally guided by moderates, the Centre's pragmatic principles leave it open to supporting either a monarchical or republican form of government. It has been an essential member of nearly every cabinet and coalition and seems inured to the dramatic electoral vagaries of other parties.

The main members of the Centre in the Reichstag are:

Heinrich Brüning. A decorated veteran, he is one of the leading economic thinkers in the Reichstag; primarily an academic, he nonetheless decided to enter public service to help veterans, and he represents the moderate center of his party.

Adam Stegerwald. He has served in numerous political offices, including prime minister of Prussia; he represents the left wing of the party and leads the powerful Christian trade unions.

Franz von Papen. A nobleman, diplomat, and general staff officer, he is one of the few Catholics who seem close to the conservative Prussian Junker class; he surprised his party in 1925 by supporting von Hindenburg over its own candidate.

Ludwig Kaas. A bishop with extremely close ties to the Vatican, he politically supports autonomy for his homeland in the Rhineland but hopes to mediate between the Centre Party's wings and ensure that they have close ties to the bishops.

Andreas Hermes. Of all the Centre Party leaders, he represents the aspirations of the smaller Catholic farmers and peasants; he is pragmatic—both a technocratic agrarian expert as well as a politician.

Helene Weber. Part of a new generation of women who have received advanced university degrees and entered politics, she has become one of the most insightful Reichstag leaders, able to build broad coalitions especially on issues related to welfare and women.

Albert Hackeslberger. An industrialist with roots in Bavaria, he is one of the leading economic thinkers in the party as well as in all of Germany, embracing liberal economic theories.

Communist Party of Germany— KPD (Communist / Bolshevik / Marxist)

The KPD (*Kommunistische Partei Deutschlands*) has become the largest communist party outside of the USSR, yet it only formed officially in 1919, after splitting from the SPD over questions related to the war (the KPD opposed war) and the Russian Revolution (the KPD supports the Bolsheviks). Committed to social revolution, the KPD launched several attempts to seize power in the Republic's early years but has since adopted a policy of building its support legally. Though often wracked by internal conflict, it has become a mass party—implacably hostile to fascism, liberalism, and social democracy. It looks to the Soviet Union, now firmly in the hands of Stalin, and the Comintern. At the moment, it decries "social fascism," denouncing the SPD as a greater threat than the Right because it dupes workers into supporting capitalism and thus provides the basis for fascism. The KPD maintains a solid electoral performance, usually polling more than 10 percent, and has every reason for confidence. The Great Depression and the constant compromises of the SPD are radicalizing younger workers.

The main members of the KPD in the Reichstag are:

Ernst Thälmann. Party leader, staunch Moscow loyalist, and advocate of a Stalinist interpretation of the party, he brooks no compromise with capitalism, the Republic, or the "social fascist" SPD.

Clara Zetkin. Eldest member of the Reichstag and personal friend of the martyred Rosa Luxemburg, she is firmly committed to the revolutionary path to socialism as carried out by the Bolsheviks.

Arthur Ewert. Directly involved with the KPD uprising in 1923, for many years he was a wanted man in Germany, but now he has close links to the Comintern, though he seems to have ended up on the wrong side of a factional struggle against Thälmann.

Walter Ulbricht. A founding member of the KPD, he is now a rising star in the party, closely associated with the street fighting of the Red Front.

Martha Arendsee. Rivaling even the venerable Zetkin, she represents the strong stance of the party on women's issues, but also serves as one of the leading communist publicists and organizers of charitable actions; she has always been willing to find coalition partners.

Willi Münzenberg. One of the few members of the Reichstag from the working class, he has emerged as the party's greatest publicist, creating a communist press empire that rivals that of Hugenberg—a fact that has led many to criticize him as the "red millionaire."

Franz Dahlem. A staunch Thälmann supporter, leader of the Ruhr Rebellion in 1923, and now an advocate of the antifascist approach, he denounces the SPD as social fascists.

Maria Reese. A recent crossover from the SPD elected to the Reichstag by the SPD in 1928, she switched to the KPD in 1929 due to the overly moderate stance of that party.

German National People's Party— DNVP (National Conservative / Fascist / Völkisch)

The DNVP (*Deutschnationale Volkspartei*) is by far the most powerful party of the Right. It is correspondingly eclectic, composed of nationalists, reactionary monarchists, *völkisch* and antisemitic elements, and pan-Germanists. The DNVP spent the Republic's early days in opposition. Between 1925 and 1928, however, the party slightly moderated its tone and actively cooperated in several right-center cabinets. But in the 1928 elections, the party suffered a disastrous showing, falling to just 14 percent. As a result, Alfred Hugenberg, from the party's right wing, became chair, and favors fundamental opposition to the Republic. The result has been a series of internal power struggles and splits. But the party is adapting. It has replaced the former kaiser with von Hindenburg as its object of veneration. It openly cooperates with the NSDAP and has integrated fascist elements into its thinking. The party has taken a drubbing but is far from out. It has vast financial resources, a press empire, and links to von Schleicher and von Hindenburg. And the campaign against the Young Plan has energized the conservative base. No one expects the DNVP, as the catchall carrier of conservative nation-

alism, to go away any time soon. Indeed, it may well succeed in tapping into the simmering discontent since the start of the Depression.

The main members of the DNVP in the Reichstag are:

Alfred Hugenberg. The most powerful and wealthy press baron in all Germany, he has just recently emerged as the leader of the party; he has actively steered it toward a more *völkisch* and anti-Republican stance.

Kuno von Westarp. Until the disastrous elections of 1928, he was the head of the DNVP, and now he is in an open rivalry with Hugenberg over the direction of the party; his views are traditional conservative monarchist.

Elard von Oldenburg. Like von Hindenburg, he is a deeply traditional Prussian Junker; indeed, he is not only wealthy but also one of the few men whom the president would consider a personal friend, offering him unique access to von Hindenburg's ear.

Paul Lejeune-Jung. Though a Catholic, he nonetheless is a member of this generally anti-Catholic party. He is closely tied to conservative Catholics in the Centre Party but also to big industry; the tensions between him and Hugenberg are well known.

Paula Müller-Otfried. While advocating for women's social and economic rights, she nonetheless expresses her party's conservative views on cultural values and even on women's participation in politics.

Oskar Hergt. A former senior official in the Prussian Finance Ministry and also former head of the DNVP, he harbors a grudge against Hugenberg, who just defeated him in an internal party power struggle.

Karl Graf zu Eulenburg. An aristocratic count from the venerable House of Eulenburg, he embodies all of the values and attitudes of the Junker class.

Martin Spahn. A respected academic and "Reform Catholic," he has an affinity for the NSDAP.

National Socialist German Workers' Party— NSDAP (National Socialist / Fascist / *Völkisch*)

The NSDAP (*Nationalsozialistische Deutsche Arbeiterpartei*) belongs to an entirely new type of ideology—a racialized version of the fascism of Italy's Benito Mussolini. It initially attracted followers of the far-right *völkisch* nationalist milieu and the anticommunist *Freikorps* paramilitary culture. Unlike traditional conservatives, however, the NSDAP appeals to the working class. Its left wing employs anti–big business, antibourgeois, and anticapitalist rhetoric. Yet, after a failed coup in 1923, and no discernible inroads into the Marxist parties' supporters, the NSDAP recently began downplaying its anticapitalism to gain the support of elites and the middle class. Now, a chauvinistic revanchist nationalism stressing antisemitism blends with anti-Marxist themes. It relentlessly denounces everything related to defeat in 1918—Marxism, the Republic, the Treaty of Versailles. It calls for the execution of the November criminals. It claims to stand above party politics—the NSDAP does not even like to call itself a party, likening itself instead to a "national movement." At the top of the NSDAP is the führer, war veteran Adolf Hitler, who ostensibly holds full command over the party. But the NSDAP received only twelve seats (2.6 percent of the vote) in 1928, mostly limited to its home base in Bavaria. Still, the party has some reason for optimism. Mussolini serves as a model for success. The creation of an elite unit (the SS) has given a more professional look to the party compared to the thuggish image of the SA. The campaign against the Young Plan has gained the party new credibility. More importantly, the Great Depression has made many wonder if Germany might indeed need a more radical solution to its problems. For most Germans, though, the party is a radical fringe with no real ability to influence Germany's future.

Special Note on Adolf Hitler: Hitler is not a German citizen. He was born in Austria-Hungary, though he fought in the German army in the war and renounced his Austrian citizenship in 1925. He is technically stateless. As a result, he cannot legally sit in the Reichstag or run for president. He can, however, be appointed chancellor through a loophole that does not specifically require that the chancellor be either a citizen or a member of the Reichstag.

The main members of the NSDAP in the Reichstag are:

Hermann Göring. The charismatic faction leader, a popular and highly decorated war hero and flying ace from the war, he has been with the party since its earliest days and was wounded at Hitler's side during the failed Munich Putsch.

Gregor Strasser. A leader in north Germany, war veteran, head of the SA and NSDAP trade unions, he represents a left wing that takes the working-class elements of the party seriously; he also calls for the creation of a People's Army to replace the Reichswehr.

Wilhelm Frick. A former faction leader, now about to be the first NSDAP member to hold a ministerial office in Germany as education and interior minister of the state of Thuringia, he has a reputation for making aggressive antisemitic speeches.

Joseph Goebbels. Though he joined only in 1924, he has established himself as a leader of the Berlin branch of the party; his inflammatory speeches are extremely popular with the local Brownshirts and he is fiercely loyal to Hitler in Munich.

Werner Willikens. A farmer by upbringing and the party's most popular man within the agrarian constituencies, his goal is to unite the various farming parties into a common front behind the NSDAP.

Ernst Graf zu Reventlow. A nobleman, expert on naval affairs, and widely read publicist, he epitomizes the power constituency within the party around Strasser who believe that the socialism aspect of the party must take precedence.

Franz Xaver Ritter von Epp. An officer and veteran of the war as well as leader of right-wing *Freikorps* in Bavaria after the war, he currently is closely associated with the violent wing of the SA.

Walter Buch. A military man by training, he joined the party immediately after his demobilization after 1918, and now inside the party he heads the powerful Inquiry and Mediation Board that maintains party discipline and loyalty to Hitler.

Social Democratic Party of Germany— SPD (Social Democratic / Socialist / Democratic Socialist / Marxist)

The SPD (*Sozialdemokratische Partei Deutschland*) has existed since 1875 and remains loyal to its Marxist roots. The Heidelberg Program of 1925 calls for the "transformation of the capitalist system of private ownership of the means of production to social ownership." However, in practice, it has moved away from revolution and has become firmly supportive of the Republic. It now plans to achieve its goals through democratic reform. As the main nonrevolutionary left-wing party, the SPD has fared best among non-Catholic workers as well as intellectuals favoring progressive social causes and increased economic equality. As the largest party, the SPD plays a pivotal role in keeping the state afloat, even when it has been excluded from coalitions. It has faced down violent opposition from the Right— including assassination of its leaders. It is also a bitter rival of the KPD. But the SPD puts its ideas of social justice into practice every chance it gets— overhauling the welfare state, expanding educational and job-training opportunities, setting up health clinics, running adult education classes and sporting facilities, and funding public libraries, swimming pools, schools, and low-income apartments. The SPD has every reason to support the Republic based on these tangible gains. Indeed, the 1928 elections resulted in the SPD again securing the chancellorship. Now in power, even under the trying conditions of the Great Depression, the SPD can hope for continued growth. An absolute majority in the next election is not unthinkable and would mean that the party could cease its constant compromising with right-wing parties.

The main members of the SPD in the Reichstag are:

Hermann Müller. The foreign minister who signed the Treaty of Versailles, he is now serving a second term as chancellor; he is a pragmatic moderate in the party, noted for his negotiating skills.

Paul Löbe. The Speaker of the Reichstag, he has a reputation for fairness but also for being on the left in his party and an active supporter of the pro-Republic paramilitary, the Reichsbanner.

Carl Severing. The interior minister, he has dedicated his career since the revolution to institutionalizing democracy at all levels, especially in the police, but due to his willingness to compromise with anyone, he is regarded as part of the right wing of the party.

Paul Levi. A former leader of the KPD, he has since become alienated from the communists, often looking for ideas from Leon Trotsky, a position that places him on the left of the SPD. His Jewish roots and sympathy for the KPD make him a frequent target of right-wing attacks.

Maria Jachucz. The first woman to ever speak in a German parliament (at the National Assembly in 1919), she is one of the great orators of the socialist movement, well known for her staunch advocacy of workers' welfare.

Carlo Mierendorff. He is one of the most outspoken anti-NSDAP politicians in the nation, directly challenging its leaders and its right to exist. He has also led the SPD's criticisms of the Reichswehr.

Arthur Crispien. When the SPD split in 1918, he initially joined the left-leaning faction before deciding to move away from the KPD. He staunchly advocates for the rights of workers, thus associating himself with the left wing.

Kurt Schumacher. The youngest member of the SPD in government, he nonetheless endorses more reformist ideas, rejecting all notions of violent revolution and instead embracing a fully democratic vision of regulating capitalism.

Phillip Scheidemann. Every person in Germany knows his name; he was the man who proclaimed the Republic and served as its first chancellor—resigning from office rather than sign the Treaty of Versailles.

INDETERMINATES

Though Germans are highly organized politically, and many parties are part of distinct milieus that try to create a closed environment for their members, not everyone in the Republic belongs to a political party. And many who do often change parties.

An historical example of this fluid indeterminacy is Otto Strasser (not in the game but brother of the NSDAP leader Gregor Strasser). Strasser joined the right-wing *Freikorps* that put down the Bavarian Soviet Republic in 1919. At the same time, he joined the SPD. In 1920 he opposed the militarist right-wing Kapp Putsch. However, he grew increasingly alienated from the SPD, particularly when it put down a workers' insurrection in the Ruhr. In 1925 he joined the NSDAP, from which he was later expelled for his radical anticapitalism and his refusal to accept Hitler's singular role as führer; he then tried to create an alternative to the NSDAP.

Like Otto Strasser, several characters are effectively indeterminate, trying to determine the best path. While they are receptive on many issues, they still have specific goals. Winning these characters over is essential for any coalition's success. Indeterminates should expect clear concessions for their alliances and feel free to shift their alliances and split their votes. Reflecting this indeterminacy, elections regularly bring surprising results as large numbers of voters alter their political allegiances based on recent experiences. There is no modern per-election polling, meaning that parties often have only a highly impressionistic idea of what the next election will bring.

Indeterminates fit into four camps: liberal (DVP, DDP, WP), agrarian (CNBP, DBP, RLB), Protestant (CSVD), and particularist (BVP, DHP). Not all will necessarily be in play. At the start of the final day of the game, all Indeterminates must clearly state to the GM and Reichstag the major party (NSDAP, DNVP, X, SPD, KPD, or possibly Camarilla) with which they are going to ally themselves. They still remain in their own party and keep their personal victory objectives, but they agree to caucus with this major party and adopt its factional victory objectives.

In addition, many characters in the larger factions are indeterminate on a number of issues, making them open to negotiations, including secret deals that may well go against the goals of their faction.

Liberal Indeterminates
German People's Party—DVP (National Liberal / Conservative Liberal)

The DVP (*Deutsche Volkspartei*) is a center-right liberal party, until recently led by its most famous member, Chancellor and Foreign Minister Stresemann. The DVP supports a mix of nationalism, constitutional monarchism, economic liberalism, and conservativism. Many consider the DVP to represent the interests of the German industrialists. But its platform is complex. It stresses Protestant values but also secular education; it supports low tariffs but opposes welfare spending; it is hostile to Marxism but also to the NSDAP. Initially lukewarm about the Republic, Stresemann gradually led it into cooperation with the Center and the Left, allowing it to wield political influence beyond its numbers. Stresemann was the Republic's only statesman of international standing. He served as foreign minister from 1923 until his death in 1929, in nine cabinets ranging from the center-right to the center-left. His recent unexpected death, however, has led to soul searching. The brewing debates over austerity and unemployment benefits may draw sharper fault lines between the DVP and the SPD. But the DVP has proven adept at shifting to the left or right based on the needs of the moment. Stresemann has left a powerful legacy of pragmatism.

The main members of the DVP in the Reichstag are:

Eduard Dingeldey. Trained in law and representing a pragmatic vision of conservative liberalism, he has made public his desire to create a mass-based party that transcends the narrow economic interests of most German parties.

Julius Curtius. A decorated veteran, lawyer, and representative of German industry generally, he represents the fusion of bourgeois economic interests and nationalist politics; like his mentor Stresemann, he is a reluctant *Vernunftrepublikaner*.

German Democratic Party—DDP (Democratic Liberal / Democratic / Republican)

The DDP (*Deutsche Demokratische Partei*) is a classic liberal party—republican, civil libertarian, free-market capitalist. In contrast to the DVP, the DDP is more leftist. Along with the SPD and the Centre Party, the DDP is committed to maintaining a democratic form of government. It considers itself a devotedly nationalist party and opposes the Treaty of Versailles, but emphasizes the need for international collaboration and the protection of ethnic minorities. Indeed, many of its members are pacifists. The party has been attacked for being a party of Jews and professors, but although Jews form one of its most loyal voter groups, its social basis lies in middle-class entrepreneurs, civil servants, teachers, scientists, and craftsmen. Nearly all German cabinets since 1918 have included ministers from the DDP. The election of 1928, however, saw a sharp drop in popular support for the party. From its 18 percent share in the first elections in 1919, it polled just 4.9 percent in 1928. The DDP now has to consider how to preserve not only the Republic but also its own popularity. While it is unthinkable that it would turn on the Republic, its alliances with the SPD may have cost it support. Perhaps a pivot to the right is necessary.

The main members of the DDP in the Reichstag are:

Theodor Heuss. Perhaps one of the most broadly educated members of the Reichstag, he is well known for his clear support of democracy as well as his willingness to find compromises in almost any situation.

Marie Elisabeth Lüders. Her special concerns have always centered on women, but her staunch feminism (demonstrated by having a child out of wedlock and refusing to marry) has made her the lightning rod of all debates on women's issues.

Economic Party—WP (Conservative Liberal / Economic Liberal)

In 1920 several medium-sized organizations combined to create the Reich Party of the German Middle Class—the so-called WP (*Wirtschaftspartei*). Their goal was to protect the economic interests of the petit bourgeois middle classes—especially home- and landowners, artisans, and traders—against continuously rising inflation and state direction of the economy. Thus the WP is not grounded in a specific ideology as such, though it combines aspects of liberal economics and conservative cultural values within a framework of nationalism. Instead, it looks toward specific social and economic policies to protect its constituencies, by defending the private sector, lowering the tax burden on the middle class, reducing state-funded housing construction, and opposing workers' representation in business and strikes. The party has been reluctant to take a clear stance, on the other hand, on basic constitutional matters, expressing neither principled opposition to nor support for the Republic. The WP entered the Reichstag only in 1924, but it has grown from a handful of mandates to twenty-five. Entering the Reichstag, though, has forced the WP to clarify its constitutional, foreign policy, and noneconomic domestic goals. Many are waiting to see where this small but influential party will ultimately align itself.

The main members of the WP in the Reichstag are:

Johann Bredt. He personifies the attitudes of his party and sees the creation of a large party built around the middle classes as the only possible means to resolve Germany's crises.

Georg Best. A leading jurist, he has moved through a number of conservative parties—the DNVP, various *völkisch* groups close the NSDAP, the Reich Party for Civil Rights and Deflation—before settling into a sometimes uneasy collaboration inside the WP.

Agrarian Indeterminates

Despite heavy industrialization, most Germans still live in small towns or villages. Agriculture dominates their lives, but beyond that there is little consensus. The diverse agricultural interests include powerful Junkers, poor landless peasants, small tenant farmers, independent farmers, and the multitude of townspeople who provide services for them. They come from every religion and region, and their local identities remain sharply evident. The political result is a constant merging and splitting of dozens of agrarian parties representing narrow interests. There is not even a fundamental agreement on support for the Republic. About the only thing they agree on is that German agriculture is in crisis. Until now, conservative parties have dominated the agrarian vote, but times are changing. The SPD and KPD have adopted substantive agrarian programs, and the NSDAP has launched an all-out effort to win over rural voters. Only the liberal parties remain somewhat aloof. If the agrarian parties were to unite, as some are attempting in a so-called Green Front, their combined influence could well be decisive; but first they need a common agenda.

Christian National Farmers' Party—CNBP (National Conservative / Christian Democratic / Agrarian)

The CNBP (*Christlich-Nationale Bauern- und Landvolkpartei* aka *Landvolk*) is a splinter from the RLB and DNVP. Its leaders view it as a Protestant counterpart to the Centre Party, with the goal of creating a national mass party grounded in the countryside and market towns. Its leaders, though generally conservative, have proven willing to work with liberals as well as conservatives to promote their constituents' interests.

The main members of the CNBP in the Reichstag are:

Martin Luther Schiele. Long a leader in the DNVP and a member of various cabinets, he took the political gamble of creating a new mass agrarian Christian democratic party because of the overbearing leadership of Hugenberg and his slavish devotion to the Junker class.

Heinrich von Sybel. Representing the right wing of the CNBP, he advocates closer cooperation with the agrarian wing of the NSDAP.

German Peasants' Party—DBP (Liberal / Republican / Secular / Agrarian)

The DBP (*Deutsche Bauernpartei*), like most agrarian parties, represents only a subsection of German agriculture. In this case, the DBP has its base in Bavaria, but unlike most Bavarian parties, it is a liberal, nonclerical association of regional farmers' parties that fundamentally supports the Republic and is willing to cooperate with any pro-Republic coalition.

The main member of the DBP in the Reichstag is **Karl Gandorfer**. A longtime advocate of small famers, he supported the revolution and served in the short-lived Bavarian Free State in 1918 to 1919, though his politics are more left-liberal and decidedly secular.

National Agrarian League—RLB (National Conservative / Authoritarian / Agrarian)

The small but influential RLB (*Reichslandbund*) has long been the dominant voice of German agriculture. Although it continues to claim to speak for all German famers, in practice it is an increasingly isolated venue for the Junker elite. Its policies, in most regards, remain firmly tied to the agrarian goals of the Kaiserreich. It is a national-conservative special interest group, in many ways acting as the agrarian wing of the DNVP, with which it tends to caucus in the Reichstag. Like the DNVP, it opposes the Republic.

The main member of the RLB in the Reichstag is **Eberhard Graf von Kalckreuth**. He is in all things national conservative, but always with a sharp focus on promoting the interests of the Junker class and opposing any and all efforts at "agro-Bolshevism," regardless of its sponsor.

Protestant Indeterminates

Christian Social People's Service— CSVD (Conservative / Christian Democratic / Political Protestantism)

The CSVD (*Christlich-Sozialer Volksdienst*) was formed only at the end of 1929. It strives to be a broad-based Protestant equivalent to the Centre Party and represents a pro-worker, anti-Marxist brand of Protestant social engagement. It grew out of a split from the DNVP but has deeper roots in the prewar antisemitic nationalist Christian Social Party. With its conservative Christian traditionalism, at first glance one might assume it sits firmly on the right. However, it combines strong Protestant and conservative ideas with progressive stances on workers' issues, state involvement, and at least cautious support for the Republic. It sees its main rival for support as the SPD and its main ally as the Centre Party. Ideally, the CSVD wants to create a broad Christian democratic movement that finds a way to balance working-class and industrial demands and to bring together liberals and social democrats, all based on Christian morality. Any success in this pursuit could rapidly turn this fledgling party into a mass people's party able to break through the ossified political divisions of the Republic.

The main member of the CSVD in the Reichstag is **Gustav Hülser.** A devout Lutheran, war veteran, professional gardener, and activist and publicist for agrarian labor in general, he encapsulates the unique contradictions of his new party.

Particularist Indeterminates

Even after the creation of a unified nation-state in 1871, Germany retained a high degree of regional loyalty (particularism). Since the numerous medieval German states had retained their independence until quite recently, many polities continued to insist on their absolute autonomy even within a united Germany. During the Republic, there was an active separatist movement in the Rhineland. Bavaria temporarily succeeded in creating its own state in 1918. And Hanover launched a (failed) referendum for independence from Prussia. Given the failure of separatist aspirations, many particularists now work instead to curb the overreach of Berlin, Prussia, and the Reichstag—agreeing with many national initiatives but demanding that they be controlled at the state level.

Bavarian People's Party—BVP (Bavarian Particularist / Conservative / Monarchist / Federalist / Christian Democratic)

The BVP (*Bayerische Volkspartei*) is more than just the Bavarian branch of the Centre Party. It pursues a more conservative, more Bavarian course, and strongly opposes the centralist nature of the Republic and Prussian hegemony. The party also displays monarchist leanings in favor of the deposed House of Wittelsbach. Indeed, the BVP flirted with separatism in the early 1920s and has retained the slogan "Bavaria for the Bavarians," though it has pragmatically come around to a more moderate line. Still, its platform calls for a new German state based on Christian democratic ideals and decentralization from Berlin. Its support comes largely from an agrarian Catholic block that is generally immune to the political overtures of every other party in Bavaria, where it dominates provincial politics. Its role in the Reichstag has been unpredictable, moving between support and opposition to the Republic, and even voting against the Centre Party. Recently, though, the BVP has taken a moderate approach. It has shown an increasing willingness to work with the Centre Party, holding cabinet ministry positions in the Reichstag coalition with the SPD. Indeed, despite its conservative tendencies, the BVP's violent opposition to the KPD is rivaled only by its hatred of the NSDAP.

The main members of the BVP in the Reichstag are:

Erich Emminger. He personifies the attitudes of a Bavarian particularist who would be happiest with an independent and conservative Free State of Bavaria, ideally under a restored Wittlesbach monarchy.

Thusnelda Lang-Brumann. She loyally supports Bavaria, but with a special interest in education and women's issues that makes her open to building broad coalitions at the national level.

German Hanoverian Party—DHP (Hanoverian Particularist / Conservative / Monarchist / Federalist / Christian Democratic)

The DHP (*Deutsch-Hannoversche Partei*) also known as the Guelph Party (*Welfenpartei*), is a conservative, federalist party that, in many ways, shares basic goals with the BVP. The party was founded in 1867 in protest of the annexation of the Kingdom of Hanover by the Kingdom of Prussia in the aftermath of the Austro-Prussian War. The DHP has consistently sought the revival of the Kingdom of Hanover and the restoration of the sequestrated assets of the former ruling House of Welf. It draws its strongest support from the rural areas around Hanover. In the Reichstag, DHP deputies long acted as allies of the anti-Prussian Centre Party. During the revolution, the DHP advocated the implementation of a Free State of Hanover within the Weimar Republic and succeeded in having a plebiscite held in the Prussian Province of Hanover on 19 May 1924. However, the referendum fell short of the one-third threshold required to enact devolution. The defeat has challenged the party, and many Protestant members are looking for a radical alternative, while many Catholics are looking to the Centre.

The main member of the DHP in the Reichstag is **Heinrich Meyer**. He represents the pragmatic attitudes of the Protestant farming constituency who desire a return to the independence or at least autonomy of Hanover—in any event, free from Prussian Berlin's domination.

5
Core Texts

To understand this polarized reality, we begin with communism as first articulated by Friedrich Engels in *Principles of Communism* (1847). This work turned out to be the draft of *The Communist Manifesto*, co-written with Karl Marx—arguably the most important political treatise of the nineteenth century. By engaging the *Principles*, we explore a theory of social organization created in the modern era, one that self-consciously saw itself as a natural extension of liberalism and a clear alternative to conservativism. Both social democracy and its offshoot communism held up the works of Engels and Marx as foundational texts, even as they disagreed—often violently—over their meaning. So influential were the core ideas of Marxism that every party had to engage them, if only to denounce them; they could not be ignored. Yet many non-Marxists went beyond denunciation—they cautiously appropriated certain Marxist ideas.

After grappling with Marxism, we proceed to our second major set of readings—National Socialism's party platform and commentary. These documents embodied the basic ideals of the Nazis: a race-based social Darwinist corporatism (with its antisemitic corollary); a loathing of class-based Marxism and individual-based liberalism; and military expansionism. Like Marxism, it was a total world philosophy that claimed to rest on historical laws grounded in nature. Like Marxism, it also offered its adherents a clear map of the world in which they struggled, allowing them to see behind the curtain to the machinations of those they blamed for their unhappiness. Like Marxism, it rose to become one of the most powerful ideologies of the twentieth century, organizing some of the world's greatest economies and spreading in one form or another to every continent.

We also look at two broad attempts to negotiate between the extremes of fascism and Marxism. One was a broad and eclectic revolutionary conservative movement. It denounced Marxism, liberalism, and traditional conservativism but generally stopped short of advocating fascism. It instead promoted radical, even revolutionary action to establish traditional cultural and social values in new and modern forms. Its supporters included Oswald Spengler, Ernst von Salomon, Arthur Moeller van den Bruck, Edgar Jung, and Carl Schmitt.

Diverse voices also supported the Republic, at one point or another including conservatives, Christian democrats, social democrats, liberals, and nationalists. Grounded in differing assumptions about the nature of society, they nonetheless agreed to work within the constitution's liberal framework but constantly sought to pull Germany in different directions —the classical tug-of-war of parliamentary democracy. Liberal democrats, primarily organized in the DDP, wholeheartedly embraced the promise of parliamentary democracy and tirelessly worked to strengthen it. Other liberals, especially in the DVP, at least initially and sometimes with fateful reservations, were more tentative in their support. The literary giant and traditional conservative Thomas Mann, for example, argued that in a time of dangerous extremes, a reasonable person had to accept practical realities over ideological idealism and tolerate the contentious nature of Germany's liberal constitution. He embodied the nuances of the *Vernunftrepublikaner*—those who (often reluctantly) regarded the Republic as the only reasonable alternative to political extremism. The Christian democrats of the Centre Party and some smaller Protestant parties such as the CSVD and CNBP but also in the particularist parties of the Bavarians and Hanoverians were torn, preferring to return to an imagined premodern golden age of Christian unity and morality. But like the *Vernunftrepublikaner*, they generally defended the Republic. And the social democrats embraced the Republic wholeheartedly as an essential step toward social democracy that must be defended at all costs against every threat from the Left or Right.

For each of the central ideologies, look especially for their views on the following: What is the central conflict in history? Where does sovereignty come from? What form should the state take? How does it relate to nationalism? How does it relate to economic relations?

Communism

Friedrich Engels, *Principles of Communism* (1847)

Friedrich Engels, the cofounder of Marxism along with Karl Marx, wrote Principles of Communism *(Grundsätze des Kommunismus) in 1847 as a draft explanation of the developing ideology. He structured it as a catechism, containing twenty-five questions and answers about communism. Engels presents core ideas of Marxism such as historical materialism, class struggle, and proletarian revolution, and* Principles of Communism *served as the basis for the* Communist Manifesto.

However, Principles *addresses issues from the first half of the nineteenth century—by 1929, at least seventy years in the past. The different contexts explain why Marxism underwent constant revision as conditions changed. As a result, there has never been a single, static Marxism but always a variety of competing Marxisms (and even socialisms), a point Engels raises in Question 24. In fact, shortly before Marx died in 1883, he wrote a letter to two leaders of French Marxism, Jules Guesde and Paul Lafargue, both of whom claimed to represent "Marxist" principles, and, frustrated at what he perceived to be their distortion of his ideas, quipped, "What is certain is that [if you are Marxists], then I myself am not a Marxist." Nevertheless, all Marxists shared a certain vocabulary, historical understanding of class struggle, and broad goals.*

Source: Engels, Frederick. *The Principles of Communism*. 1847. In *Selected Works*, by Karl Marx and Frederick Engels, trans. Paul Sweezy, vol. 1, 81–97. Moscow: Progress Publishers, 1969.

Study Questions
Conflict*: What does Engels claim is the main source of conflict throughout history? What are the implications for race-based, nation-based, or rational choice theories of struggle?*

Proletariat and bourgeoisie*: Who are the proletariat and bourgeoisie? What makes each of them a class? How do they stand in relationship to each* *other? How does the proletariat differ from other and earlier historical lower classes?*

Democracy and the state: What is the nature of the state and democracy? Whom do they serve? Can democracy be used in any manner to serve the proletariat? If so, how?

Revolution: Can positive change occur peacefully? How does capitalism lead to revolution? What will the proletarian revolution look like?

Industrialization: How does industrialization relate to Engels' understanding of class struggle? What evils does Engels trace to modern industrialism? How could these evils be avoided?

Internationalism: To what extent has modern capitalism stripped workers of their national character? Does Engels believe that the struggle of the proletariat with the bourgeoisie can be carried out internationally, all at once? What are the implications for nationalism?

Property: When Engels argues that the proletarian is without property, he does not mean workers do not own their clothes and toothbrushes. What does he mean? Why does he believe that proletarians will be motivated to destroy the whole system of individual private property?

Communists: What does Engels say the relationship of the communists to the proletarians as a whole is? In what ways are they different from other working-class parties? What are their immediate aims?

Culture, family, and religion: What will happen to the family and religion as they now exist?

The countryside and the city: How does communism relate to agriculture and the city?

1—What is Communism?

Communism is the doctrine of the conditions of the liberation of the proletariat.

2—What is the proletariat?

The proletariat is that class in society which lives entirely from the sale of its labor and does not draw profit from any kind of capital; whose weal and woe, whose life and death, whose sole existence depends on the demand for labor—hence, on the changing state of business, on the vagaries of unbridled competition. The proletariat, or the class of proletarians, is, in a word, the working class of the 19th century.

3—Proletarians, then, have not always existed?

No. There have always been poor and working classes; and the working class have mostly been poor. But there have not always been workers and poor people living under conditions as they are today; in other words, there have not always been proletarians, any more than there have always been free unbridled competitions.

4—How did the proletariat originate?

The Proletariat originated in the industrial revolution, which took place in England in the last half of the last [18th] century, and which has since then been repeated in all the civilized countries of the world.

This industrial revolution was precipitated by the discovery of the steam engine, various spinning machines, the mechanical loom, and a whole series of other mechanical devices. These machines, which were very expensive and hence could be bought only by big capitalists, altered the whole mode of production and displaced the former workers, because the machines turned out cheaper and better commodities than the workers could produce with their inefficient spinning wheels and handlooms. The machines delivered industry wholly into the hands of the big capitalists and rendered entirely worthless the meagre property of the workers (tools, looms, etc.). The result was that the capitalists soon had everything in their hands and nothing remained to the workers. This marked the introduction of the factory system into the textile industry.

Once the impulse to the introduction of machinery and the factory system had been given, this system spread quickly to all other branches of industry, especially cloth- and book-printing, pottery, and the metal industries.

Labor was more and more divided among the individual workers so that the worker who previously had done a complete piece of work now did only a part of that piece. This division of labor made it possible to produce things faster and cheaper. It reduced the activity of the individual worker to simple, endlessly repeated mechanical motions which could be performed not only as well but much better by a machine. In this way, all these industries fell, one after another, under the dominance of steam, machinery, and the factory system, just as spinning and weaving had already done.

But at the same time, they also fell into the hands of big capitalists, and their workers were deprived of whatever independence remained to them. Gradually, not only genuine manufacture but also handicrafts came within the province of the factory system as big capitalists increasingly displaced the small master craftsmen by setting up huge workshops, which saved many expenses and permitted an elaborate division of labor.

This is how it has come about that in civilized countries at the present time nearly all kinds of labor are performed in factories—and, in nearly all branches of work, handicrafts and manufacture have been superseded. This process has, to an ever greater degree, ruined the old middle class, especially the small handicraftsmen; it has entirely transformed the condition of the workers; and two new classes have been created which are gradually swallowing up all the others. These are:

i. The class of big capitalists, who, in all civilized countries, are already in almost exclusive possession of all the means of subsistence and of the instruments (machines, factories) and materials necessary for the production of the means of subsistence. This is the bourgeois class, or the bourgeoisie.

ii. The class of the wholly propertyless, who are obliged to sell their labor to the bourgeoisie in order to get, in exchange, the means of subsistence for their support. This is called the class of proletarians, or the proletariat.

5—Under what conditions does this sale of the labor of the proletarians to the bourgeoisie take place?

Labor is a commodity, like any other, and its price is therefore determined by exactly the same laws that apply to other commodities. In a regime of big industry or of free competition—as we shall see, the two come to the same thing—the price of a commodity is, on the average, always equal to its cost of production. Hence, the price of labor is also equal to the cost of production of labor.

But, the costs of production of labor consist of precisely the quantity of means of subsistence necessary to enable the worker to continue working, and to prevent the working class from dying out. The worker will therefore get no more for his labor than is necessary for this purpose; the price of labor, or the wage, will, in other words, be the lowest, the minimum, required for the maintenance of life.

However, since business is sometimes better and sometimes worse, it follows that the worker sometimes gets more and sometimes gets less for his commodities. But, again, just as the industrialist, on the average of good times and bad, gets no more and no less for his commodities than what they cost, similarly on the average the worker gets no more and no less than his minimum.

This economic law of wages operates the more strictly the greater the degree to which big industry has taken possession of all branches of production.

6—What working classes were there before the industrial revolution?

The working classes have always, according to the different stages of development of society, lived in different circumstances and had different relations to the owning and ruling classes.

In antiquity, the workers were the slaves of the owners, just as they still are in many backward countries and even in the southern part of the United States.

In the Middle Ages, they were the serfs of the landowning nobility, as they still are in Hungary, Poland, and Russia. In the Middle Ages, and indeed right up to the industrial revolution, there were also journeymen in the cities who worked in the service of petty bourgeois masters. Gradually, as manufacture developed, these journeymen became manufacturing workers who were even then employed by larger capitalists.

7—In what way do proletarians differ from slaves?

The slave is sold once and for all; the proletarian must sell himself daily and hourly.

The individual slave, property of one master, is assured an existence, however miserable it may be, because of the master's interest. The individual proletarian, property as it were of the entire bourgeois class which buys his labor only when someone has need of it, has no secure existence. This existence is assured only to the class as a whole.

The slave is outside competition; the proletarian is in it and experiences all its vagaries.

The slave counts as a thing, not as a member of society. Thus, the slave can have a better existence than the proletarian, while the proletarian belongs to a higher stage of social development and, himself, stands on a higher social level than the slave.

The slave frees himself when, of all the relations of private property, he abolishes only the relation of slavery and thereby becomes a proletarian; the proletarian can free himself only by abolishing private property in general.

8—In what way do proletarians differ from serfs?

The serf possesses and uses an instrument of production, a piece of land, in exchange for which he gives up a part of his product or part of the services of his labor.

The proletarian works with the instruments of production of another, for the account of this other, in exchange for a part of the product.

The serf gives up, the proletarian receives. The serf has an assured existence, the proletarian has not. The serf is outside competition, the proletarian is in it.

The serf liberates himself in one of three ways: either he runs away to the city and there becomes a handicraftsman; or, instead of products and services, he gives money to his lord and thereby becomes a free tenant; or he overthrows his feudal lord and himself becomes a property owner. In short, by one route or another, he gets into the owning class and enters into competition. The proletarian liberates himself by abolishing competition, private property, and all class differences.

9—In what way do proletarians differ from handicraftsmen?

In contrast to the proletarian, the so-called handicraftsman, as he still existed almost everywhere in the past [18th] century and still exists here and there at present, is a proletarian at most temporarily. His goal is to acquire capital himself wherewith to exploit other workers. He can often achieve this goal where guilds still exist or where freedom from guild restrictions has not yet led to the introduction of factory-style methods into the crafts nor yet to fierce competition. But as soon as the factory system has been introduced into the crafts and competition flourishes fully, this perspective dwindles away and the handicraftsman becomes more and more a proletarian. The handicraftsman therefore frees himself by becoming either bourgeois or entering the middle class in general, or becoming a proletarian because of competition (as is now more often the case). In which case he can free himself by joining the proletarian movement, i.e., the more or less communist movement.

10—In what way do proletarians differ from manufacturing workers?

The manufacturing worker of the 16th to the 18th centuries still had, with but few exception, an instrument of production in his own possession—his loom, the family spinning wheel, a little plot of land which he cultivated in his spare time. The proletarian has none of these things.

The manufacturing worker almost always lives

in the countryside and in a more or less patriarchal relation to his landlord or employer; the proletarian lives, for the most part, in the city and his relation to his employer is purely a cash relation.

The manufacturing worker is torn out of his patriarchal relation by big industry, loses whatever property he still has, and in this way becomes a proletarian.

11—What were the immediate consequences of the industrial revolution and of the division of society into bourgeoisie and proletariat?

First, the lower and lower prices of industrial products brought about by machine labor totally destroyed, in all countries of the world, the old system of manufacture or industry based upon hand labor.

In this way, all semi-barbarian countries, which had hitherto been more or less strangers to historical development, and whose industry had been based on manufacture, were violently forced out of their isolation. They bought the cheaper commodities of the English and allowed their own manufacturing workers to be ruined. Countries which had known no progress for thousands of years—for example, India—were thoroughly revolutionized, and even China is now on the way to a revolution.

We have come to the point where a new machine invented in England deprives millions of Chinese workers of their livelihood within a year's time.

In this way, big industry has brought all the people of the Earth into contact with each other, has merged all local markets into one world market, has spread civilization and progress everywhere and has thus ensured that whatever happens in civilized countries will have repercussions in all other countries.

It follows that if the workers in England or France now liberate themselves, this must set off revolution in all other countries—revolutions which, sooner or later, must accomplish the liberation of their respective working class.

Second, wherever big industries displaced manufacture, the bourgeoisie developed in wealth and power to the utmost and made itself the first class of the country. The result was that wherever this happened, the bourgeoisie took political power into its own hands and displaced the hitherto ruling classes, the aristocracy, the guildmasters, and their representative, the absolute monarchy.

The bourgeoisie annihilated the power of the aristocracy, the nobility, by abolishing the entailment of estates—in other words, by making landed property subject to purchase and sale, and by doing away with the special privileges of the nobility. It destroyed the power of the guildmasters by abolishing guilds and handicraft privileges. In their place, it put competition—that is, a state of society in which everyone has the right to enter into any branch of industry, the only obstacle being a lack of the necessary capital.

The introduction of free competition is thus public declaration that from now on the members of society are unequal only to the extent that their capitals are unequal, that capital is the decisive power, and that therefore the capitalists, the bourgeoisie, have become the first class in society.

Free competition is necessary for the establishment of big industry, because it is the only condition of society in which big industry can make its way.

Having destroyed the social power of the nobility and the guildmasters, the bourgeois also destroyed their political power. Having raised itself to the actual position of first class in society, it proclaims itself to be also the dominant political class. This it does through the introduction of the representative system which rests on bourgeois equality before the law and the recognition of free competition, and in European countries takes the form of constitutional monarchy. In these constitutional monarchies, only those who possess a certain capital are voters—that is to say, only members of the bourgeoisie. These bourgeois voters choose the deputies, and these bourgeois deputies, by using their right to refuse to vote taxes, choose a bourgeois government.

Third, everywhere the proletariat develops in step with the bourgeoisie. In proportion, as the bourgeoisie grows in wealth, the proletariat grows in numbers. For, since the proletarians can be employed only by capital, and since capital extends only through employing labor, it follows that the growth of the proletariat proceeds at precisely the same pace as the growth of capital.

Simultaneously, this process draws members of the bourgeoisie and proletarians together into the great cities where industry can be carried on most profitably, and by thus throwing great masses in one spot it gives to the proletarians a consciousness of their own strength.

Moreover, the further this process advances, the more new labor-saving machines are invented, the greater is the pressure exercised by big industry on wages, which, as we have seen, sink to their minimum and therewith render the condition of the proletariat increasingly unbearable. The growing dissatisfaction of the proletariat thus joins with its rising power to prepare a proletarian social revolution.

12—What were the further consequences of the industrial revolution?

Big industry created in the steam engine, and other machines, the means of endlessly expanding industrial production, speeding it up, and cutting its costs. With production thus facilitated, the free competition, which is necessarily bound up with big industry, assumed the most extreme forms; a multitude of capitalists invaded industry, and, in a short while, more was produced than was needed.

As a consequence, finished commodities could not be sold, and a so-called commercial crisis broke out. Factories had to be closed, their owners went bankrupt, and the workers were without bread. Deepest misery reigned everywhere.

After a time, the superfluous products were sold, the factories began to operate again, wages rose, and gradually business got better than ever.

But it was not long before too many commodities were again produced and a new crisis broke out, only to follow the same course as its predecessor.

Ever since the beginning of this [19th] century, the condition of industry has constantly fluctuated between periods of prosperity and periods of crisis; nearly every five to seven years, a fresh crisis has intervened, always with the greatest hardship for workers, and always accompanied by general revolutionary stirrings and the direct peril to the whole existing order of things.

13—What follows from these periodic commercial crises?

First: That, though big industry in its earliest stage created free competition, it has now outgrown free competition;

that, for big industry, competition and generally the individualistic organization of production have become a fetter which it must and will shatter;

that, so long as big industry remains on its present footing, it can be maintained only at the cost of general chaos every seven years, each time threatening the whole of civilization and not only plunging the proletarians into misery but also ruining large sections of the bourgeoisie;

hence, either that big industry must itself be given up, which is an absolute impossibility, or that it makes unavoidably necessary an entirely new organization of society in which production is no longer directed by mutually competing individual industrialists but rather by the whole society operating according to a definite plan and taking account of the needs of all.

Second: That big industry, and the limitless expansion of production which it makes possible, bring within the range of feasibility a social order in which so much is produced that every member of society will be in a position to exercise and develop all his powers and faculties in complete freedom.

It thus appears that the very qualities of big industry which, in our present-day society, produce misery and crises are those which, in a different form of society, will abolish this misery and these catastrophic depressions.

We see with the greatest clarity:

i. That all these evils are from now on to be ascribed solely to a social order which no longer corresponds to the requirements of the real situation; and
ii. That it is possible, through a new social order, to do away with these evils altogether.

14—What will this new social order have to be like?

Above all, it will have to take the control of industry and of all branches of production out of the hands of mutually competing individuals, and instead institute a system in which all these branches of production are operated by society as a whole—that is, for the common account, according to a common plan, and with the participation of all members of society.

It will, in other words, abolish competition and replace it with association.

Moreover, since the management of industry by individuals necessarily implies private property, and since competition is in reality merely the manner and form in which the control of industry by private property owners expresses itself, it follows that private property cannot be separated from competition and the individual management of industry. Private property must, therefore, be abolished and in its place must come the common utilization of all instruments of production and the distribution of all products according to common agreement—in a word, what is called the communal ownership of goods.

In fact, the abolition of private property is, doubtless, the shortest and most significant way to characterize the revolution in the whole social order which has been made necessary by the development of industry—and for this reason it is rightly advanced by communists as their main demand.

15—Was not the abolition of private property possible at an earlier time?

No. Every change in the social order, every revolution in property relations, is the necessary consequence of the creation of new forces of production which no longer fit into the old property relations.

Private property has not always existed.

When, towards the end of the Middle Ages, there arose a new mode of production which could not be carried on under the then existing feudal and guild forms of property, this manufacture, which had outgrown the old property relations, created a new property form, private property. And for manufacture and the earliest stage of development of big industry, private property was the only possible property form; the social order based on it was the only possible social order.

So long as it is not possible to produce so much that there is enough for all, with more left over for expanding the social capital and extending the forces of production—so long as this is not possible, there must always be a ruling class directing the use of society's productive forces, and a poor, oppressed class. How these classes are constituted depends on the stage of development.

The agrarian Middle Ages give us the baron and the serf; the cities of the later Middle Ages show us the guildmaster and the journeyman and the day laborer; the 17th century has its manufacturing workers; the 19th has big factory owners and proletarians.

It is clear that, up to now, the forces of production have never been developed to the point where enough could be developed for all, and that private property has become a fetter and a barrier in relation to the further development of the forces of production.

Now, however, the development of big industry has ushered in a new period. Capital and the forces of production have been expanded to an unprecedented extent, and the means are at hand to multiply them without limit in the near future. Moreover, the forces of production have been concentrated in the hands of a few bourgeois, while the great mass of the people are more and more falling into the proletariat, their situation becoming more wretched and intolerable in proportion to the increase of wealth of the bourgeoisie. And finally, these mighty and easily extended forces of production have so far outgrown private property and the bourgeoisie, that they threaten at any moment to unleash the most violent disturbances of the social order. Now, under these conditions, the abolition of private property has become not only possible but absolutely necessary.

16—Will the peaceful abolition of private property be possible?

It would be desirable if this could happen, and the communists would certainly be the last to oppose it. Communists know only too well that all conspiracies are not only useless, but even harmful. They know all too well that revolutions are not made intentionally and arbitrarily, but that, everywhere and always, they have been the necessary consequence of conditions which were wholly independent of the will and direction of individual parties and entire classes.

But they also see that the development of the proletariat in nearly all civilized countries has been violently suppressed, and that in this way the opponents of communism have been working toward a revolution with all their strength. If the oppressed proletariat is finally driven to revolution, then we communists will defend the interests of the proletarians with deeds as we now defend them with words.

17—Will it be possible for private property to be abolished at one stroke?

No, no more than existing forces of production can at one stroke be multiplied to the extent necessary for the creation of a communal society.

In all probability, the proletarian revolution will transform existing society gradually and will be able to abolish private property only when the means of production are available in sufficient quantity.

18—What will be the course of this revolution?

Above all, it will establish a democratic constitution, and through this, the direct or indirect dominance of the proletariat. Direct in England, where the proletarians are already a majority of the people. Indirect in France and Germany, where the majority of the people consists not only of proletarians, but also of small peasants and petty bourgeois who are in the process of falling into the proletariat, who are more and more dependent in all their political interests on the proletariat, and who must, therefore, soon adapt to the demands of the proletariat. Perhaps this will cost a second struggle, but the outcome can only be the victory of the proletariat.

Democracy would be wholly valueless to the proletariat if it were not immediately used as a means for putting through measures directed against private property and ensuring the livelihood of the proletariat. The main measures, emerging as the necessary result of existing relations, are the following:

i. Limitation of private property through progressive taxation, heavy inheritance taxes, abolition of inheritance through collateral lines (brothers, nephews, etc.), forced loans, etc.

ii. Gradual expropriation of landowners, industrialists, railroad magnates and shipowners, partly through competition by state industry, partly directly through compensation in the form of bonds.

iii. Confiscation of the possessions of all emigrants and rebels against the majority of the people.

iv. Organization of labor or employment of proletarians on publicly owned land, in factories and workshops, with competition among the workers being abolished and with the factory owners, in so far as they still exist, being obliged to pay the same high wages as those paid by the state.

v. An equal obligation on all members of society to work until such time as private property has been completely abolished. Formation of industrial armies, especially for agriculture.

vi. Centralization of money and credit in the hands of the state through a national bank with state capital, and the suppression of all private banks and bankers.

vii. Increase in the number of national factories, workshops, railroads, ships; bringing new lands into cultivation and improvement of land already under cultivation—all in proportion to the growth of the capital and labor force at the disposal of the nation.

viii. Education of all children, from the moment they can leave their mother's care, in national establishments at national cost. Education and production together.

ix. Construction, on public lands, of great palaces as communal dwellings for associated groups of citizens engaged in both industry and agriculture and combining in their way of life the advantages of urban and rural conditions while avoiding the one-sidedness and drawbacks of each.

  x. Destruction of all unhealthy and jerry-built dwellings in urban districts.

  xi. Equal inheritance rights for children born in and out of wedlock.

  xii. Concentration of all means of transportation in the hands of the nation.

It is impossible, of course, to carry out all these measures at once. But one will always bring others in its wake. Once the first radical attack on private property has been launched, the proletariat will find itself forced to go ever further, to concentrate increasingly in the hands of the state all capital, all agriculture, all transport, all trade. All the foregoing measures are directed to this end; and they will become practicable and feasible, capable of producing their centralizing effects to precisely the degree that the proletariat, through its labor, multiplies the country's productive forces.

Finally, when all capital, all production, all exchange have been brought together in the hands of the nation, private property will disappear of its own accord, money will become superfluous, and production will so expand and man so change that society will be able to slough off whatever of its old economic habits may remain.

19—Will it be possible for this revolution to take place in one country alone?

No. By creating the world market, big industry has already brought all the peoples of the Earth, and especially the civilized peoples, into such close relation with one another that none is independent of what happens to the others.

Further, it has co-ordinated the social development of the civilized countries to such an extent that, in all of them, bourgeoisie and proletariat have become the decisive classes, and the struggle between them the great struggle of the day. It follows that the communist revolution will not merely be a national phenomenon but must take place simultaneously in all civilized countries—that is to say, at least in England, America, France, and Germany.

It will develop in each of these countries more or less rapidly, according as one country or the other has a more developed industry, greater wealth, a more significant mass of productive forces. Hence, it will go slowest and will meet most obstacles in Germany, most rapidly and with the fewest difficulties in England. It will have a powerful impact on the other countries of the world, and will radically alter the course of development which they have followed up to now, while greatly stepping up its pace.

It is a universal revolution and will, accordingly, have a universal range.

20—What will be the consequences of the ultimate disappearance of private property?

Society will take all forces of production and means of commerce, as well as the exchange and distribution of products, out of the hands of private capitalists and will manage them in accordance with a plan based on the availability of resources and the needs of the whole society. In this way, most important of all, the evil consequences which are now associated with the conduct of big industry will be abolished.

There will be no more crises; the expanded production, which for the present order of society is overproduction and hence a prevailing cause of misery, will then be insufficient and in need of being expanded much further. Instead of generating misery, overproduction will reach beyond the elementary requirements of society to assure the satisfaction of the needs of all; it will create new needs and, at the same time, the means of satisfying them. It will become the condition of, and the stimulus to, new progress, which will no longer throw the whole social order into confusion, as progress has always done in the past. Big industry, freed from the pressure of private property, will undergo such an expansion that what we now see will seem as petty in comparison as manufacture seems when put beside the big industry of our own day. This development of industry will make available to society a sufficient mass of products to satisfy the needs of everyone.

The same will be true of agriculture, which also suffers from the pressure of private property and is held back by the division of privately owned land into small parcels. Here, existing improvements and scientific procedures will be put into practice, with a resulting leap forward which will assure to society all the products it needs.

In this way, such an abundance of goods will be able to satisfy the needs of all its members.

The division of society into different, mutually hostile classes will then become unnecessary. Indeed, it will be not only unnecessary but intolerable in the new social order. The existence of classes originated in the division of labor, and the division of labor, as it has been known up to the present, will completely disappear. For mechanical and chemical processes are not enough to bring industrial and agricultural production up to the level we have described; the capacities of the men who make use of these processes must undergo a corresponding development.

Just as the peasants and manufacturing workers of the last century changed their whole way of life and became quite different people when they were drawn into big industry, in the same way, communal control over production by society as a whole, and the resulting new development, will both require an entirely different kind of human material.

People will no longer be, as they are today, subordinated to a single branch of production, bound to it, exploited by it; they will no longer develop *one* of their faculties at the expense of all others; they will no longer know only *one* branch, or one branch of a single branch, of production as a whole. Even industry as it is today is finding such people less and less useful.

Industry controlled by society as a whole, and operated according to a plan, presupposes well-rounded human beings, their faculties developed in balanced fashion, able to see the system of production in its entirety.

The form of the division of labor which makes one a peasant, another a cobbler, a third a factory worker, a fourth a stock-market operator, has already been undermined by machinery and will completely disappear. Education will enable young people quickly to familiarize themselves with the whole system of production and to pass from one branch of production to another in response to the needs of society or their own inclinations. It will, therefore, free them from the one-sided character which the present-day division of labor impresses upon every individual. Communist society will, in this way, make it possible for its members to put their comprehensively developed faculties to full use. But, when this happens, classes will necessarily disappear. It follows that society organized on a communist basis is incompatible with the existence of classes on the one hand, and that the very building of such a society provides the means of abolishing class differences on the other.

A corollary of this is that the difference between city and country is destined to disappear. The management of agriculture and industry by the same people rather than by two different classes of people is, if only for purely material reasons, a necessary condition of communist association. The dispersal of the agricultural population on the land, alongside the crowding of the industrial population into the great cities, is a condition which corresponds to an undeveloped state of both agriculture and industry and can already be felt as an obstacle to further development.

The general co-operation of all members of society for the purpose of planned exploitation of the forces of production, the expansion of production to the point where it will satisfy the needs of all, the abolition of a situation in which the needs of some are satisfied at the expense of the needs of others, the complete liquidation of classes and their conflicts, the rounded development of the capacities of all members of society through the elimination of the present division of labor, through industrial education, through engaging in varying activities, through the participation by all in the enjoyments produced by all, through the combination of city and country—

these are the main consequences of the abolition of private property.

21—What will be the influence of communist society on the family?

It will transform the relations between the sexes into a purely private matter which concerns only the persons involved and into which society has no occasion to intervene. It can do this since it does away with private property and educates children on a communal basis, and in this way removes the two bases of traditional marriage—the dependence rooted in private property, of the women on the man, and of the children on the parents.

And here is the answer to the outcry of the highly moral philistines against the "community of women." Community of women is a condition which belongs entirely to bourgeois society and which today finds its complete expression in prostitution. But prostitution is based on private property and falls with it. Thus, communist society, instead of introducing community of women, in fact abolishes it.

22—What will be the attitude of communism to existing nationalities?

The nationalities of the peoples associating themselves in accordance with the principle of community will be compelled to mingle with each other as a result of this association and thereby to dissolve themselves, just as the various estate and class distinctions must disappear through the abolition of their basis, private property.

23—What will be its attitude to existing religions?

All religions so far have been the expression of historical stages of development of individual peoples or groups of peoples. But communism is the stage of historical development which makes all existing religions superfluous and brings about their disappearance.

24—How do communists differ from socialists?

The so-called socialists are divided into three categories.

Reactionary Socialists: The first category consists of adherents of a feudal and patriarchal society which has already been destroyed, and is still daily being destroyed, by big industry and world trade and their creation, bourgeois society. This category concludes, from the evils of existing society, that feudal and patriarchal society must be restored because it was free of such evils. In one way or another, all their proposals are directed to this end.

This category of reactionary socialists, for all their seeming partisanship and their scalding tears for the misery of the proletariat, is nevertheless energetically opposed by the communists for the following reasons:

   i. It strives for something which is entirely impossible.

  ii. It seeks to establish the rule of the aristocracy, the guildmasters, the small producers, and their retinue of absolute or feudal monarchs, officials, soldiers, and priests—a society which was, to be sure, free of the evils of present-day society but which brought it at least as many evils without even offering to the oppressed workers the prospect of liberation through a communist revolution.

 iii. As soon as the proletariat becomes revolutionary and communist, these reactionary socialists show their true colors by immediately making common cause with the bourgeoisie against the proletarians.

Bourgeois Socialists: The second category consists of adherents of present-day society who have been frightened for its future by the evils to which it necessarily gives rise. What they want, therefore, is to maintain this society while getting rid of the evils which are an inherent part of it.

To this end, some propose mere welfare measures—while others come forward with grandiose systems of reform which, under the pretense of re-organizing society, are in fact intended to preserve the foundations, and hence the life, of existing society.

Communists must unremittingly struggle against these bourgeois socialists because they work for the enemies of communists and protect the society which communists aim to overthrow.

Democratic Socialists: Finally, the third category consists of democratic socialists who favor some of the same measures the communists advocate, as described in Question 18, not as part of the transition to communism, however, but as measures which they believe will be sufficient to abolish the misery and evils of present-day society.

These democratic socialists are either proletarians who are not yet sufficiently clear about the conditions of the liberation of their class, or they are representatives of the petty bourgeoisie, a class which, prior to the achievement of democracy and the socialist measures to which it gives rise, has many interests in common with the proletariat.

It follows that, in moments of action, the communists will have to come to an understanding with these democratic socialists, and in general to follow as far as possible a common policy with them—provided that these socialists do not enter into the service of the ruling bourgeoisie and attack the communists.

It is clear that this form of co-operation in action does not exclude the discussion of differences.

[*The final question, 25, is specific to the immediate conditions of the 1840s and has been omitted.*]

"Programmatic Statement for the National and Social Liberation of the German People" (1930)

The program was intended to address concerns about the NSDAP's growth and to clarify the KPD's stance on the Young Plan as well as the entire international Versailles system. The new program sought to prove to workers that only the KPD could actually offer what National Socialism promised: the tearing-up of the Versailles Treaty and Young Plan; restoration of Germany's lost territories; prosperity for all Germans; victory over French and Polish imperialism; and the restoration of national dignity. Although never descending into outright chauvinism or pan-German power fantasies, the program's rhetoric is undoubtedly nationalistic in flavor.

Source: "Programmerklärung der KPD zur nationalen und sozialen Befreiung des deutschen Volkes." *Die Rote Fahne* 13, no. 197 (24 August 1930). Translated by Robert Goodrich.

Study Questions

Context: *How had the KPD altered Engels's vision of socialism to fit the context of 1930?*

Nationalism: *While Engels was unambiguous that the nation-state and nationalism were products of bourgeois liberalism, how does the 1930 program address the issue?*

Young Plan: *The Young Plan is mentioned eighteen times in this document. Why? And what is the KPD's position?*

National Socialism: *Much of the document addresses the NSDAP. How does the KPD characterize the NSDAP? How do they differentiate themselves from the NSDAP?*

Social democracy: *What is the KPD's stance on social democracy (the SPD)?*

Liberalism, the bourgeoisie, and parliament: *What is the stance of the KPD on liberalism? Why do they reject working with the existing power structures in coalitions?*

Soviet: What exactly does the KPD mean by a "Soviet Germany?" What would that look like and how will they get there? What do they mean by "dictatorship of the proletariat?"

While Social Democracy wants to sustain and perpetuate the existent state of misery, while the Hitler party with deceitful phrases heralds a nebulous "Third Reich" that in reality would look even worse than the present wretchedness, we communists say clearly what we want. We conceal nothing. We make no promises that we will not unequivocally keep. Every laborer, every female worker, every young proletarian, every office worker, every member of the cities' indigent middle classes, every working peasant in the country, every honest productive person in Germany, should with full clarity be convinced of our goal. The only way to the national liberation of the broad masses is a Soviet Germany.

The German fascists (National Socialists) are presently engaged in the most aggressive advances against the German working class. In a period of German enslavement through the Treaty of Versailles, growing crisis, unemployment, and the misery of the masses, the fascists attempt, through unbridled demagogy and the shrieking of radical phrases under the banner of resistance against the Policy of Fulfillment and the Young Plan, to win over significant layers of the petty bourgeoisie, déclassée intellectuals, students, office workers, and peasants, as well as groups of backward, unenlightened workers. The partial successes of National Socialist agitation are the result of twelve years of treacherous policies by Social Democracy, which, through suppression of the revolutionary movement, participation in capitalist rationalization, and complete capitulation before the imperialists (France, Poland), have prepared the ground for National Socialist demagogy.

Against this National Socialist demagogy the Communist Party of Germany sets its program of struggle against fascism, its policy of true representation of the interests of the working masses of Germany.

The fascists (National Socialists) maintain that they are fighting for the national liberation of the German people. They purport to be against the Young Plan, which brings misery and hunger to the working masses of Germany. These assurances by the fascists are deliberate lies. The German bourgeoisie has adopted the predatory Young Plan with the intention of passing all its burdens on to the working people.

The fascists provide practical help in the implementation of the Young Plan by condoning and encouraging the transfer of its burdens onto the working masses, by assisting in the implementation of the customs and tax laws dictated by the Young Plan (approval of the National Socialist Reichstag faction to all submissions for customs and tax increases; Frick's negro-tax in Thuringia), by attempting to forestall and stifle all strike movements against wage reductions. [*"Negro-tax" was the mocking name for Frick's (NSDAP) proposed flat-rate poll tax. The name derived from comparisons to tax practices in Germany's former colonies, where the local African populations had been taxed on a similar universal, flat-rate basis.*]

The governing parties and Social Democracy have sold off the belongings, life, and existence of the working German people to the highest-bidding foreign imperialists. The Social Democratic leaders, Hermann Müller, Severing, Grzesinski, and Zörgiebel, are not only the executioner's assistants of the German bourgeoisie, but simultaneously the willing agents of French and Polish imperialism.

All actions of treacherous, corrupt Social Democracy represent continuous high treason against the vital interests of the working masses of Germany.

Only we communists are fighting against both the Young Plan and the Versailles plunderers' peace, the starting point of the enslavement of all working people in Germany, as well as against all international treaties, agreements, and plans (the Locarno Treaty, Dawes Plan, Young Plan, German-Polish Agreement, etc.) that result from the Versailles Peace Treaty. We communists are against any fulfillment of reparations payments, against any payment of international debts.

We solemnly declare before all the peoples of the Earth, before all foreign governments and capitalists, that in the event of our seizure of power we will declare all obligations arising from the Treaty of Versailles to be null and void, that we will not render a single pfennig in interest payments on the imperialist bonds, loans, and capital investments in Germany.

We lead and organize the struggle against taxes and duties, against rising rents and municipal tariffs, against wage cuts, unemployment, and every attempt to transfer the burdens of the Young Plan onto the working populace in city and country.

The fascists (National Socialists) maintain that they are against the borders drawn by the Versailles Peace, against the separation of a number of German territories from Germany. In reality, however, fascism suppresses the peoples subjected to it everywhere it is in power (in Italy the Germans and Croats; in Poland the Ukrainians, Byelorussians, and Germans; in Finland the Swedes, etc.). The leaders of German fascism, however, Hitler and his accomplices, do not raise their voices against the forcible annexation of South Tyrol by fascist Italy. Hitler and the German National Socialists keep silent over the needs of the German peasant communities of South Tyrol, who groan under the yoke of Italian fascism.

Hitler and his party have concluded behind the backs of the German people a sordid secret pact with the Italian fascist regime, on the basis of which the German territory of the South Tyrol is handed over unconditionally to the foreign conquerors. With this despicable act Hitler and his party have sold off the national interests of Germany's working masses to the victorious powers of Versailles, in the same fashion as German Social Democracy has been continuously doing for twelve years. We communists declare that we do not accept the forcible incorporation of a people or part of a population into other national state-structures, that we do not recognize a single border that is drawn without the consent of the working masses and the actual majority of the population.

We communists are opposed to the territorial rupturing and plundering of Germany carried out as a consequence of the dictated peace of Versailles.

The fascists (National Socialists) maintain that their movement is directed against imperialism. In reality, however, they enter into agreements with imperialists (England, Italy). They turn against the struggle for freedom of colonial peoples (India, China, Indochina); demand colonies for Germany; and chase after new wars, above all seeking intervention against the Soviet Union, the only country whose victorious working class has triumphantly defended itself by force of arms against all assaults by world capital, against all raids by the Versailles imperialists. Wherever imperialism enslaves, strangles, and shoots down the oppressed masses of the people, the German fascists work through their representatives: in China through the Kapp putschists Wetzel and Kriebel, in South America through the military mission of General Kuntz, in Austria through the Liebknecht murderer Papst.

We communists are the only party that seeks the overthrow of imperialism and the liberation of the people from the power of finance capital. Therefore we call on the working masses of Germany to fight above all against the enemy in their own country for the overthrow of capitalist rule and the establishment of Soviet power in Germany, to tear up the Versailles Peace Treaty and to do away with its consequences.

The fascists (National Socialists) maintain that they are a "national," a "socialist," and a "workers'" party. We retort that they are antipopulist and antilabor, antisocialist, a party of the most extreme reaction, of the exploitation and enslavement of the working people. A party anxious to take from the working people everything that even the bourgeois and Social Democratic governments could not take from them. A party of murderous, fascist dictatorship, a party for the reestablishment of the regime of the Junkers and officers, a party for the restoration of the "hereditary" privileges of countless German princes, for the reinstatement of officers and high officials to their titles and posts.

The fascists (National Socialists) maintain that they are opponents of today's state and social order. At the same time, however, they participate alongside the parties of big business in the government of the

Weimar Republic in Thuringia. They share ministerial seats with the capitalist Peoples' Party [the DVP] and with the landlords of the Economic Party. In Saxony they bargain with everyone from the businessmen's parties to the "Peoples' National Association" over the formation of a coalition government. They declare themselves willing to participate in a national government with all bourgeois Young Plan parties. They control police departments in Thuringia. They are subsidized by capitalists. They tolerate in their own ranks not only Hohenzollern princes, Coburg dukes, and noble lords, but also numerous manorial landowners, industrialists, and millionaires, including the exploiter Kirdorf and other agitators like the textile manufacturer Mutschmann.

Every party in Germany, with the single exception of the Communist Party, is pursuing coalition politics in the Reich, in Prussia, in Thuringia, and in the other individual states. Every party, other than the Communists, is a coalition party, a governing party, a ministerial party.

Only we communists are opposed to any collaboration with the bourgeoisie; only we are for the revolutionary overthrow of the contemporary capitalist social order, for the abolition of all rights and privileges of the ruling classes, for the elimination of all exploitation.

The National Socialists maintain that the economic crisis and the plundering of the masses are merely consequences of the Young Plan, that the surmounting of the crisis is already assured so long as Germany casts off the shackles of the Versailles Treaty. This is a gross fraud. To liberate the German people, it is not enough simply to break the power of foreign capital, but the rule of their own bourgeoisie in their own country must be overthrown at the same time. The crisis rages not only in the Germany of the Young Plan, but also in the victorious imperial powers with America at the forefront. Wherever the capitalists and their agents, the Social Democrats, are at the helm, the masses are exploited in the same way. Only in the Soviet Union are industry and agriculture on the ascendant. Only in the Soviet Union is unem-

ployment eliminated, wages raised, and the sociopolitical accomplishments of the working people expanded to unprecedented heights. In every capitalist country, in every country of fascism and Social Democracy, there grows misery and hunger, wage cuts and unemployment, reaction and terror.

The Communist Party of Germany deploys the harshest political and defensive mass struggle against nationally treacherous, antisocialist, antilabor fascism.

We fight for the working masses' salvation from the looming catastrophe.

We communists declare that, after the overthrow of the power of the capitalists and large landowners, after the establishment of a proletarian dictatorship in Germany, our first course will be to implement the following program in fraternal alliance with the proletarians of all other countries, which we set against National Socialist demagogy:

We will tear up the rapacious Versailles "peace treaty" and the Young Plan which subjugate Germany; we will annul all international debts and reparations payments which the capitalists have imposed on the working people of Germany.

We communists will champion the full right to self-determination for all nations and, in consensus with the revolutionary workers of France, England, Poland, Italy, Czechoslovakia, etc., will secure the opportunity of joining to Soviet Germany those German territories that express their desire for it.

We communists will conclude between Soviet Germany and the Union of Soviet Socialist Republics a firm political and economic alliance, on the basis of which the factories will supply Soviet Germany's industrial products to the Soviet Union, to receive foodstuffs and raw materials from the Soviet Union in return.

We declare before the working people of Germany: if today's Germany is vulnerable and isolated, then Soviet Germany, which will be buttressed by more than nine-tenths of its population and will enjoy the sympathy of the working peoples of all countries, need not fear invasion by foreign imperialists. We refer the working people of Germany to the fact that, only thanks to the support of the workers of all countries, has the Soviet Union successfully managed to repulse the interventions of world imperialism with the aid of its invincible Red Army.

In contrast to the hypocritical fascist phrases against large bank and commercial capital, in contrast to the empty National Socialist war of words against parasites and corruption, we will implement the following program:

Upon gaining power we will mercilessly put an end to the activities of the banking magnates, who openly impose their will over the country today. We will implement the proletarian nationalization of the banks and nullify the burden of debt to German and foreign capitalists.

The wholesalers, the magnates of commercial capital, are today driving the small merchants to ruin, throwing thousands of employees out into the streets, destroying the livelihoods of hundreds of thousands of the middle classes, extorting the peasants, and pushing up prices for mass-consumption items. Upon gaining power we will put an end to the activities of the commercial magnates, nationalize the wholesaling system, and create strong consumer cooperatives that will truly represent the interests of all working peoples and liberate them from rapacious profiteers. We will smash with an iron fist any speculation which takes advantage of the misery of the working people.

We will destroy capitalist forms of the municipal economy [*essential services such as water and electricity*], expropriate the large landowners without compensation, and billet the workers and the poor populations of the city into the houses of the rich.

We will scale the costs for rent, gas, water, electricity, transport, and all public utilities in accordance with the class principle, reducing them to the minimum for proletarians and less well-off working people.

We will put an end to the bourgeoisie's fiscal policy. Through the seizure of power, the expropriation without compensation of the industrial enterprises, banks, large landowners, and wholesalers, the working class will create all the preconditions for the class budget of the proletarian state. We will unconditionally ensure social security of all kinds (unemployment, disability, health, old age, and accident insurance; assistance for the war disabled and for soldiers' surviving dependents) at the state's expense.

We will exempt the treasury of the German Soviet Republic from all unproductive expenditures on police and church, pensions and annuities. We will liberate it from being hounded by imperial princes, kings, dukes, nobles, marshals, generals, admirals; from ministerial salaries and ministerial pensions; from remuneration for reactionary officials; from corruption and luxury expenses of every description.

We will break the rule of the large landowners; we will expropriate their land and property without compensation and turn both over to the landless peasants; we will produce Soviet goods with the most state-of-the-art machinery; we will equate the working conditions of the rural proletariat with those of the urban working classes, and incorporate many millions of working peasants in the construction of socialism.

With an iron proletarian broom we will sweep away all parasites, industrial magnates, bankers, Junkers, big businessmen, generals, bourgeois politicians, traitor workers, speculators, and profiteers.

We will smash the machinery of power intended for the repression and enslavement of the working people. From the workshops all the way up to the German Soviet government—the proletariat, in alliance with all working people, will rule everywhere on a foundation of the truest, most extensive Soviet democracy.

Through the introduction of the seven-hour day and the four-day working week, through a firm economic alliance with the Soviet Union and through uplifting the purchasing power of the masses, we will eradicate unemployment.

We will give everyone the opportunity to work. We will place all the productive forces of industry and agriculture exclusively into the service of the working people. We will guarantee full political equality to working women and working youth, equal pay for equal work.

We will raise wages by abolishing business profits, the unproductive costs of the capitalist economic system, and reparations payments. With bolshevist ruthlessness we will implement against all bourgeois loafers the principle: whoever does not work should also not eat.

We communists bring to the working people the program of their social liberation from the yoke of capital. We will kindle the masses' enthusiasm for victory over the bourgeoisie, for the social and at the same time national liberation of the working German people. Only the hammer of proletarian dictatorship can shatter the chains of national subjugation and the Young Plan. Only the social revolution of the working class can resolve Germany's national question.

If every worker, every poor peasant, every office worker, every working middle-class person—men and women, youth and adults alike—suffering under the crisis of capitalism bands together in the Communist Party of Germany, then they will form a force of such insurmountable strength that not only will they be able to topple the rule of capital, but any resistance against them—both internal as well as external—is rendered completely futile.

Therefore we call on all working people who are still under the spell of the cunning fascist swindlers to break unflinchingly and conclusively with National Socialism, to enlist in the army of proletarian class struggle. Therefore we communists call for all workers who are still aligned with perfidious Social Democracy to break with this party of coalition politics, Versailles Peace, Young Plan, and the slavery of the working masses of Germany, to form a revolutionary front of millions with the communists and fight for proletarian dictatorship.

Down with the Young Plan!
Down with the government of capitalists and Junkers!
Down with fascism and Social Democracy!
Long live the dictatorship of the proletariat!
Long live Soviet Germany! ▪

Nazism

Nazism, though eclectic, had a clear centralizing element—that the entirety of German life should be based on the *Volk* organized as an organic racial community, the *Volksgemeinschaft*. Grasping the Nazi understanding of *Volk* is essential to unlocking the underlying coherency of the philosophy. It is a difficult word to translate due to its specific connotations in German, and every party used it. It can translate as "people" in the sense of people in a crowd, or as people invested with sovereignty in the sense of a nation, or as an ethnic group, or as a group related by blood (in the Nazi sense, a social Darwinist racial understanding of ethnicity).

In German philosophy of the late eighteenth and nineteenth centuries, *Volksgeist* was used in the sense of "national spirit," not necessarily in reference to the German nation, but still strongly correlated with the development of a German national identity in the wake of the dissolution of the Holy Roman Empire. A *völkisch* movement originated at this time, proposing the formation of a German nation-state as a solution to the "German Question." Johann Gottlieb Fichte, in his eighth *Address to the German Nation* from 1808, asked, "What is a *Volk*, in the higher sense of the term, and what is love of fatherland?" He answered that it could only be that "special spiritual nature of human environment . . . from which he himself, with all his thoughts and deeds . . . has proceeded—the *Volk*, from which he is descended and among which he was educated and grew up to be what he now is."[1] The new nationalist movement combined sentimental patriotic interest in German folklore, local history, and a "back-to-the-land" anti-urban populism with many parallels with Romanticism.

Throughout much of the nineteenth century, it was not universally agreed that there was such a thing as a single German *Volk*. The "Germans" were, rather, seen as the equivalent of what would now be called the Germanic peoples—a large ethnolinguistic phylum comprising a number of peoples such as the Germanic "stems" or tribes of the Franks, Swabians, Bavarians, Thuringians, Saxons, and so on. It also included Scandinavians, Anglo-Saxons, Dutch, Swiss, and Austrians. Only towards the end of the 19th century did a vision of German nationalism emerge that linked it to a radically racialized redefinition of the *Volk* infused with Social Darwinism—the nation, for these *völkisch* thinkers, was a homogeneous organism of racially pure, Germanic "Aryans." *Volk* thus had a broad set of meanings, referring sometimes to the entirety of the German nation, or to the Aryan race, or to a liberal conception of the people.

In *Mein Kampf,* Hitler even denounced usage of the word *völkisch,* which he considered too vague due to its overuse. But he never developed an alternative, and he used the term with great frequency, especially in compound words: *Volksdeutsche* (racial Germans living outside of Germany), *Volksgenosse* (racially German citizens), *Völkischer Beobachter* (*People's Observer,* the official NSDAP paper); *Volksgeimeinschaft* (community of race-related people); *Herrenvolk* (master race), and so on.

The Twenty-Five Points (1920)

The NSDAP program, commonly called the Twenty-Five Points, represented the party's views at its inception in 1919–20. At that time, it had a strong anticapitalist message. However, the Hitler wing of the party moved to a pro-capitalist stance while the Strasser wing remained opposed. Hitler, though, refused to allow any alterations to the program, even as he made often radical changes in his strategy and tactics. Its organizing principle was the Volk.

Source: Feder, Gottfried, ed. *The Programme of the NSDAP, the National Socialist German Workers' Party, and Its General Conceptions.* Translated by E. T. S. Dugdale. Munich: Franz Eher Verlag, 1932.

Study Questions

Conflict, nationalism, and race*: How does Nazism link German nationalism and racism? How do racism and nationalism combine to create a theory of conflict? What is the racial nature of a "German"? What* are the specific goals of the party related to German military expansion? In what ways is the ideology explicitly militaristic? How does it view irredentism and expansionism? What political movements are they linked to? What is their goal?

Antisemitism*: What does Nazism claim is the role of Jews in history and modern Germany? What international movements are they allegedly linked to? What steps are proposed to combat the alleged threat?*

Social class*: How does Nazism relate to the Marxist concept of class struggle? What does it see as the role of class in Germany, and how does that differ from the Marxist view? Since Nazism is also a theory of struggle, what does it replace class struggle with? How does that struggle relate to national struggle?*

Sex and gender*: What are the proper roles of men and women? How does this view tie back into attitudes toward nationalism?*

Religion*: What is meant by "positive Christianity?" Does Nazism support religious freedom? How does the party seem to relate to the Christian parties (the Centre, BVP, CNBP, and CSVD)?*

Economics*: Who did Nazism blame for Germany's economic suffering and what did it offer as a solution? How did Nazism approach private property and the free market? How did Nazism view economics in relation to power?*

Agriculture*: What is Nazism's stance on land reform?*

Workers*: Is Nazism a workers' party? How does it attempt to appeal specifically to workers? Why does it make this appeal?*

Anticommunism*: What aspects of Marxism did Nazism reject and why? What did Nazism see as the link between communism and Jews? What programs did it support that the social democrats and communists also supported?*

Anticapitalism*: How did Nazism argue that capitalism was dangerous? What did it see as the link between capitalism and Jews?*

Totalitarianism vs. parliamentarism*: What is the relationship of the individual to the nation and wider community? What is the role of the state in this rela-*

tionship? What is the critique of democratic or parliamentary states?

The Program of the German Workers' Party is a program for our time.

The leadership rejects the establishment of new aims after those set out in the Program have been achieved, for the sole purpose of making it possible for the Party to continue to exist as the result of the artificially stimulated dissatisfaction of the masses.

1. We demand the uniting of all Germans within one Greater Germany, on the basis of the right to self-determination of nations.
2. We demand equal rights for the German *Volk* with respect to other nations, and the annulment of the peace treaty of Versailles and St. Germain.
3. We demand land and soil (Colonies) to feed our People and settle our excess population.
4. Only Nationals (*Volksgenossen*) can be Citizens of the State. Only persons of German blood can be Nationals, regardless of religious affiliation. No Jew can therefore be a German National.
5. Any person who is not a Citizen will be able to live in Germany only as a guest and must be subject to legislation for Aliens.
6. Only a Citizen is entitled to decide the leadership and laws of the State. We therefore demand that only Citizens may hold public office, regardless of whether it is a national, state or local office.

   We oppose the corrupting parliamentary custom of making party considerations, and not character and ability, the criterion for appointments to official positions.
7. We demand that the State make it its duty to provide opportunities of employment first of all for its own Citizens. If it is not possible to maintain the entire population of the State, then foreign nationals (non-Citizens) are to be expelled from the Reich.
8. Any further immigration of non-Germans is to be prevented. We demand that all non-Germans who entered Germany after August 2, 1914, be forced to leave the Reich without delay.
9. All German Citizens must have equal rights and duties.
10. It must be the first duty of every Citizen to carry out intellectual or physical work. Individual activity must not be harmful to the public interest and must be pursued within the framework of the community and for the general good.

    We therefore demand:
11. The abolition of all income obtained without labor or effort.

    Breaking the Servitude of Interest.
12. In view of the tremendous sacrifices in property and blood demanded of the nation by every war, personal gain from the war must be termed a crime against the nation. We therefore demand the total confiscation of all war profits.
13. We demand the nationalization of all enterprises (already) converted into corporations (trusts).
14. We demand profit-sharing in large enterprises.
15. We demand the large-scale development of old-age pension schemes.
16. We demand the creation and maintenance of a sound middle class; the immediate communalization of the large department stores, which are to be leased at low rates to small tradesmen. We demand the most careful consideration for the owners of small businesses in orders placed by national, state, or community authorities.
17. We demand land reform in accordance with our national needs and a law for expropriation without compensation of land for public purposes. Abolition of ground rent and prevention of all speculation in land.
18. We demand ruthless battle against those who harm the common good by their activities. Persons committing base crimes against the

People, usurers, profiteers, etc., are to be punished by death without regard to religion or race.

19. We demand the replacement of Roman Law, which serves a materialistic World Order, by German Law.

20. In order to make higher education—and thereby entry into leading positions—available to every able and industrious German, the State must provide a thorough restructuring of our entire public educational system. The courses of study at all educational institutions are to be adjusted to meet the requirements of practical life. Understanding of the concept of the State must be achieved through the schools (teaching of civics) at the earliest age at which it can be grasped. We demand the education at the public expense of specially gifted children of poor parents, without regard to the latter's position or occupation.

21. The State must raise the level of national health by means of mother-and-child care, the banning of juvenile labor, achievements of physical fitness through legislation for compulsory gymnastics and sports, and maximum support for all organizations providing physical training for young people.

22. We demand the abolition of hireling troops and the creation of a national army.

23. We demand laws to fight against deliberate political lies and their dissemination by the press. In order to make it possible to create a German press, we demand:

    a. all editors and editorial employees of newspapers appearing in the German language must be German by race;

    b. non-German newspapers require express permission from the State for their publication. They may not be printed in the German language;

    c. any financial participation in a German newspaper or influence on such a paper is to be forbidden by law to non-Germans and the penalty for any breach of this law will be the closing of the newspaper in question, as well as the immediate expulsion from the Reich of the non-Germans involved.

    Newspapers which violate the public interest are to be banned. We demand laws against trends in art and literature which have a destructive effect on our national life, and the suppression of performances that offend against the above requirements.

24. We demand freedom for all religious denominations, provided that they do not endanger the existence of the State or offend the concepts of decency and morality of the Germanic race.

    The Party as such stands for positive Christianity, without associating itself with any particular denomination. It fights against the Jewish-materialistic spirit within and around us, and is convinced that a permanent revival of our nation can be achieved only from within, on the basis of: Public Interest before Private Interest.

25. To carry out all the above we demand: the creation of a strong central authority in the Reich. Unquestioned authority by the political central Parliament over the entire Reich and over its organizations in general. The establishment of trade and professional organizations to enforce the Reich basic laws in the individual states.

The Party leadership promises to take an uncompromising stand, at the cost of their own lives if need be, on the enforcement of the above points. ▪

Joseph Goebbels, *Those Damned Nazis: Something to Think About* (1929)

This widely distributed Nazi pamphlet first appeared in 1929 and summarized the basic lines of Nazi thinking and propaganda in 1929. Goebbels effectively guides readers in a manner similar to Engels's catechism. Be sure to understand the answers to his questions on how he understands his five key concepts: nationalism, socialism, workers, Jews, and revolution.

Source: Goebbels, Joseph, and Mjölnir. *Die verfluchten Hakenkreuzler: Etwas zum Nachdenken.* [1929]. Munich: Verlag Fritz Eher, 1932. Translated by Randall Bytwerk. https://research.calvin.edu/german-propaganda-archive/haken32.htm.

Why Are We Nationalists?

We are nationalists because we see the nation as the only way to bring all the forces of the nation together to preserve and improve our existence and the conditions under which we live.

The nation is the organic union of a people to protect its life. To be national is to affirm this union in word and deed. To be national has nothing to do with a form of government or a symbol. It is an affirmation of things, not forms. Forms can change, their content remains. If form and content agree, then the nationalist affirms both. If they conflict, the nationalist fights for the content and against the form. One may not put the symbol above the content. If that happens, the battle is on the wrong field and one's strength is lost in formalism. The real aim of nationalism, the nation, is lost.

That is how things are today in Germany. Nationalism has turned into bourgeois patriotism and its defenders are battling windmills. One says Germany and means the monarchy. Another proclaims freedom and means Black-White-Red [the colors of the German flag]. Would our situation today be any different if we replaced the republic with a monarchy and flew the black-white-red flag? The colony would have different wallpaper, but its nature, its content, would stay the same. Indeed, things would be even worse, for a facade that conceals the facts dissipates the forces today fighting against slavery.

Bourgeois patriotism is the privilege of a class. It is the real reason for its decline. When 30 million are for something and 30 million are against it, things balance out and nothing happens. That is how things are with us. We are the world's pariah not because we do not have the courage to resist, but rather because out entire national energy is wasted in eternal and unproductive squabbling between the Right and the Left. Our way only goes downward, and today one can already predict when we will fall into the abyss.

Nationalism is more wide-reaching than internationalism. It sees things as they are. Only he who respects himself can respect others. If as a German nationalist I affirm Germany, how can I hold it against a French nationalist who affirms France? Only when these affirmations conflict in vital ways will there be a power-political struggle. Internationalism cannot undo this reality. Its attempts at proof fail completely. And even when the facts seem to have some validity, nature, blood, the will to life, and the struggle for existence on this hard earth prove the falsity of fine theories.

The sin of bourgeois patriotism was to confound a certain economic form with the national. It connected two things that are entirely different. Forms of the economy, however firm they may seem, are changeable. The national is eternal. If I mix the eternal and the temporal, the eternal will necessarily collapse when the temporal collapses. This was the real cause for the collapse of liberal society. It was rooted not in the eternal, but in the temporal, and when the temporal declined it took the eternal down with it. Today it is only an excuse for a system that brings growing economic misery. That is the only reason why international Jewry organizes the battle of the proletarian forces against both powers, the economy and the nation, and defeats them.

From this understanding, the young nationalism draws its absolute demand. The faith in the nation is a matter for everyone, never a group, a class or an economic clique. The eternal must be distinguished from the temporal. Maintaining a rotten economic system has nothing to do with nationalism, which is an affirmation of the Fatherland. I can love Germany and hate capitalism. Not only can I, I must. Only the annihilation of a system of exploitation carries with it the core of the rebirth of our people.

We are nationalists because, as Germans, we love Germany. Because we love Germany, we want to preserve it and fight against those who would destroy it. If a communist shouts "Down with nationalism!" he means the hypocritical bourgeois patriotism that sees the economy only as a system of slavery. If we make clear to the man of the Left that nationalism and capitalism, that is the affirmation of the fatherland and the misuse of its resources, have nothing to do with each other, indeed that they go together like fire and water, then even as a socialist he will come to affirm the nation, which he will want to conquer.

That is our real task as National Socialists. We were the first to recognize the connections, and the first to begin the struggle. Because we are socialists we have felt the deepest blessings of the nation, and because we are nationalists we want to promote socialist justice in a new Germany.

A young fatherland will rise when the socialist front is firm.

Socialism will become reality when the fatherland is free.

Why Are We Socialists?

We are socialists because we see in socialism, that is the union of all citizens, the only chance to maintain our racial inheritance and to regain our political freedom and renew our German state.

Socialism is the doctrine of liberation for the working class. It promotes the rise of the fourth class and its incorporation in the political organism of our fatherland, and is inextricably bound to breaking the present slavery and regaining German freedom. Socialism, therefore, is not merely a matter of the oppressed class, but a matter for everyone, for freeing the German people from slavery is the goal of contemporary policy. Socialism gains its true form only through a total fighting brotherhood with the forward-striving energies of a newly awakened nationalism. Without nationalism it is nothing, a phantom, a mere theory, a castle in the sky, a book. With it, is everything, the future, freedom, the fatherland!

The sin of liberal thinking was to overlook socialism's nation-building strengths, thereby allowing its energies to go in anti-national directions. The sin of Marxism was to degrade socialism into a question of wages and the stomach, putting it in conflict with the state and its national existence. An understanding of both these facts leads us to a new sense of socialism, which sees its nature as nationalistic, state-building, liberating and constructive.

The bourgeoisie is about to leave the historical stage. In its place will come the class of productive workers, the working class, that has been up until today oppressed. It is beginning to fulfill its political mission. It is involved in a hard and bitter struggle for political power as it seeks to become part of the national organism. The battle began in the economic realm; it will finish in the political. It is not merely a matter of wages, not only a matter of the number of hours worked in a day—though we may never forget that these are an essential, perhaps even the most significant part of the socialist platform—but it is much more a matter of incorporating a powerful and responsible class in the state, perhaps even to make it the dominant force in the future politics of the fatherland. The bourgeoisie does not want to recognize the strength of the working class. Marxism has forced it into a straitjacket that will ruin it. While the working class gradually disintegrates in the Marxist front, bleeding itself dry, the bourgeoisie and Marxism have agreed on the general lines of capitalism, and see their task now to protect and defend it in various ways, often concealed.

We are socialists because we see the social question as a matter of necessity and justice for the very existence of a state for our people, not a question of cheap pity or insulting sentimentality. The worker has a claim to a living standard that corresponds to what he produces. We have no intention of begging for that right. Incorporating him in the state organism is not only a critical matter for him, but for the whole nation. The question is larger than the eight-hour day. It is a matter of forming a new state consciousness that includes every productive citizen. Since the political powers of the day are neither willing nor able to create such a situation, socialism must be fought for. It is a fighting slogan both inwardly and outwardly. It is aimed domestically at the bourgeois parties and Marxism at the same time, because both are sworn enemies of the coming workers' state. It is directed abroad at all powers that threaten our national existence and thereby the possibility of the coming socialist national state.

Socialism is possible only in a state that is united domestically and free internationally. The bourgeoisie and Marxism are responsible for failing to reach both goals, domestic unity and international freedom. No matter how national and social these two forces present themselves, they are the sworn enemies of a socialist national state.

We must therefore break both groups politically. The lines of German socialism are sharp, and our path is clear.

We are against the political bourgeoisie, and for genuine nationalism!

We are against Marxism, but for true socialism!

We are for the first German national state of a socialist nature!

We are for the National Socialist German Workers' Party!

Why a Workers' Party?

Work is not mankind's curse, but his blessing. A man becomes a man through labor. It elevates him, makes him great and aware, raises him above all other creatures. It is in the deepest sense creative, productive, and culture-producing. Without labor, no food. Without food, no life.

The idea that the dirtier one's hands get, the more degrading the work, is a Jewish, not a German, idea. As in every other area, the German first asks how, then what. It is less a question of the position I fill,

and more a question of how well I do the duty that God has given me.

We call ourselves a workers' party because we want to rescue the word work from its current definition and give it back its original meaning. Anyone who creates value is a creator, that is, a worker. We refuse to distinguish kinds of work. Our only standard is whether the work serves the whole, or at least does not harm it, or if it is harmful. Work is service. If it works against the general welfare, then it is treason against the fatherland.

Marxist nonsense claimed to free labor, yet it degraded the work of its members and saw it as a curse and disgrace. It can hardly be our goal to abolish labor, but rather to give new meaning and content. The worker in a capitalist state—and that is his deepest misfortune—is no longer a living human being, a creator, a maker.

He has become a machine. A number, a cog in the machine without sense or understanding. He is alienated from what he produces. Labor is for him only a way to survive, not a path to higher blessings, not a joy, not something in which to take pride, or satisfaction, or encouragement, or a way to build character.

We are a workers' party because we see in the coming battle between finance and labor the beginning and the end of the structure of the twentieth century. We are on the side of labor and against finance. Money is the measuring rod of liberalism, work and accomplishment that of the socialist state. The liberal asks: What are you? The socialist asks: Who are you? Worlds lie between.

We do not want to make everyone the same. Nor do we want levels in the population, high and low, above and below. The aristocracy of the coming state will be determined not by possessions or money, but only by the quality of one's accomplishments. One earns merit though service. Men are distinguished by the results of their labor. That is the sure sign of the character and value of a person. The value of labor under socialism will be determined by its value to the state, to the whole community. Labor means creating value, not haggling over things. The soldier is a worker when he bears the sword to protect the national economy. The statesman also is a worker when he gives the nation a form and a will that help it to produce what it needs for life and freedom.

A furrowed brow is as much a sign of labor as a powerful fist. A white collar worker should not be ashamed to claim with pride that of which the manual laborer boasts: labor. The relations between these two groups determine their mutual fate. Neither can survive without the other, for both are members of an organism that they must together maintain if they are to defend and expand their right to exist.

We call ourselves a workers' party because we want to free labor from the chains of capitalism and Marxism. In battling for Germany's future, we freely admit to it, and accept the odium from the liberal bourgeoisie that results. We know that we will succeed in bringing new blessings out of their curses.

God gave the nations territory to grow grain. The seed becomes grain and the grain becomes bread. The middleman of it all is labor.

He who despises labor but accepts its benefits is a hypocrite.

That is the deepest meaning of our movement: it gives things back their original significance, unconcerned that today they may be in danger of sinking into the swamp of a collapsing worldview.

He who creates value works, and is a worker. A movement that wants to free labor is a workers' party.

Therefore we National Socialists call ourselves a workers' party.

When our victorious flags fly before us, we sing:

We are the army of the swastika,
Raise high the red flags!
We want to clear the way to freedom
For German Labor!

Why Do We Oppose the Jews?

We oppose the Jews because we are defending the freedom of the German people. The Jew is the cause and beneficiary of our slavery. He has misused the social misery of the broad masses to deepen the dreadful split between the Right and Left of our people, to divide Germany into two halves thereby concealing the true reason for the loss of the world war and falsifying the nature of the revolution.

The Jew has no interest in solving the German question. He cannot have such an interest. He depends on it remaining unsolved. If the German people formed a united community and won back its freedom, there would be no place any longer for the Jew. His hand is strongest when a people lives in domestic and international slavery, not when it is free, industrious, self-aware and determined. The Jew caused our problems, and lives from them.

That is why we oppose the Jew as nationalists and as socialists. He has ruined our race, corrupted our morals, hollowed out our customs and broken our strength. We owe it to him that we today are the pariah of the world. He was the leper among us as long as we were German. When we forgot our German nature, he triumphed over us and our future.

The Jew is the plastic demon of decomposition. Where he finds filth and decay, he surfaces and begins his butcher's work among the nations. He hides behind a mask and presents himself as a friend to his victims, and before they know it he has broken their neck.

The Jew is uncreative. He produces nothing, he only haggles with products. With rags, clothing, pictures, jewels, grain, stocks, cures, peoples and states. He has somehow stolen everything he deals in. When he attacks a state he is a revolutionary. As soon as he holds power, he preaches peace and order so that he can devour his conquests in comfort.

What does antisemitism have to do with socialism? I would put the question this way: What does the Jew have to do with socialism? Socialism has to do with labor. When did one ever see him working instead of plundering, stealing and living from the sweat of others? As socialists we are opponents of the Jews because we see in the Hebrews the incarnation of capitalism, of the misuse of the nation's goods.

What does antisemitism have to do with nationalism? I would put the question this way: What does the Jew have to do with nationalism? Nationalism has to do with blood and race. The Jew is the enemy and destroyer of the purity of blood, the conscious destroyer of our race. As nationalists we oppose the Jews because we see the Hebrews as the eternal enemy of our national honor and of our national freedom.

But the Jew, after all, is also a human being. Certainly, none of us doubts that. We only doubt that he is a decent human being. He does not get along with us. He lives by other laws than we do. The fact that he is a human being is not sufficient reason for us to allow him to subject us in inhumane ways. He may be a human being—but what kind of a human being is he! If someone slaps your mother in the face, do you say: "Thank you! He is after all a human being!" That is not a human being, it is a monster. Yet how much worse has the Jew done to our mother Germany, and is still doing today!

There are also white Jews. True, there are scoundrels among us, even though they are Germans, who act in immoral ways against their own racial and blood comrades. But why do we call them white Jews? You use the term to describe something inferior and contemptible. Just as we do. Why do you ask us why we oppose the Jews when you without knowing it oppose them too?

Antisemitism is not Christian. That means that it is Christian to allow the Jews to go on as they are, stripping the skin from our bodies and mocking us. To be a Christian means to love one's neighbor as oneself! My neighbor is my racial and blood brother. If I love him, I have to hate his enemies. He who thinks German must despise the Jews. The one requires the other.

Christ himself saw that love did not always work. When he found the moneychangers in the temple, he did not say: "Children, love one another!" He took up a whip and drove them out.

We oppose the Jews because we affirm the German people. The Jew is our greatest misfortune.

It is not true that we eat Jews for breakfast.

It is true that slowly but surely, he is stealing all that we have.

Things would be different if we behaved as Germans.

Revolutionary Demands

We do not enter parliament to use parliamentary methods. We know that the fate of peoples is determined by personalities, never by parliamentary majorities. The essence of parliamentary democracy is the majority, which destroys personal responsibility and glorifies the masses. A few dozen rogues and crooks run things behind the scenes. Aristocracy depends on accomplishment, the rule of the most able, and the subordination of the less capable to the will of the leadership. Any form of government—no matter how democratic or aristocratic it may outwardly appear—rests on compulsion. The difference is only whether the compulsion is a blessing or a curse for the community.

What we demand is new, decisive, and radical, revolutionary in the truest sense of the word. That has nothing to do with rioting and barricades. It may be that that happens here or there. But it is not an inherent part of the process. Revolutions are spiritual acts. They appear first in people, then in politics and the economy. New people form new structures. The transformation we want is first of all spiritual; that will necessarily change the way things are.

This revolutionary act is beginning to be visible in us. The result is a new type of person visible to the knowing eye: the National Socialist. Consistent with his spiritual attitude, the National Socialist makes uncompromising demands in politics. There is no if and when for him, only an either-or.

He demands:

The return of German honor. Without honor, one has no right to life. A nation that has pawned its honor has pawned its bread. Honor is the foundation of any people's community. Losing our honor is the true cause of the loss of our freedom.

In place of a slave colony, we want a restored German national state. The state is not an end in itself for us, but rather a means to an end. The true end is the race, the sum of all the living, creative forces of the people. The structure that today calls itself the German republic is not a way to maintain our racial inheritance. It has become an end in itself with no real connection to the people and their needs. We want to abolish the slave colony and replace it with a people's state in freedom.

We want work and bread for every productive national and blood comrade. Pay should be according to accomplishment. That means more pay for German workers! That will stop the senseless fighting in which we engage today.

First provide housing and food for the people, then pay reparations! No democrat, no republican, has the right to complain about this demand, for it was first raised by a banner carrier of November Germany. We only want to make the slogan a reality.

Provide essentials first! First we must meet the critical needs of the people, then we can produce luxury goods. Provide work for those willing to work! Give the farmers land! The German foreign policy that today sells what we have at below-market rates must be completely transformed and must focus radically on the German need for space, drawing the necessary power-political conclusions.

Peace among productive workers! Each should do his duty for the good of the whole community. The state then has the responsibility of protecting the individual, guaranteeing him the fruits of his labor. The people's community must not be a mere phrase, but a revolutionary achievement following from the radical carrying out of the basic life needs of the working class.

A ruthless battle against corruption! A war against exploitation, freedom for the workers! The elimination of all economic-capitalist influences on national policy.

A solution to the Jewish question! We call for the systematic elimination of foreign racial elements from public life in every area. There must be a sanitary separation between Germans and non-Germans on racial grounds exclusively, not on nationality or even religious belief.

Down with democratic parliamentarianism! Establish a parliament based on occupations which determines production. Policies will be determined by a political body that earns its place by the laws of strength and selection.

The return of loyalty and faith in economic life. The complete reversal of the injustice that has robbed millions of Germans of their possessions.

The right of personality before that of the mob. Germans always will have preference before foreigners and Jews.

A battle against the destructive poison of international Jewish culture! A strengthening of German forces and German customs. The elimination of corrupt Semitic principles and racial decay.

The death penalty for crimes against the people! The gallows for profiteers and usurers!

An uncompromising program implemented by men who will implement it passionately. No slogans, only living energy.

That is what we demand!

The Conservative Revolutionary Movement

The conservative revolutionary movement, prominent in the years following the war, advocated a specifically German (or Prussian in particular) nationalism, argued against Marxism as well as liberalism, and promoted a synthesis of "German" socialism and revolutionary conservatism without clearly defining either.

The movement based its ideas on organic rather than materialistic thinking, on quality instead of quantity, and on *Volksgemeinschaft* (ethnic community) rather than Marxist class conflict or liberal "mob rule." Its promoters produced a profusion of radical nationalistic literature that consisted of war diaries, combat fiction, political journalism, and manifestos and philosophical treatises outlining their ideas for the transformation of German cultural and political life. Outraged by liberalism and egalitarianism and rejecting the commercial culture of industrial and urban civilization, they championed the destruction of the liberal order (by revolutionary means if necessary) in order to make way for the establishment of a new order, founded on conservative principles. They rejected the kind of reactionary conservatism that aimed solely to restore the monarchy. But they were not fascists, though many of their ideas were taken up by the NSDAP. The movement had particular influence among Germany's middle-class youth and found adherents in all conservative parties.

The conservative revolutionaries were basically formed by their experiences of the war and the consequent revolution. This abrupt break with the past left them disillusioned. The horrors of trench warfare, the filth, the hunger, the negation of heroism by the effort to simply stay alive, and the random death led many to despair that there was no meaning to the war, or to life itself. They also had to contend with the stab-in-the-back conspiracy theory. They found solace in a glorification of the camaraderie of the front—the brotherhood of soldiers, regardless of background. The war may have been pointless, but a new society could be built on the sense of common purpose they had found in the trenches. This new reality would be built by men who abjured reason, glorified force, prophesied the age of an imperial dictator, and condemned all existing institutions.

Their utopian idealism motivated many Germans to reject the pragmatism and compromise necessary for the Republic; instead, they denounced any effort at becoming a *Vernunftrepublikaner* as un-German.

Study Questions

For each of the documents in this section, consider how they approach the issues below. Look for their points of agreement, but also for their differences in emphasis as well as substance.

Democracy*: What is their stance on parliamentary democracy in general and its appropriateness for Germany in particular? How do they explain the relationship between democracy and equality?*

Liberalism*: How do they contrast liberalism and democracy? How do they distinguish between democracy and parliamentarism? What is the "crisis of the state" in modern mass democracy? Are they attempting to drive a wedge between liberalism and democracy and thereby undermine the regime's claims to legitimacy and pave the way for a more overtly authoritarian system? Are they arguing for a more exclusionary form of the state, for instance one that might practice exclusivity on ethnic or national grounds?*

Idealism*: What is their vision of an ideal society? Do they look to any past or contemporary models?*

Reform or revolution*: Conservativism since Edmund Burke has generally been based on the principles of respecting tradition and allowing only gradual change. How do these conservative revolutionaries retain and reject those principles?*

Legitimacy*: On what do they base the legitimacy of their truth claims? Do they rely on secular or religious theories of truth?*

Oswald Spengler, *The Decline of the West* (1918)

When The Decline of the West *appeared in the summer of 1918, it was a wild success. Spengler insisted that all civilizations must rise and, more important for his argument, also fall. The Occident (the West and Germany with it) was in its moment of decline. The national climate in Germany seemed to validate Spengler's thesis. His ideas comforted Germans because they rationalized their downfall as part of larger world-historical processes.*

Source: Spengler, Oswald. *Der Untergang des Abendlandes: Gestalt und Wirklichkeit*. Munich: C. H. Beck, 1920. Pages 1–29. Translated by Robert Goodrich.

Is there a logic to history? Beyond everything coincidental and unpredictable in the singular events, is there a, so to speak, metaphysical structure of historical mankind that is essentially independent from the commonly visible, popular, intellectual-political forms of the surface? Something this lower order reality rather creates in the first place? To the understanding eye, do the great moments in world history appear again and again in a form that allows us to draw conclusions? And if so, what are the limits of such conclusions? . . . (1)

The decline of the West, initially a spatially and temporally limited phenomenon like that corresponding to the decline of antiquity, is, as one can see, a philosophical theme, which, understood in all its gravity, includes all great questions of existence. . . . (4)

But "mankind" has no goal, no idea, no plan, just as little as the genus of butterflies or orchids has a goal. "Mankind" is an empty word. . . . (28)

There are blossoming and aging cultures, peoples, languages, truths, gods, landscapes, just as there are young and old oaks and pines, blossoms, branches, leaves, but there is no aging "mankind." Every culture has its own possibilities of expression that appear, ripen, wither, and never return. There are many sculptures, paintings, mathematics, physics that are completely different from one another in their deepest being, each of a limited life span, each self-contained, just as each plant species has its own flowers and fruits, its own type of growth and decline. These cultures, living beings of the highest order, grow up in a sublime purposelessness, like flowers in the field. Like plants and animals, they belong to Goethe's living nature, not to Newton's dead nature. I see in world history the image of an eternal shaping and transformation, a wonderful development and decay of organic forms. The professional historian, however, sees it in the form of a tapeworm that tirelessly "starts" epochs. (29)

Oswald Spengler, *Prussianism and Socialism* (1919)

Spengler addressed the connection of the Prussian character with right-wing socialism. He contended that German socialism began not with Marxism but rather with the German national struggle of the World War, with its ethos of creativity, discipline, concern for the greater good, productivity, and self-sacrifice. Spengler claimed that these socialistic Prussian qualities were present across Germany and that the merger of German nationalism with this form of socialism, while resisting Marxist and internationalist socialism, was in the interests of Germany. His views of socialism were clearly corporatist.

Source: Spengler, Oswald. *Preussentum und Sozialismus*. Munich: C. H. Beck, 1920. Pages 97–99. Translated by Robert Goodrich.

In the future, shall business rule the state, or the state rule business? . . .

Prussiandom and socialism stand together against the inner England, against the worldview that infuses our entire life as a people, crippling it and stealing its soul. . . . There is salvation either for conservatives and workers together, or for neither.

The working class must liberate itself from the illusions of Marxism. Marx is dead. As a form of existence, socialism is just beginning, but the socialism of the German proletariat is at an end. For the worker, there is only Prussian socialism or nothing. . . .

For conservatives, there is only conscious socialism or destruction. But we need liberation from the forms of Anglo-French democracy. We have our own. . . .

The meaning of socialism is that life is controlled not by the opposition between rich and poor, but by the rank that achievement and talent bestow. That is our freedom, freedom from the economic despotism of the individual. . . .

My hope is that no one remains lowly who was born with the ability to command, and that no one commands who was not called to do so based on his talent. Socialism means being able to, not wanting to. What matters is not the quality of intentions but the quality of accomplishments. I turn to our youth. I call upon all who have marrow in their bones and blood in their veins. Train yourselves! Become men! We need no more ideologues, no more talk of education and cosmopolitanism and Germany's spiritual mission. We need hardness, we need a valiant skepticism, we need a class of socialistic masters by nature. Once again: socialism means power, power, and power over and over again. Plans and schemes are nothing without power. The way to power has already been laid out: the valuable parts of the German workforce in combination with the best representatives of the Old Prussian state idea, both determined to found a strictly socialist state, to democratize in the Prussian manner; both forged together by the same sense of duty, by the awareness of a great obligation, by the will to obey in order to rule, to die in order to win, by the strength to make tremendous sacrifices in order to accomplish what we were born for, what we are, what could not be without us.

We are socialists. We do not want it to have been in vain. ▓

Ernst von Salomon, "We and the Intellectuals" (1930)

Salomon joined a series of ultranationalist paramilitary movements after the war—fighting in the Freikorps; *supporting the Kapp Putsch; working in the terrorist Organization Consul and participating in the assassination of Foreign Minister Rathenau; and planting a bomb in the Reichstag building as part of the Rural People's Movement. This activism, linked to a longing for the active purpose of the war experience, is clear in his essay.*

Source: Salomon, Ernst von. "Wir und die Intellektuellen." *Die Kommenden: Überbündische Wochenschrift der deutschen Jugend* 18, no. 5 (2 May 1930): 206–7. Translated by Robert Goodrich.

The intellectual speaks and writes "I." He feels no connections. His work is dissolution. It is the dissolution of the mass of individual beings into separate individual beings, which from now on stand not below and not above the *Volk*, but apart. The means to achieve this is the misunderstood concept "education" [*Bildung*]. According to German sentiment, education means to give form, internal and external. But form can be given only where there is content, and only the idea gives content. But the idea always shows a connectedness. The thought stands alone and is generated in a brain. The idea is something connected. It grows out of the tensions between person and person. Where there is tension, there is also connectedness. For the intellectual, education is at best highly developed thought acrobatics and always just a characteristic of the "I." The presumptuousness attached to the concept of "education" could arise only through this conception by the intellectual, and this conception could flourish only in the empty space in which the intellectual lives.

The emphasized "we" of the newer generation is a clear rejection of intellectualism. The "we" of the young nationalist generation occurs consciously. We—that is, the still small group of men and, in the broad sense of the term, male youth who, beyond mere rejection, are already putting new values in place of the old or in the empty spaces. We have no intellectuals—we say it with pride; we say it because we are mockingly accused of this alleged deficiency. The spiritual in nationalism is of a different kind than the spiritual of the past period. It is linked to blood. It knows no dialectics, and where it looks for new connections, it does so in the sense of a responsibility toward the whole. The spiritual of the misunderstood education knows no whole and has its goal and its apex in the "prominent figures." We know something connected, from which we draw strength, and this connected thing is not rooted in the word, but in action and in the willingness to act. The individuals who leap out from of our ranks and whom we praise do not stand aside as a result, because they have the strength for the leap in the consciousness of being connected with the community and they are never detached in the most exalted moments, but above us, before us; they are leaders. The knowledge of the unconditionality of leadership and the purification of this concept from all slag—that is what separates us primarily from liberalism. The liberal system has no leadership. Instead of leaders, it had intellectuals. Marxism knows no leadership. Its first leaders and masters were intellectuals of foreign origin, and what was then endured with discomfort as "leaders" were elected, flung-up philistines; the Marxist himself calls them "bigwigs." The system, which collapsed in the November days of 1918, had "representatives" who derived their leadership from "tradition" alone. This system was thoroughly liberal and therefore collapsed, for that reason and because the ruling forces, which stood invisibly behind the events and waited for the failure of the leaders, either wanted a collapse or, due to their merchant mentality, had no idea of leadership themselves. Or else—and this is a special chapter—[they] saw in any leadership a danger that could ruin their business.

Be that as it may, we are facing a new situation. The structure of our movement is special. It is rooted in what emerges from the natural character of a *Volk*. Every movement must be, and not just every movement, but every animated thing that simply wants to grow. But from our commitment to what emerges from the natural character of a *Volk*, we draw conclusions that are unique. That only those who are conscious of their *völkisch* character can belong to the German *Volk* is a consequence. That all ideas that one lives can only be permitted to serve the *Volk* is another. That to discern all phenomena of diverse life, to test them and recognize or reject them, depending on whether they have value or valuelessness for what we live, that is a third. We reject intellectualism. It has been weighed and found to be too light. Our "we" grows out of our will and our service. And our will and our service belong to the final fanaticism of the German *Volk*. Because, according to our distressing conviction, it is different from the others, therefore this "we." ▪

Arthur Moeller van den Bruck, *The Third Empire* (1923)

Moeller's title, The Third Empire *(also translated as* The Third Reich*), referenced the chiliastic view of history put forth by medieval theologian Joachim von Fiore. By linking this vision to a specific nation, Moeller arrived at the idea of a "Third Rome," a concept that he had encountered in Fyodor Dostoevsky and Dmitri Merezhkovsky. Moelller considered the Holy Roman Empire the first empire; the second was the recently collapsed Kaiserreich (though on account of the exclusion of Austria, he regarded this as only a "transitional empire"). The greater German "Third Empire"—the "final empire"—would represent the fulfillment of German history and the harmonious incorporation of all oppositional social and political tendencies—a political realization of Hegel's telos.*

Source: Moeller van der Bruck, Arthur. *Das dritte Reich.* Berlin: Ring Verlag, 1923. Translated by Robert Goodrich.

This book contains a critique of parties. And it is addressed to the Germans in all parties. It deals with their ideologies and with people as party types.

The attempt made in this book was only possible

from a point of view that is not dedicated to any party, but rather covers the whole range of problems that run through the politics of our time, from the extreme left to the extreme right: only from a third point of view, which includes every other partisan German—from the point of view of a third party that already exists. Only such an attempt, attacking the parties, could go beyond them to address the nation. Only such an attempt could show the German breakdown and conflict, which have resulted from the deeply fateful consequences of the parties that have brought them into our political life. Only such an attempt could again establish the spiritual plane of political thinking which had been abandoned by party politics but which, nevertheless, for the sake of the nation, must be maintained, conservatively asserted, and revolutionarily taken by storm.

In place of party patronage, we set the idea of the Third Reich. It is an old and grand German concept. It emerged with the fall of our first Reich. Early on, it was associated with the expectation of a thousand-year Reich. But a political concept always lived therein, which probably referred to the future, but not so much to the end of times as to the dawn of a German age in which the German *Volk* would finally fulfill its destiny on earth.

In the years that followed the collapse of our second Reich, we had our experience with Germans. We experienced in these years as well that the nation has its enemy within itself, in its credulity, in its carefreeness, in its good faith, and, if we want to express these peculiarities of the soul ideologically, in an innate, extremely fatal, and, as it seems, utterly unshakeable optimism. The German people had scarcely been defeated, as no other historical people had ever been defeated, when a sentiment arose in its people: we will soon rise again! We heard the German fools assure us: there is nothing to worry about for Germany! And we saw the German dreamers nod in agreement: nothing can happen to me.

If we speak of a third Reich to this *Volk*, then we must give ourselves a clear and cold account that not even the slightest certainty is connected with it. The concept of the third Reich is a worldview concept that transcends reality. It is no coincidence that the notions that arise with the term itself, with the name of the third Reich, and also with a book that derives its title from it, are ideologically exposed from the outset, are strangely cloudy, emotional, and floating away, and completely otherworldly. The German *Volk* is only too inclined toward self-delusion. The concept of the third Reich could become the greatest of all self-delusions it has ever made. It would be very German if they trusted it and if they felt calmed by it. They could be ruined by it.

This must be said here. We cannot abandon the concept of the third Reich, as our highest and ultimate concept of a worldview, but it can only be fruitful as a concept of reality if it succeeds in moving away from the illusionary and fully integrates the political realities of our state and national life, under which we as a European people should live, and if it is as skeptical and pessimistic as befits this present moment.

There are Germans who assure that the new Reich, which arose in rubble from the events of November 9th, was already the third Reich, democratic and republican and thus logically completed. They are our opportunists and eudaimonists. There are other Germans who do not deny their disappointment, but still trust the common sense of history. There are rationalists and pacifists. They all draw the conclusions of their respective party-political or utopian wishes, but not those of the reality that surrounds us, and they do not want to admit that we are a bound and mistreated nation that perhaps stands close to, very close to and on the verge of dissolution. But our reality is: the triumph of all the *Völker* of the world over the German nation. Our reality is: the primacy of parliamentarism in our country based on the model of the West. Our reality is: rule of the parties. The third Reich, if it ever is to be, will not descend beneficently from above. The third Reich, which will end the strife, will not arise in a peace that is realized in an ideological way. The third Reich will be a realm of stability that will succeed politically for us within the European chaos.

This is an outlook on the future that the Germans

of November 9th did not include in their party-political account. It was only the events that led to the 11th of January and those that followed that brought about a change, not in the parties, but in the people. Only then did the nation start to become suspicious. There were Germans who went mad at the equanimity with which they had accepted all blows up to then. And there were other Germans who defended themselves. Therefore, the 11th of January was a turning point. It once again opened the prospect of liberation for the deceived nation. It seemed to want to end *Erfüllungspolitik*, which, while appearing to be foreign policy, had been entirely party policy. It returned us to our own resolve. And it gave us back our will. The parties, of course, have been the least participatory in the excitement that has raged through the aroused nation since that day. And already the suspicion has arisen that they might fail again, as they have always failed. Parliamentarism has become an institution of public life that seems to have understood its special task in weakening as much as possible all political demands and national passions in the name of the *Volk*. And we can trust it to once again seize the next opportunity and play its worst hand for an agreement that again betrays our possibilities.

When the revolution overwhelmed the war, when it buried all hopes and seemed to shed all prospects, we asked ourselves about the meaning of the events. And we found it, in the midst of nonsense, in the concept of the politicization of the German nation, which will matter now and afterward. We said at the time that this war was our war of education. Today we ask ourselves in doubt: was it really? We hope with bitterness: it will have to be! . . . (ii–iv)

Today we do not call this revolution conservative. We call it nationalist.

It desires the conservation of all that is worth conserving in Germany. It wills the preservation of Germany for Germany's sake. And it knows what it wills.

Nationalism does not say, as patriotism does, that Germany is worth preserving because it is German. For the nationalist, the nation is not an end in itself that is clear and visible from the past and lies before us already fulfilled. Nationalism is entirely directed toward the future of the nation. It is conservative because it knows that there is no future without being rooted in the past. And it is political because it knows that it can only be sure of the past and the future insofar as it secures the nation in the present. But spiritually it is directed beyond this present. If we were to look at German history only in terms of the past, then the notion would be quite obvious that it is now closed. Nowhere is it written that a *Volk* has an eternal right to life, to which it can refer for the sake of a miserable present in which it still wants to have its share. The hour comes for all *Völker* when they die by murder or suicide, and no greater end could be imagined for a great *Volk* than destruction in a world war that had to muster the whole earth to conquer a single country.

Nationalism comprehends nations by their destinies. It comprehends these from the contrasts between the *Völker*, which gives each *Volk* its own particular mission. In its own way, German nationalism is an expression of German universalism and is directed entirely at the European whole, but not, as middle-aged Goethe put it, to "float away into universality," but to assert the nation as something distinct. It is the expression of a German will for self-preservation and instead permeated by experience, which the old Goethe affirmed when he spoke of the fact that art and science were only "a tiresome consolation" and that a "proud consciousness" could not replace "belonging to a well-respected and feared *Volk*." Romantic nationalism thinks only of itself. German nationalism thinks in context. It thinks in terms of the shifting foci of history. It does not want to preserve what is German because it is German, which could very easily mean, as we saw, wanting to preserve something that has been. Rather, it wants to preserve what is German in what is becoming, in what is emerging around us, in the revolutionary restructuring processes of the ascending age. It wants to preserve Germany because it is the Middle, because only from here can Europe be rushed into equilibrium—and from here, not from the West, where Pannwitz retrospectively relocated the creative center of our continent, and not from the East, where Spengler prematurely gave its inheritance. It wants to preserve Germanness, not to give it up, as recommended by the weaklings of the interstate party who are degenerate phenomena on the fringes of the race: not to exchange it for the "supranational formation" of Fr. W. Foerster, in which the degeneration of German idealism was completed, which had the trusting expectation of a weakened brain that it would turn "the land of the European Middle" "again into a center of humanity," which the apostate can still discern among the French—but instead to give the nation the consciousness that, from this German element, it still has a task that no other *Volk* can take away. It is our ancient and eternal task continued in the Austrian and the Prussian and again the Bismarckian. We have finally discovered once and for all that we can serve this task in the East only if we have our backs free in the West. And to liberate ourselves is our most immediate and most German task that has remained for us after the error of our Western revolution. Fr. W. Foerster called Bismarck the mistake of German history. But Bismarck, who was the founder of the second Reich, will, based on his accomplishment, also have been the founder of the third. . . . (245–46).

Democratic engagement and a proletarian stake are part of the participation that the nationalism of the nation seeks to create, and to create within it. But the nationalist movement differs from the self-conception of a purely formal democracy, just as it does from that of a class-conscious proletariat, primarily in that it is thoroughly a movement upward and not from below. Participation presupposes consciousness, consciousness of the values in which the nation is to participate. This consciousness can never be conveyed unless it is met by an urge from below. In this sense, nationalism wants penetration downward. But the mediation itself remains consciousness from above. . . . (249).

The democratic person, who still tends toward cosmopolitan points of view, and especially the proletarian person who still indulges internationalist trains of thought, like to play with the idea that there should be some indeterminate region beyond language and country, in which the differences between the values of one *Volk* and those of the other *Volk* disappear. Conversely, the nationalistic person operates in reverse, starting with values as the most particular thing that a nation possesses, as the breath of its essence, wherein it takes form and which, like everything essential, rests on a weight that cannot tolerate any displacement (250). ▪

Edgar J. Jung, "Germany and the Conservative Revolution" (1932)

Jung had volunteered for the military in the war, fought in the suppression of the Bavarian Soviet Republic, taken up arms in the resistance to the French occupation of the Palatinate, and participated in the assassination of Rhenish separatist Franz Josef Heinz. Jung believed the breakdown of liberal democracy was inevitable and regarded the Republic as teetering on the brink of revolutionary turmoil, with a real prospect of either a "Red Revolution" sponsored by the Soviet Union or a "Brown Revolution" by the Nazis, both of which he strongly opposed.

Source: Jung, Edgar J. "Deutschland und die konservative Revolution." In *Deutsche über Deutschland*, 369–82. Munich: Albert Langen, 1932. Translated by Robert Goodrich.

The German revolution in which we find ourselves will hardly take on manifest forms like the French one in the storming of the Bastille. It will be protracted like the Reformation, but it will determine the face of humanity all the more thoroughly. It will ruthlessly revise all human values and dissolve all mechanical forms. It will be opposed to the intellectual driving forces, formulas, and goals brought about by the French Revolution. It will be the great conservative counterrevolution that prevents the dissolution of Occidental humanity, establishing a new order, a new ethos, and a new Occidental unity under German leadership. But just as the new leadership rests not on violence but on voluntary authority vis-à-vis responsible noble people, so the new leadership of

Europe will lie beyond the conceptual world that is called conquest, imperialism, militarism, or denationalization. Just as the French Revolution shifted the center of gravity of Europe to the West, so the German revolution will allow the heart of Europe, its center, to regain its rights again. The most rigid will to insist on the Versailles "system" will not save France from the bitter realization which the World War brought her and which is now turning into brutal politics of violence: the realization that the most biologically strong *Volk* in Europe are the Germans.

We call the conservative revolution the reinstatement of all those elementary laws and values without which man loses his connection with nature and with God and cannot build up any true system. In place of equality comes intrinsic value, in place of social sentiment the just integration into the tiered society, in place of mechanical elections the organic growth of leadership, in place of bureaucratic compulsion the inner responsibility of real self-administration, in place of mass happiness the right of the personality of the *Volk*.

The basic attitude of the new person, who establishes this order, which only restores the personality and its own essence by placing it in a humble relationship to the whole, merging microcosmic value and macrocosmic priority, is a religious one. This contemplation does not want to venture either into the philosophy of religion or even into the theological. It should only express that the humble person, who can be master precisely because he feels himself to be an instrument of God, will be the bearer of the coming new formation. I measure the suitability of a person to pave the way for the German revolution by the degree of inner humility, which is proportional to the unbroken pride in relation to the mass currents of the time. The great separation that is arising is not about moral judgments, about social attitudes, about national sentiments. It is about who is a true master because he can be a servant. It deals with the question of the extent to which the individual—regardless of externally acting laws—sets laws himself. The terrible moral decay of our time cannot be explained at all by the level of faith found in the churches, obedience to state laws, or any superficial code of honor. Rather, the chaos stems from the fact that there is no "caste" that inexorably gives itself laws that are also inexorably exercised. This is one side. The other is: equal measure for all. Who wonders under the rule of this equal measure that in the end the "concept of honor" of the mob destroys that of the upper class? What can a word of honor be worth in a time when a street whore is distributing words of honor? Who wonders about the disappointments in supposed friends at a time when even the worst blood easily pushes its way into social classes that are simply incompatible with the conceptual world of those unjustified upstarts? Who is shocked at the general dishonor when there is no longer a class that keeps its ranks pure with iron severity? And where, finally, is that active role model, without which no ethos of social interaction can develop in broad circles of the people, as English society communicated even to the simplest man?

Humility in the face of the higher, voluntarily accepted responsibility, and in exchange the right to rule, that is the expression of that basic religious attitude that only a man of good race can muster. From this attitude, this new belief, will grow a compelling world of religious forms. If it was said above that the German conservative revolution is in all respects the opposite of the French one, then this opinion also includes the hope that the conservative revolution will erect a new altar to God, just as the French one did to the goddess reason.

The Third Reich will therefore not be possible as a continuation of the great process of secularization, but only as its end. It will be Germanic-Christian or not at all. It encompasses the turning away from the national forms of Western character, from the narrowing of a misguided nationalism. The new nationalism is a religious-cultural concept because it pushes toward totality and does not tolerate any restriction to the purely political. The language of the German Revolution will be worldly—with all of and precisely because of this nationalistic attitude. In the struggle for self-preservation we will speak for the first time a language that reaches the hearts of other

Völker. For the German cause will become the cause of all *Völker* who, unlike France, do not want to inhibit the course of history by setting themselves and their intellectual property as the final climax for all times. Thus, the moment of foreign policy liberation already lies in the voluntary acceptance of the German revolution as a European task. Revolution means the rule of a new social value principle. Every revolution must therefore be a "world revolution"; its specific form may remain within the limits drawn by the *völkisch* character. But should we rave about the place in the sun, proclaim our right to life or should we step frankly and freely before the world and tell it that without our contributions there would be no face of humanity that shows orderly spiritual traits, and should we really not succeed—we, the *Volk* of Luther, Kant, Beethoven and Goethe—in doing something decisive for the political reorganization of the world?

German does not lend itself to use as a spiritual world language, a conclusion that is not meant philologically. It is true that the language of a Hegel, a Marx, a Nietzsche has become politically alive in the world. It is true that today in Italy, France, and other countries one listens to the voices of the German conservative revolution. Much more attention is paid to the powerful mass protest represented by National Socialism. It is committed to the Third Reich, but it is an open question whether in the deep, comprehensive sense as cherished by the men who have revived the idea of the sacred kingdom. One can be of the opinion that it will succeed in penetrating National Socialism with the intellectual renaissance that the last decade has given Germany. But it is also permissible to believe that National Socialism has a limited historical task: the shattering of a rotten world and the preparation of a great fallow period during which the new seeds are to grow. One thing is certain: the longing of all the masses who are sacrificing for National Socialism today arises from the great conservative heritage that rests in them and forces them to act in this way. Whether—to stay with this racial hygienic image—the appearance of this longing, which is called National Socialism today, bears predominantly the features of the conservative revolution or liberal liquidation, will remain unanswered at this point. The enormous energies pulsing through the awakening German *Volk* are indestructible. Let prophets, enemies, and friends passionately contest the future of National Socialism; let them announce imminent fulfillment or setbacks; we, who carry immovably in our hearts the approaching kingdom and the will to realize it, cannot be led astray from its basic direction by either a setback or a tumultuous mass success.

We are accused of running alongside or behind political forces, of being Romantics who do not see reality and who would enhance ourselves in dreams of a backward-looking ideology of the Reich. But form and formlessness are two eternal social principles, just as the struggle between microcosm and macrocosm continues in an eternal pendulum motion. The appearances that history produces are always new, the great principles of order (mechanistic or organic) always remain the same. If we therefore tap in to the Middle Ages and see therein the great form, we not only do not misjudge the past, but we see it more realistically than those who are unable to look behind the curtain. A Romantic is someone who sets up historical models against the laws of an era. The Romantics of the nineteenth century painted such pictures and failed to recognize that the wave of liberalism was unbroken. But if they tried to revive a new reality from the center of the soul, against the pseudo-reality of the liberal worldview, it was not for that reason that they were unrealistic. Their reality was greater and deeper because their perceptual senses were more finely developed.

Things are different for us. The time has come when the dissolution is complete, when the reality of the liberal worldview has revealed itself to be illusory, when the mastery of life through abstraction and intellectual domination has proven impossible. Once again, we see the world as it is not only because we ourselves are of this world, but because we have a presentiment of the metaphysical and feel it as a cosmic law in us. That is why our hour has come: the hour of the German revolution. ▪

Carl Schmitt, *On the Contradiction between Parliamentarism and Democracy* (1926)

Schmitt has been recognized as one of the leading thinkers of conservativism to this day, and his works were considered the most articulate presentation of secular conservativism of his time. He was a practicing jurist and grounded his political theories in tradition and the precedent-oriented framework of his profession. Yet he was, until his twenties, a devout Catholic. He thus brought to his ideas many of the concepts of political Catholicism.

Source: Schmitt, Carl. "Preface." In *Die geistesgeschichtliche Lage des heutigen Parlamentarismus*, 10–23. Berlin: Duncker und Humbolt, 1926. Translated by Robert Goodrich.

That the parliamentary enterprise today is the lesser evil, that it will continue to be preferable to Bolshevism and dictatorship, that it would have unforeseeable consequences were it to be discarded, that it is "socially and technically" a very practical thing—all these are interesting and in part also correct observations. But they do not constitute the intellectual foundations of a specifically intended institution. Parliamentarism exists today as a method of government and a political system. Just as everything else that exists and functions tolerably, it is useful—no more and no less. It counts for a great deal that even today, it functions better than other untried methods, and a minimum of order that is today actually at hand would be endangered by frivolous experiments. Every reasonable person would concede such arguments. But they do not carry weight in an argument about principles. Certainly, no one would be so undemanding that he regarded an intellectual foundation or a moral truth as proven by the question, What else?

The situation of parliamentarism is critical today because the development of modern mass democracy has made public discussion an empty formality. Many norms of contemporary parliamentary law—above all, provisions concerning the independence of representatives and the openness of session—as a result function like a superfluous decoration, useless and even embarrassing, as though someone had painted the radiator of a modern central heating system with red flames in order to give the appearance of a blazing fire. The parties (which according to the text of the written constitution officially do not exist) do not face each other today discussing opinions, but as social or economic power groups calculating their mutual interests and opportunities for power, and they actually agree on compromises and coalitions on this basis. The masses are won over through a propaganda apparatus whose maximum effect relies on an appeal to immediate interests and passions. Argument, in the real sense that is characteristic for genuine discussions, ceases. In its place there appears a conscious reckoning of interests and chances for power in the parties' negotiations; in the treatment of the masses, poster-like, insistent suggestion or—as Walter Lippmann says in his very shrewd, although too psychological, American book *Public Opinion*—the "symbol" appears. The literature on the psychology, technique, and critique of public opinion today is very large. One may therefore assume it is well known today that it is no longer a question of persuading one's opponent of the truth or justice of an opinion but rather of winning a majority in order to govern with it. What [Camillo di] Cavour identified as the great distinction between absolutism and constitutional regimes, that in an absolute regime a minister gives orders whereas in a constitutional one he persuades all those who should obey, must today be meaningless. Cavour says explicitly, I (as constitutional minister) persuade that I am right, and it is only in this connection that his famous saying is meant: "The worst chamber is still preferable to the best antechamber." Today parliament itself appears a gigantic antechamber in front of the bureaus or committees of invisible rulers. It is like a satire if one quotes [Jeremy] Bentham today: "In Parliament ideas meet, and contact between ideas gives off sparks and leads to evidence." Who still remembers the time when [Lucien-Anatole] Prévost-Paradol saw the value of parliamentarism over the "personal regime" of Napoléon III, in that through the transfer of real power it forced the true holders of power to reveal themselves, so that government, as a result of this, always represents the strongest power in a "wonderful" coordination of appearance and reality? Who still believes in this kind of openness? And in parliament as its greatest platform?

The arguments of [Edmund] Burke, Bentham, [François] Guizot, and John Stuart Mill are thus antiquated today. The numerous definitions of parliamentarism which one still finds today in Anglo-Saxon and French writings and which are apparently little known in Germany, definitions in which parliamentarism appears as essentially "government by discussion," must accordingly also count as moldy. Never mind. If someone still believes in parliamentarism, that person will at least have to offer new arguments for it. A reference to Friedrich Naumann, Hugo Preuss, and Max Weber is no longer sufficient. With all due respect to these men, no one today would share their hope that parliament alone guarantees the education of a political elite. Such convictions have in fact been shaken and they can only remain standing today as an idealistic belief so long as they can bind themselves to belief in discussion and openness.

The belief in parliamentarism, in government by discussion, belongs to the intellectual world of liberalism. It does not belong to democracy. Both liberalism and democracy have to be distinguished from one another so that the patchwork picture that makes up modern mass democracy can be recognized.

Every actual democracy rests on the principle that not only are equals equal, but unequals will not be treated equally. Democracy requires therefore first homogeneity and second—if the need arises—elimination or eradication of heterogeneity. To illustrate this principle, it is sufficient to name two different examples of modern democracy: contemporary Turkey, with its radical expulsion of the Greeks and its reckless Turkish nationalization of the country, and the Australian commonwealth, which restricts unwanted entrants through its immigration laws and like other dominions takes only immigrants who conform to the notion of a "right type of settler." A de-

mocracy demonstrates its political power by knowing how to refuse or keep at bay something foreign and unequal that threatens its homogeneity. The question of equality is precisely not one of abstract, logical, arithmetical games. It is about the substance of equality. It can be found in certain physical and moral qualities, for example in civic virtue, in *arête*, the classical democracy of *vertus* (*vertu*). In the democracy of English sects during the seventeenth century, equality was based on a consensus of religious convictions. Since the nineteenth century, it has existed above all in membership in a particular nation, in national homogeneity. Equality is only the possibility and the risk of inequality. There may be isolated examples perhaps for the idyllic case of a community in which relationship itself is sufficient, where each of its inhabitants possesses this happy independence equally and each one is so similar to every other physically, psychically, morally, and economically that a homogeneity without heterogeneity exists, something that was possible in primitive agrarian democracies or for a long time in the colonial states. Finally, one has to say that a democracy—because inequality always belongs to equality—can exclude one part of those governed without ceasing to be a democracy, that until now, people who in some way were completely or partially without rights and who were restricted from the exercise of political power, let them be called barbarians, uncivilized, atheists, aristocrats, counterrevolutionaries, or even slaves, have belonged to a democracy. Neither in the Athenian city democracy nor in the British Empire are all inhabitants of the state territory politically equal. Of the more than four hundred million inhabitants of the British Empire, more than three hundred million are not British citizens. If English democracy, universal suffrage, or universal equality is spoken of, then these hundreds of millions in English democracy are just as unquestionably ignored as were slaves in Athenian democracy. Modern imperialism has created countless new governmental forms, conforming to economic and technical developments, which extend themselves to the same degree that democracy develops within the motherland. Colonies, protectorates, mandates, intervention treaties, and similar forms of dependence make it possible today for a democracy to govern a heterogeneous population without making them citizens, making them dependent on a democratic state and at the same time held apart from this state.

Until now there has never been a democracy that did not recognize the concept *foreign* and that could have realized the equality of all men. If one were serious about a democracy of mankind and really wanted to make every person the political equal of every other person, it would be an equality in which every person took part as a consequence of birth or age and nothing else. Equality would have been robbed of its value and substance, because the specific meaning that it has as political equality, economic equality, and so forth—in short, as equality in a particular sphere—would have been taken away. Every sphere has its specific equality and inequalities, in fact. However great an injustice it would be not to respect the human worth of every individual, it would nevertheless be an irresponsible stupidity, leading to the worst chaos and therefore to even worse injustice, if the specific characteristics of various spheres were not recognized. In the domain of the political, people do not face each other as abstractions but as politically interested and politically determined persons, as citizens, governors or governed, politically allied or opponents—in any case, therefore, in political categories. In the sphere of the political, one cannot abstract out what is political, leaving only universal human equality; the same applies in the realm of economics, where people are not conceived as such, but as producers, consumers, and so forth—that is, in specifically economic categories.

An absolute human equality, then, would be an equality understood only in terms of itself and without risk; it would be an equality without the necessary correlate of inequality, and as a result, conceptually and practically meaningless, an indifferent equality. Now such an equality certainly does not exist anywhere, so long as the various states of the earth, as was said above, distinguish their citizens politically from other persons and exclude politically dependent populations that are unwanted on whatever grounds by combining dependence in international law with the definition of such populations as alien in public law. In contrast, it appears that, at least inside the different modern democratic states, universal human equality has been established; although there is of course no absolute equality of all persons, since foreigners and aliens remain excluded, there is nevertheless a relatively far-reaching human equality among the citizenry. But it must be noted that in this case, national homogeneity is usually that much more strongly emphasized, and that general human equality is once again neutralized through the definitive exclusion of all those who do not belong to the state, of those who remain outside it.

The equality of all persons as persons is not democracy but a certain kind of liberalism, not a state form but an individualistic, humanitarian ethic and *Weltanschauung*. Modern mass democracy rests on the confused combination of both. Despite all the work on [Jean-Jacques] Rousseau and despite the correct realization that Rousseau stands at the beginning of modern democracy, it still seems to have gone unnoticed that the theory of the state set out in *The Social Contract* contains these two different elements incoherently next to each other. The façade is liberal: the state's legitimacy is justified by a free contract. But the subsequent depiction and the development of the central concept, the "general will," demonstrates that a true state, according to Rousseau, exists only where the people are so homogeneous that there is essentially unanimity.

A popular presentation sees parliamentarism in the center today, threatened from both sides by Bolshevism and fascism. That is a simple but superficial constellation. The crisis of the parliamentary system and of parliamentary institutions in fact springs from the circumstances of modern mass democracy. These lead first of all to a crisis of democracy itself because the problem of a substantial equality and homogeneity, which is necessary to democracy, cannot be resolved by the general equality of mankind. It leads further to a crisis of parliamentarism that must certainly be distinguished from the crisis of democracy. Both crises have appeared today at the same time and each one aggravates the other, but they are conceptually and in reality different. As democracy, modern mass democracy attempts to realize an identity of governed and governing, and thus it confronts parliament as an inconceivable and outmoded institution. If democratic identity is taken seriously, then in an emergency no other constitutional institution can withstand the sole criterion of the people's will, however it is expressed. Against the will of the people, especially an institution based on discussion by independent representative has no autonomous justification for its existence, even less so because the belief in discussion is not democratic but originally liberal. Today one can distinguish three crises: the crisis of democracy (M. J. Bonn directs his attention to this without noticing the contradiction between liberal notions of human equality and democratic homogeneity); further, a crisis of the modern state (Alfred Weber); and finally, a crisis of parliamentarism. The crisis of parliamentarism presented here rests on the fact that democracy and liberalism could be allied to each other for a time, just as socialism and democracy have been allied; but as soon as it achieves power, liberal democracy must decide between its elements, just as social democracy, which is finally in fact a social, liberal democracy inasmuch as modern mass democracy contains essentially liberal elements, must also decide. In democracy there is only the equality of equals, and the will of those who belong to the equals. All other institutions transform themselves into insubstantial social-technical expedients that are not in a position to oppose the will of the people, however expressed, with their own values and their own principles. The crisis of the modern state arises from the fact that no state can realize a mass democracy, a democracy of all people, not even a democratic state.

Bolshevism and fascism, by contrast, are, like all dictatorships, certainly antiliberal but not necessarily antidemocratic.

Even if Bolshevism is suppressed and fascism held at bay, the crisis of contemporary parliamentarism would not be overcome in the least. For it has not appeared as a result of the appearance of those two opponents; it was there before them and will persist after them. Rather, the crisis springs from the consequences of modern mass democracy and, in the final analysis, from the contradiction of a liberal individualism burdened by moral pathos and a democratic sentiment governed essentially by political ideals. A century of historical alliance and common struggle against royal absolutism has obscured the awareness of this contradiction. But the crisis unfolds today ever more strikingly, and no cosmopolitan rhetoric can prevent or eliminate it. It is, in its depths, the inescapable contradiction of liberal individualism and democratic homogeneity. ▪

Republicanism

Many Germans passionately defended the Republic as a great leap forward that the Kaiserreich had hindered, a final and long-overdue reckoning with feudalism. Grounded in parliamentary democracy, based on the rule of law enshrined in the constitution, validated as the legitimate expression of popular sovereignty based on universal franchise, and directly articulating the civil liberties of all citizens, the Republic was for democratic liberals the unanticipated fulfillment of a long-thwarted dream. The DDP best embodied the Republic-affirming liberal perspective, as seen in its party platform from 1919.

On the other hand, Weimar was dubbed "a republic without republicans." While clearly an exaggeration, the remark accurately suggests that many of the Republic's leaders such as Walther Rathenau and Gustav Stresemann only reluctantly supported it, at least initially. They viewed the Republic as the best from a list of poor possibilities. These were the pragmatic Republicans (*Vernunftrepublikaner*), especially in the DVP, which the historian Peter Gay described as Republican "by intellectual choice rather than passionate conviction."[2] The term *Vernunftrepublikaner* was first linked to Stresemann by Wilhelm Kahl, his colleague in the DVP, but it also describes Thomas Mann, Max Weber, and Friedrich Meinecke. All sought to preserve prewar aristocratic trappings within the new republican framework.

Just as important as liberalism for the democracy, both social democracy and Christian democracy firmly embraced a republic as the only form capable of fulfilling their goals. The SPD, for all its revolutionary rhetoric, had become "revisionist"—that is to say, its practice was firmly entrenched in the framework of the Republic, which it ardently defended. Similarly, the Centre Party, while maintaining its ideological purity in keeping with various encyclicals from Rome and guidance from the German episcopate, nonetheless had become a party dedicated to secular parliamentarianism. For all its concerns about secularism, liberalism, and individualism, it remained the only party to serve in every cabinet throughout the Weimar Republic.

Democratic Liberalism: The DDP Party Platform (1919)

The DDP was central to the founding of the Republic, to the drafting of its constitution, and in the Weimar Coalition. Its platform from 1919, expresses the fundamental goals of democratic liberalism. Equality before the law and civil justice were at the heart of its agenda, but its foreign policy pledged support for German nationals abroad and the unification of all Germans into a single national state, though within the parameters of the League of Nations. It was thoroughly secular and embraced an ill-defined sense of solidarity between labor and capital.

Source: "Programm der Deutschen Demokratischen Partei." 1919. In *Quellensammlung zur Kulturgeschichte*, vol. 3, edited by Wolfgang Treue, 122–26. Berlin: Musterschmidt Wissenschaftlicher Verlag, 1955. Translated by Robert Goodrich.

The German Democratic Party arose at the hour of the greatest need in our country. Not following the model of the old parties, but unifying the whole people in the spirit of modern democracy, it will steadfastly pursue the aim of a state in the continuous process of social and cultural development. The party's permanent principles are freedom and justice.

The whole people, with no differences of class, occupation, or religion—for democracy it means adjustment of interests; it means the removal of ever-permanent obstacles between the rulers and the ruled; it means equal rights for all in the organization of the state as well as of society. Let the individual be free in his spiritual development and economic activity. More ardently than ever, let us devote ourselves to our sorely tried nation. We believe in the German people; and we have faith that through its own strength, it will rise again from the misfortunes of the present hour. According to these principles we form our program.

I. The State

1. *Domestic Policy*. The relation of the individual to the state is determined by the conception of civic duty. It is this duty that gives definite meaning to the rights of fellow citizens. The equal rights of all form the cornerstone of this citizen state. Its cohesion through a sense of duty ensures the unified will of the state. For this reason, we advocate the idea of a people's state that must at the same time be a constitutional state.

The German Democratic Party stands for the Weimar Constitution. It finds its highest political task in the protection and execution of this constitution, and in the education of the people to civic consciousness. The German Democratic Party therefore demands the gradual development of the German Republic to even greater unity, with the greatest possible autonomy for the different states.

We demand, unconditionally, equality of opportunity for all in legislation and administration. The legislation still existing that limits the rights of women must be repealed. The administrative organization must be built up on a free foundation, retaining the specially trained public servants, but also freely granting participation of the lay element of the community in the solution of state problems.

The present standing army of mercenaries imposed on us by the Peace of Versailles is at variance with the nature of a democratic military organization. This demands instead the system of universal military service, which is as adaptable to the defense of national independence as it is unadapted to become a tool for military aggression; and it also helps the physical well-being and civic education of youth.

2. *Foreign Policy*. The imperial idea, which controls the relations of the individuals within the state, shall also determine the relation of the states one to another within the empire. Not might and power, but right and justice shall determine the relationships of the peoples in the future. The party therefore stands for the self-determination of peoples.

In accordance with this principle, we demand the immediate revision of the peace treaties of Versailles and of St. Germain, for otherwise a lasting peace is impossible. Until revision occurs, we must attempt honorably to fulfil the terms of the treaty. But we will never acknowledge the dictation of force as a permanent legal order. No German stock shall be denied the possibility of joining its own people. We can never recognize the separation of sections of the German people from the fatherland as the permanent decision of history. We therefore will fight for their return to Germany. Together with the protection of Germans abroad and their intimate reciprocal relationship with the fatherland, this is the center of German foreign policy. During the period of separation, it is a national duty to help those of our own people who are subject to foreign rule to preserve their nationality. We also regard the protection of national minorities in Germany as a matter of honor.

No civilized nation can refuse to help in opening up and developing the backward countries. Germany's part in the spiritual uplift of humanity warrants participation in colonial activity. We will always resist the theft of our colonies, which took place under flimsy pretexts.

The final realization of our ideas can come only through a unified league of all free states working together. We therefore champion the idea of a league of nations, the first duty of which shall be to maintain the peaceful cooperation of nations and which shall at the same time become an international community.

II. Cultural Questions

The building of the new Germany can be successful only through steady, clear-sighted attention to the intellectual welfare of the people, without suppression of personality, with regard to individual differences, and with respectful consideration for every honorable conviction. On such a foundation alone can develop the highest creation of the human spirit: the cultural state . . . .

2. *Science, Art, and Literature*. Science, art, and literature give comfort and adornment to the structure of the cultural state. They should be unrestricted in life and in the press. Their right and duty to increase the culture and good breeding of the people

should be recognized; they should induce intellectual progress, refinement, and recreation; and with a feeling of constant responsibility toward the community as a whole, awaken and deepen the same feeling.

3. *Religion and the Church.* The crowning of the cultural state, however, is the fullest freedom in the cultivation of philosophy and individual conviction. No limitations will be put on existing churches or the establishment of new churches or of free religious communities. After their separation, the church and state will still have historical, intellectual, and practical relations. The separation must be brought about gradually, but thoroughly. Grants hitherto made to the churches by the state shall, with due consideration to the circumstances, be stopped. Religious communities whose importance entitles them to such a position shall be given the rights of public corporations in the future.

III. Economic Affairs

The German Democratic Party is a party of work; it is a party of the whole people, not of special classes; a party of mutual understanding, neither preserving nor increasing conflicts of interest. Its goal in the sphere of economics is the state of social justice. This is not to be reached by any single formula. The socialization of the means of production in the sense of their general acquisition by the state would be a fatal bureaucratization of industry; it would threaten a reduction of the products of industry disastrous to the whole people. We repudiate this and stand firmly for private control as the normal form of industry.

Therefore we demand, first, that monopolistic power in the hands of an individual or a small group not be tolerated. Hence, for land, that most important monopoly of the people, our policy is to resist land speculation and to divide large estates immediately in order to establish a system of independent peasant families doing their own work.

In like manner, that reconstruction that alone can make possible the fulfilment of our future tasks depends on a new advance of industry and commerce.

Bureaucratic measures and unnecessary regulations must be eliminated. But here, too, the common interest is superior to that of the individual. So the state must exercise its supreme power in industry, commerce, banking, and insurance, wherever natural monopoly exists, wherever trusts have in fact already limited or ended economic freedom. We reject loosely conceived experiments that regulate everything according to a single scheme.

Second, we demand that social injustice in the distribution of property and income be done away with.

Third, we demand that efforts be made to oppose the tendency to make a machine of the worker. A master-and-servant relationship, against which the individual is helpless, has grown up. The specialization of industry threatens to rob labor of its soul. Hence, handwork and small industry, in which the direct relation of the individual to the product of his labor is preserved, shall be protected and encouraged. This independent working class forms the bridge from the class of dependent workers to the free employer. The development of large-scale industry, on the other hand, makes the individual more and more an involuntary wheel in a huge machine, in which he no longer realizes the worth and meaning of his work. The specialization of labor and machinery, the development of which brought this about, cannot be abandoned, for that would mean a decrease of production, a lower standard of living, and millions losing their means of existence. So a remedy must be sought in the democratization of industry. The employer's power of decision and readiness to assume responsibility must be retained, but the joy of work on the part of the worker is also a factor in production of the highest importance. Therefore we need a labor law in which employer and employee stand on equal terms. We require further a labor constitution, raising those mere dependents to conscious cooperators. The factory must pass from the master-and-servant relation to a cooperative community. The industrial serf must become an industrial citizen. In such fashion, the democratic state of social justice will establish the dignity of the individual in industry. ▨

Pragmatic Republicanism: Thomas Mann, "On the German Republic" (1922)

Thomas Mann, Germany's most celebrated living author of his day, provided a pragmatic perspective on the Republic. He was neither an immediate supporter of the Republic nor an obvious opponent of the conservatives. Although originally opposed to the Republic, he came to recognize liberalism as the only option against authoritarian extremism—especially after the assassination of Minister Rathenau. Mann's lecture at the Beethoven Hall in Berlin on 13 October 1922, the text of which appeared in numerous newspapers immediately afterward, developed his distinctive defense of the Republic based on close readings of Novalis and Walt Whitman. Thereafter, his political views gradually shifted toward liberal democratic principles. In this speech, Mann attempted to convince university students—a notoriously right-wing demographic and former admirers of his—that they needed to leave their idealistic nationalism behind. Consider how Mann attempts to defend his conservativism in light of his support for the Republic; how he links the Republic to history; and how he critiques the Revolutionary Conservative Movement in general and Spengler in particular.

Source: Mann, Thomas. *Von deutscher Republik*. Berlin: S. Fischer, 1923. Translated by Robert Goodrich.

War is romantic. Nobody has ever denied its inherent mystical-poetic element. But today, to deny that it is an utterly debased romanticism, a disgusting distortion of the poetic, is obstinacy. And to prevent national sentiment from falling completely into ill repute, to keep it from becoming nothing but a curse, it will be necessary that, instead of being the epitome of all warmongering and sabre-rattling, it comes to be understood in relationship to its artistic and almost infatuating nature, indispensable as a part of the cult of peace. . . . (10–11).

I am not a pacifist, either of the groveling or the greasy type. Pacifism is not my thing—not as a worldview, as vegetarianism for the soul, or as a bourgeois rationalization of the good life. It was not Goethe's thing, either, or would not have been, and yet he was a man of peace. I am no Goethe; but a little, distantly related somehow or other. My side is also peace, for it is the realm of culture, art, and thought, whereas brutality triumphs in war. Not that alone, I know, but given the way humans are, the way things are today in the world, war is not much else. Today, the world, the *Völker* are old and clever, their epic and heroic stage lies far in the past; any attempt to return to it means a wild rebellion against the laws of time, spiritual insincerity. War is a lie, its results are lies; it is stripped of all honor regardless of whatever honor the individual may bring to it, and therefore it restlessly deludes itself that a blood orgy of egoism, corruption, and misdeeds are the triumph of every element of the *Volk* that is brutal and vulgar and adamantly opposed to culture and thought. . . . (11).

My aim, which I state quite openly, is to win you, as far as that is necessary, to the Republic and to what is called democracy and what I call humanity. . . . (13).

Our students, our student fraternities by no means lack democratic tradition. There have been times when the national idea was at odds with the monarchical and dynastic; when they were in irreconcilable opposition; when patriotism and republic, far from being opposed, appeared much more frequently as one and the same thing; and the cause of freedom and the fatherland had the passionate support of the noblest youth. Today youth, or at least considerable and important sections of youth, seem to have sworn eternal hatred against the Republic without being reminded about what might have been once—for such a reminder would have to quietly diminish the unconditionally of this hate. . . . (13–14).

The Republic is a fate, and indeed one to which *amor fati* is the only proper stance. That is a none too solemn word for the thing, for fate is not a trivial thing; so-called liberty is no fun and games, at least I do not consider it to be. Its other name is responsibility—and therewith it is clearer that it is rather much more a heavy burden, indeed especially for those with intellectual gifts. . . . (15–16).

The state has become the business of everyone;

we are the state, and this situation is profoundly hated by considerable sections of youth and citizens. They want nothing to do with it. They deny it at every opportunity, and primarily because it emerged not on the path of victory, of free will, of national exaltation, but in defeat and collapse, making it seem indissoluble from weakness, foreign domination, shame. "We are not the Republic," these patriots tell me, averting their faces. "The Republic is foreign domination—insofar as weakness is nothing other than an administrative, characteristically foreign power that has the upper hand." True, true. But it is also true that "a man can ennoble everything, make it worthy of himself, by dint of willing it" (that is quite true, quite beautiful and almost sly—an expression of dexterity in life. And secondly, it is not true—it is, to make it perfectly clear, utterly and in no way true—that the Republic as a domestic fact (I refer here to the constitutional meaning) is a creature of defeat and shame. It is one of exaltation and honor. . . . (17).

Youth and citizens, your resistance to the Republic, to democracy, is a fear of words. Yes, you buck and shy at these words like restive horses; superstitious nervousness robs you of your reason as soon as they are spoken. But they are words: relativities, temporally contextual forms, necessary tools; and to think they must refer to some foreign humbug is mere childishness. The Republic—as though that were not always still Germany! Democracy—as though one could not be more at home in the homeland than in any shining, rattling, brandishing empire! Have you heard the *Meistersinger von Nürnberg* lately? Well, Nietzsche expresses in a sparkling manner that it was "directed against civilization" and incited "the Germans against the French." But meanwhile it is democracy, through and through, democratic to the degree and as exemplarily as Shakespeare's *Coriolanus* is aristocratic. It is, I repeat, German democracy, and with the most respectable pomp, in its fervidly romantic way, it proves that this word combination, far from being contrary to nature or revealing a wooden-iron logic, is actually so organically properly formulated as perhaps only one other possible one: "German *Volk*." . . . (18).

What you will now respond to me, I know full well. You will say: "But no! That is precisely not it. The German spirit—what has that got to do with democracy, republic, socialism, not to mention Marxism? This economic materialism with its base talk of 'ideological superstructure,' rubbish from the nineteenth century, this is just childish nonsense now. How unfortunate if it were realized at the moment of its spiritual demise! And is it not the same with the other fine things for which you strangely try to stir up enthusiasm in the German youth? Do you see the stars above us? Do you know and honor our gods? Do you know the heralds of the German future? Goethe and Nietzsche, were they liberals? Hölderlin and George are ultimately democratic spirits, in your whimsical opinion?" No, they were not. Of course, of course, you are right. Dear friends, how ashamed I am. I was not thinking of Goethe and Nietzsche, Hölderlin and George. Or, rather, I was thinking of them to myself, and only asking myself which is more absurd—to plead for the Republic in their name, or to preach for restoration in their name? . . . (20–21).

Now you are angry. Yes, if only the presence of high-placed persons did not restrain your animation, you would shout at me: "What: And your book? Your antipolitical, antidemocratic meditations of the year '18? Renegade and turncoat! You are eating your own words. Clumsy clod, step down from the podium and don't dare claim that the words of an unprincipled self-denier can have the power to convince!"

Dear friends, I am still here. I still have something to say that seems to me good and important. As for the betrayal and clumsiness, consider this, that it is not quite accurate. I revoke nothing. I take back nothing essential. I told the truth and tell it today. . . . I will rather answer you that I am indeed a conservative, that my natural task in this world is not of a revolutionary but of a sustaining kind. . . . (21).

We want to bring in our opinion about Spengler's work here; it is the place to do it. His *Decline* is the product of enormous potency and willpower, scientific and rich in insights, an intellectual novel of great entertainment power and reminiscent of Schopenhauer's *World as Will and Idea*, not only through its musical style of composition. This sets the book quite high. Nevertheless, we have our democratic opinion about it, find its attitude wrong, presumptuous, and "convenient" to the point of extreme inhumanity. It would be different if this attitude hid irony, as we initially believed; if his prophecy was a polemical means of defense. One can really prophesy something like "civilization"—according to Spengler, the biologically inevitable final state of every culture, and now also the Occidental one—not so that it will come to pass, but so that it will not come to pass, thus preventively, in the sense of spiritual evocation; and so, I thought, was the case here. But when I found out that this man wanted to have his calcified prophecy taken seriously and positively and instructed youth in its spirit—that is, told them not to waste their hearts and passions on things of culture, art, poetry, and education, but to stick to what is the only future and what one must want in order to still be able to want anything, namely mechanics, technology, economics, or at most politics—when I became aware that he actually clenched a devilish fist of cold "natural law" against the will and longing of man, then I turned away from so much hostility and put his book out of sight so as not to have to admire the harmful, the deadly. . . . (31–32).

As for us, we will do well to concern ourselves with ourselves and with our own affairs—yes, let us say it with modest joy—our own national affairs. I will call it again by its name that is somewhat old-fashioned and yet even today still bright with youthful allure: humanity. Between aesthetic isolation and undignified downfall of the individual in general; between mysticism and ethics; private and public; between a death-bound negation of the ethical, of the civic, of values and a transparent ethical philistine rationalism; it is truly the German mean, the beautiful and human, of which our best have dreamed. And we pay homage to its positive legal form, whose meaning and aim we understand to be the unification of our political and national life, as we form our as yet unguided tongues to the cry: "Long live the Republic!" (39). ◼

Social Democracy: An Exchange between Rudolf Hilferding and Siegfried Aufhäuser (1927)

The following two documents are an exchange at the SPD party congress in 1927 between two wings of the party. Hilferding represented the more conservative views of the party's right, and the fact that he delivered the keynote speech, "On the Tasks of Social Democracy in the Republic," which was afterward published as a separate pamphlet (and later banned by the Third Reich), indicates the dominance of his views in the party. Yet Aufhäuser, too, was deeply respected in the party, especially for his influence in the trade unions, and he issued a rebuttal of sorts during the debate on Hilferding's presentation from the party's left. Both ultimately defended democracy, but they understood that defense differently in relationship to the conditions in Germany in that year. At the time, Prussia, Germany's largest state, was an SPD stronghold, but at the national level the Reichstag was dominated by a right-center coalition that excluded the SPD. Consider how Social Democrats defined liberal democracy and its relationship to socialism.

Source: Hilferding, Rudolf. "Die Aufgaben der Sozialdemokratie in der Republik," 172–75, 180–81; and Siegfried Aufhäuser, 198–200. In *Sozialdemokratischer Parteitag in Kiel* 1927: Protokoll mit dem Bericht der Frauenkonferenz. Berlin: Dietz, 1927. Translated by Robert Goodrich.

Rudolf Hilferding, The Tasks of Social Democracy in the Republic

Viewed historically, democracy has always been the cause of the proletariat. I have always been amazed by the assertion . . . that democracy is a matter for the bourgeoisie. This view denotes a lack of knowledge of the history of democracy and a wish to extract that history from the writings of a few theoreticians in a colorless, intellectual fashion. In reality, there is no sharper political struggle than that of the proletariat against the bourgeoisie, for democracy. Not to see that this fight belongs among the great deeds of the proletarian class struggle is to deny the whole past of socialism. It is historically false and misleading to speak of "bourgeois democracy." Democracy was our cause. We had to wage a stubborn campaign to wring democracy out of the bourgeoisie. What a lot of proletarian blood has flowed to attain universal and equal suffrage, for instance!

But what if the rulers do not respect democracy? Is that a problem for us? Is it not evident that the moment an attempt is made to destroy the foundations of democracy, not only every Social Democrat but every republican will employ every means available to maintain those foundations? Then there is the question of the use of force. . . . If the foundations of democracy are destroyed, we are defending ourselves and we have no choice but to employ all methods of defense. . . . We want to defend democracy, and for that reason we are grateful to the Reichsbanner for its work. . . . If you haven't understood that the preservation of democracy and the Republic are in the highest interests of the party, you have not grasped the ABC of political thinking. There are people who go around saying: beware of democratic illusions! I am of a very different opinion. The real danger is rather . . . that there have been proletarian strata in other countries who have failed to recognize the importance of freedom, of democracy. In Italy Mussolini achieved power because the Italian proletariat did not know how good it was to have freedom and democracy. . . . The danger, not for the Republic —I admit that—but for the real content and extent of democracy has been tremendously heightened by the very fact that the German Nationalists [DNVP] have kept their monarchist ideas in cold storage for the last two years. . . . The fight between the Republic and the monarchy does not stand in the foreground when formulated directly in those terms; but it has changed into a fight between fascism and democracy. We should be committing the worst of mistakes if we said to the proletariat: you don't need to worry much about politics any more, only material questions come into consideration at present. . . .

Thanks to Otto Braun and Karl Severing [leaders of the SPD in Prussia], the waves of both Bolshevism and fascism have been broken in Prussia. That has been a world-historical achievement. History will eventually record what Severing, that little metalworker from Bielefeld, has achieved for Central Europe, indeed for the whole of Europe. . . . We were seriously concerned, after Severing's departure, as to whether we could find an appropriate replacement. Our worries were unjustified. Severing's successor [Braun] is an outstanding success. Prussia is a proud stronghold in the camp of the Republic, and our only task is to make it a proud stronghold in the camp of socialism. But when one reads some of the resolutions put forward here, one might think that the most important task of the proletarian class struggle in Germany was to overthrow the Prussian government. No, the most important task of the class struggle is the overthrow of the right-wing government of the German Reich.

Siegfried Aufhäuser, Reply to Hilferding

It has been pointed out numerous times what value the republican oaths of the German Nationalists [DNVP] brings us, when we know that they care only about the fulfillment of their economic demands and those of the circles that stand behind them. What is stated in our resolution is nothing other than that this government represents less an act against the Republic than an antisocial act against the working class. I take back no word of that. Hilferding plainly stated . . . that the confrontation today is not mainly monarchy against republic but capitalism against social democracy. Why should we not be permitted to express this in a resolution? Hilferding and others, who are against this out of regard for building future governments, are showing, to state it plainly, regard for the Centre Party. But if the Centre Party decides it is appropriate to look for a different coalition in the Reichstag, it will not matter how plainly we describe the situation today. The Centre Party is not as sensitive as some people assume. Moreover, I do not see this consideration toward us from the Centre Party. We have seen that they have attacked us more sharply than ever in the last few weeks, and they have asserted that they are ready for a merciless struggle against Social Democracy within the government. . . .

Comrade Scheidemann says that we should not forget that this is our Republic. Why then have we been excluded from the new government? It is not our fault. It happened for economic reasons. If we want to conquer these positions in our Republic, we must be ready to take up the struggle against the opponents of the Republic and its false friends who rule it. . . . I therefore protest against the claim that those who want to conduct the struggle mercilessly are inferior republicans to those who don't want to express themselves so plainly. It is not true that our resolution weakens the republican idea. We are merely describing the situation, not expressing an opinion, when we say that it is not the form of the state that is decisive for the present bourgeois government but the wishes of powerful economic circles. . . .

I say that we are all equally ready to defend and to extend the People's State. But we do not therefore need to awaken any kind of democratic illusions. Where does it lead, when Hilferding says he refuses to describe present-day democracy as bourgeois? We have learned from Hilferding himself what a difference there is between social and bourgeois democracy. . . .

What use is a purely abstract democracy when one doesn't think about the human beings who have to be prepared for a given goal and a given decision? There are now new proletarian strata, such as employees and professionals. We shall not win these new strata by taking part in the government. We must meet them with our own social democratic program plainly visible, just as we did previously in the case of manual workers. We shall only win over these strata if we reject responsibility for things Social Democracy cannot tolerate. . . . We find ourselves in an oppositional position, and the more plainly the party congress proclaims this fact to the whole working population, the sooner we shall arrive at the great victories Hilferding desires. ■

Christian Democracy: National Political Manifesto (1927)

The manifesto came after the collapse of the Centre-led minority cabinet of Wilhlem Marx in 1926, following a vote of no confidence by the SPD, which had previously tolerated the cabinet. The question confronting the Centre was whether or not it wanted to take a turn to the right and form a right-wing coalition against the SPD. The problem was that it was in a coalition government with the SPD in Prussia, and such a move would have isolated it in Germany's largest state and forced it to adopt a stance more critical of parliamentary democracy by working with the anti-Republican DNVP. The manifesto reflects a power struggle inside the Centre between its left wing (led by Stegerwald) and right wing (led by von Papen and Kaas), but it concludes with a decisive affirmation of the Republic. Consider the stance of the Centre vis-à-vis the Republic and how it balances its Catholic conservativism within a secular liberal constitutional framework.

Source: "Nationalpolitisches und Sozialpolitisches Manifest der Zentrumsfraktion des Reichstages vom 22 Januar 1927." In *Politisches Jahrbuch, 1927/28*, edited by Georg Schreiber, 83–89. München-Gladbach: Volksverein-Verlag, 1928. Translated by Robert Goodrich.

Large circles of the German *Volk* have followed the political and parliamentary developments of the last weeks with growing disconcert. Public opinion in the country is no longer able to make sense of the rancor and conflict of the parties. They want to see a clear path and trustworthy leadership in the political confusions of our times. Both can be won only if we direct our political actions toward a higher goal and decisively express what is politically necessary.

Since the day of the collapse, the Centre Party has known its political message well and has remained consistently loyal to it in the years of heavy responsibility. All of our efforts were about saving the German *Volk* and the construction of the German state.

Republican Constitution

The foundations of our new German state were laid out in Weimar. A new political will broke through in the work on the Weimar Constitution, one that strives in international affairs for national validation on the path of understanding with the other nations, and in domestic affairs for the achievement of a deeper consciousness of the *Volk* via a comprehensive social regeneration of our national life. For us, there is no other civil reality except those of the German Republic and its symbols, which saved the unity of the German *Volk* during desperate times. It remains into the distant future the only promising path. The German Centre Party helped to create this constitution. We stand by it, in that we protect, develop, and cultivate its meaning and constantly attempt to maintain this constitution in an organic connection to the broader *Volk* and its living energies. The German Republic should liberate us in foreign affairs, and in domestic affairs unleash the energies that make the German state into a true state of the *Volk*. The energies of science, art, education of the *Volk*, the family, and other communities must arise from the root soil of our German spirit of the *Volk* and flow into the higher unity of the state, in which service to our *Volk* become a reality. The spirit of German heritage and identity, however, must also be constantly rejuvenated on the basis of Christian faith. On this must be built the moral education of our *Volk*, especially the education of our youth. With the formation of the *school system*, we must guarantee freedom of conscience and the rights of parents.

Reichswehr

The only instrument of power of our state remains the Reichswehr. It is necessity of the state. It is a component of the German Republic. There is no political sovereignty of the state without power. From this grow the internal justification and tasks of the army of the German *Volk*. Today we must do away with certain fears that the Reichswehr is subservient only to specific political groups. Our Reichswehr is not permitted to serve either a party or a class or any other such special interest. It belongs to the German

Volk united in the German Republic. The problem of recruitment must be solved in a form that allows access to military service for the sons of our *Volk* who are truly loyal to the constitution.

Social Policy

The social restructuring in our *Volk* since the World War has been powerful and deep reaching. It has increased the number of dependent and dispossessed masses in our *Volk* and made palpable the necessity to be aware of domestic cohesion in our *Volk*. The German future demands that West and East, South and North, city and country, entrepreneur and worker come to a greater understanding in the common task of economic, social, and cultural development and find with mutual respect worthy forms of dealing with the contradictions of special interests. Important legislative proposals stand ahead, which should complete and carry forward the entire work of German social policy. Our state social policy must expand to become social state policy. Yet not laws alone, but rather a true social regeneration in spirit and will is necessary if we are to earn new hope and trust from the oppressed and desperate masses.

Foreign Affairs

All of the construction work in domestic affairs and all the social reform work will be successful only if there is success in including the German *Volk* once again as an entirety in a European interstate system of laws. In addition, and as has always been our goal, foreign policy and the relationships of Germany to the nations of the world must be fulfilled in a new spirit of commitment to treaties, of a willingness to reach consensus, of loyal cooperation in the creation of the solidarity of nations. Germany is a member of the League of Nations. And now we must organize our politics so that they correspond to the community of nations. The essence of our own nation may and should not be obscured in the integration into the practical solidarity of nations. Our yearning is for freedom and the independent ability to determine our destiny. No civilized nation can live without secure borders, can tolerate that its territory remains occupied by a foreign power. With tenacious persistence regarding the methods of the policy and without injuring the national essential interests, every German policy will therefore work toward a final evacuation of the Rhineland as soon as possible.

Germany has entered into international obligations in London and Geneva. We stand by these obligations and recognize in the legal validity of the Treaties of Locarno the essential preconditions of any potentially auspicious foreign policy. The fruits of this policy, which we have constantly represented in long, fateful years, have ripened. No one who wishes to seriously accept responsibility can overlook this as our political baseline and cannot hesitate to acknowledge it. The next task for a greater understanding between Germany and France, which we have especially laid upon ourselves, can succeed only if both sides work at all times in the spirit of European solidarity and put aside naked power considerations. We renew this dedication to peaceful development precisely now, where fears, which emerge without justification, must be repressed.

Within this moral framework, the Centre Party recognized the national and social policies necessary for the times. We are animated by the desire to gather together as quickly as possible the energies for a government that contains within itself the best possible guarantee for a solidification of the domestic cohesion of our *Volk* in the sense of the political state and society.

The Social-Political Manifesto

The economic policy of our party was never the one-sided promotion of one estate or one occupational group. We fundamentally reject that now, as before. Precisely in the equalization of overlapping interests in the framework of the common good, and with the goal of promoting it, do we recognize the only correct path for economic advancement. In this, we strive to especially assist the suffering branches of our economy, and are not afraid to impose sacrifices there where the common good demands it.

The Centre delegation in the Reichstag took a position in a detailed economic program this year on all-important questions of agriculture and industry, commerce and trade, and pointed toward practical ways to promote the economy. We will restrict ourselves here therefore to those questions that have come to the fore due to contemporary political developments.

We consider the retention of as many independently owned enterprises in the crafts, trades, and commerce to be a national economic, social, state necessity. We strive for this goal not only with trade legislation favorable to the middle estates. In the framework of our general and constant efforts for just representation and lowering of state levies, we will push for relief for the economically weak in all estates.

The Centre Party considers an especially important task for the political economy at this time to be the incremental removal of housing controls. We can and want to realize this goal only in that housing construction is simultaneously increased, all exorbitant rents are fought against, and the inevitable increase in rents are balanced with corresponding wages and salaries.

Out of economic, social, general political, and especially political demographic reasons, the Centre Party, now as before, expressly takes care of *agriculture* and its interests through promotion of agrarian technologies and through relevant trade and tax policies. Today we do not think lastly about the small and weak in agricultural, about the agrarian laborers, about the tenant farmers and about the non-firstborn sons of farmers. To improve their situation, especially through the cultivation of wastelands and increased settlement, is our pressing duty of the day.

The Centre Is and Remains the Party of Social Reform

For us, a top priority is the realization of a condition wherein the legal recognition of the equal status of the employee and the employer finds its real impact. The expansion of our labor legislation should serve this urgent commandment of the day, the next step in which is unitary legislation on protection in the workplace, including the special protection of mining work, which, above all else, will regulate the work hours, compatible with international agreements.

For the official and legal representation of occupations, a form must finally be found that realizes the employees' right to participation in the economy, as provided for in Article 165 of the national constitution.

The Centre takes every opportunity to promote, via legislation as well as in all other areas of conflict between capital and labor, the spirit of respect on both sides and the will for mutual consideration.

The Centre Party pursues these goals on the national as well international level.

The Centre Party sees in *social insurance* the indispensable means for the maintenance of the health of the labor force of the insured population. Here, it is not a matter of social costs but of social responsibilities, regardless of how heavy these might be felt in places today.

The expansion of our social insurance via unemployment insurance, the simplification of its structure and procedures, an organic connection between the insurance branches, the improvement of the situation of invalids, and the health insurance of mariners are the next goals of the Centre's politics.

We also strive for and welcome international agreements in these areas as contributions to the ordering of the economy and for the promotion of labor peace at home and abroad.

An essential complement of the social-political measures is the

Promotion of Social Welfare Work

In accordance with its nature and historical development, it must carefully take into consideration the special needs of the individual in need of assistance. It must keep itself distant from the schematics of universal state care just as much as from the haphazardness of old-fashioned charity. Its highest task must be to train the individual in need of assistance to be self-sufficient and where possible, make him independent of the aid of others. The authorities will not be able to solve the tasks of social welfare work

alone. They require the help and additional support of the organs of social welfare work that are free and independent of the state. These are the foundations on which the Centre Party wants to craft legislation and administration in the area of social welfare work.

The care of wounded veterans and their surviving dependents, those on a small or state pension, draws our special attention. And not least of all the unemployed. It is precisely in this last area that social policies and social welfare work encounter each other, and even more! We in the Centre Party see the issue of unemployment and combatting it not only as a problem for the national economy, social policy, and welfare; rather, we see here an issue of the highest political meaning for the state—for the nation touched by it as well as for the entire word. National and international economics, the peaceful political development within every single state as well as between the states, the maintenance of currency, the realization of international obligations—all this relates to the solution of the unemployment problem. This also indicates, however, the great difficulties that lie ahead and even more, the importance of the solution. At this moment, we consider it the pressing task for all of our social welfare activity to cooperate in this effort as best we can through the promotion and improvement of employment agencies, through public work projects, and through financial support as well as through care of those individual circles that have been especially disadvantaged. ▨

SUPPLEMENTAL DOCUMENTS

Optional Documents

Depending on the instructor's needs, you may be required to read or view particular books, movies, music, or works of art, which may include

> Erich Maria Remarque, *All Quiet on the Western Front* (1929); or the film version, Lewis Milestone, dir., *All Quiet on the Western Front* (1930)
>
> Ernst Krenek, *Johnny Strikes Up* (*Jonny spielt auf*, 1926)
>
> George Grosz, *Shut up and Soldier on* (*Maul halten und Weiterdienen*, 1927)

Foundational Documents (1919)

Weimar Constitution (11 August 1919)

Source: German National Assembly. Constitution of the German Reich (Weimar Constitution). Translated by Howard Lee McBain and Lindsay Rogers. https://en.wikisource.org/wiki/Weimar_constitution. Edited by Robert Goodrich.

Preamble

The German *Volk*, united in every respect and inspired by the determination to restore and confirm the Reich in liberty and justice, to serve peace at home and peace abroad, and to further social progress, has given itself this constitution.

Chapter I: Organization and Functions of the Reich

SECTION I: THE REICH AND THE STATES

ARTICLE 1: The German Reich is a Republic. The political power emanates from the people.

ARTICLE 4: The universally recognized rules of international law are accepted as integral and obligatory parts of the law of the German Reich.

ARTICLE 5: Political power shall be exercised, in matters pertaining to the Reich, through the organs of the Reich on the basis of the Reich constitution, and, in matters pertaining to the states, through the organs of the states on the basis of the constitutions of the states.

ARTICLE 10: The Reich may by law prescribe fundamental principles with respect to:

1. Rights and duties of religious associations.
2. Education, including higher education and scientific libraries. . . .
4. Land titles, land distribution, land colonization and homesteads, entail, housing, and distribution of the population.

SECTION II: THE REICHSTAG

ARTICLE 20: The Reichstag shall be composed of the representatives of the German people.

ARTICLE 21: The deputies shall be representatives of the entire people. They are subject only to their conscience and are not bound by instructions.

ARTICLE 22: The deputies shall be elected by the universal, equal, direct and secret suffrage of all men and women over twenty years of age, according to the principles of proportional representation.

ARTICLE 23: The Reichstag shall be elected for a four year term.

ARTICLE 25: The Reich president may dissolve the Reichstag, but only once for the same cause.

ARTICLE 32: A resolution of the Reichstag requires a simple majority of the votes cast, except as the constitution requires another majority.

ARTICLE 33: The Reichstag and the committees of the Reichstag may demand the presence of the chancellor and of every minister. The chancellor, the ministers, and their deputies shall have access to the sittings of the Reichstag and of its committees. They shall be subject to the rulings of the presiding officer.

ARTICLE 34: The Reichstag shall have the right to, and upon the proposal of one-fifth of its members must, set up inquiry committees. These committees shall in public sitting inquire into such evidence as they or the petitioners consider necessary. The public may be excluded from sittings of an inquiry committee.

SECTION III: THE REICH PRESIDENT AND THE REICH CABINET

ARTICLE 41: The Reich president shall be elected by the whole German people.

ARTICLE 42: The Reich president shall take the following oath on assuming office:

I swear that I will devote my energy to the good of the German people, that I will advance the people's interests, will protect the people from injury, will maintain the constitution and the laws, will fulfill my duties conscientiously, and will exercise justice toward all.

The addition of a religious oath is permissible.

ARTICLE 43: The term of office of the president shall be seven years. Reelection is permissible.

Before the expiration of his term the Reich president may be removed from office by popular vote on resolution of the Reichstag. The resolution of the Reichstag requires a two-thirds majority vote. By such resolution the Reich president is suspended from further exercise of his functions. If the popular vote fails to remove the Reich president such vote shall be regarded as a new election of the Reich president and a dissolution of the Reichstag shall follow.

ARTICLE 44: The Reich president may not at the same time be a member of the Reichstag.

ARTICLE 47: The Reich president shall have supreme command over the entire military forces of the Reich.

ARTICLE 48: If a state fails to carry out the duties imposed upon it by the Reich constitution or Reich laws, the Reich president may compel performance with the aid of armed force.

If public safety and order be seriously disturbed or threatened within the German Reich, the Reich president may take the necessary measures to restore public safety and order; if necessary, with the aid of armed force. For this purpose he may temporarily suspend in whole or in part the fundamental rights enumerated in Articles 114, 115, 117, 118, 123, 124 and 153.

The Reich president must immediately communicate to the Reichstag all measures taken by virtue of Paragraph 1 or Paragraph 2 of this Article. On de-

mand of the Reichstag these measures must be abrogated.

If there be danger in delay, the government of a state may, for its own territory, take such temporary measures as are indicated in Paragraph 2. On demand by the Reich president or by the Reichstag such measures shall be abrogated.

ARTICLE 49: The Reich president shall exercise the pardoning power for the Reich. For Reich amnesties a Reich law is necessary.

ARTICLE 50: All orders and decrees of the Reich president, including those concerning the armed force, require for their validity the counter-signature of the chancellor or of the competent Reich minister. Responsibility is accepted by the act of counter-signature.

ARTICLE 51: In case of disability the Reich president shall be represented first of all by the chancellor. If the disability will presumably continue for a longer time, the matter of a substitute shall be determined by Reich law.

In case of a premature vacancy in the presidency, the same course shall be followed until a new election has been held.

ARTICLE 52: The Reich cabinet consists of the Reich chancellor and the Reich ministers.

ARTICLE 53: The chancellor and, upon his recommendation, the Reich ministers shall be appointed and removed by the Reich president.

ARTICLE 54: The chancellor and Reich ministers must have the confidence of the Reichstag for the exercise of their offices. Any one of them must resign if the Reichstag withdraws its confidence by express resolution.

ARTICLE 55: The chancellor shall preside over the Reich cabinet, and shall conduct its business according to rules of procedure which shall be determined by the Reich cabinet and approved by the Reich president.

ARTICLE 56: The chancellor shall lay down the general course of policy and shall be responsible therefore to the Reichstag. In accordance with this general policy each Reich minister shall independently conduct the branch of administration entrusted to him, and shall be under personal responsibility to the Reichstag.

SECTION V: REICH LEGISLATION

ARTICLE 68: Bills shall be introduced by the Reich cabinet, or by members of the Reichstag. Reich laws shall be enacted by the Reichstag.

ARTICLE 76: The constitution may be amended by legislative action. However, resolutions of the Reichstag for amendment of the constitution are valid only if two-thirds of the legal members are present and if two-thirds of those present give their assent.

Chapter II: Fundamental Rights and Duties of Germans

SECTION I: THE INDIVIDUAL

ARTICLE 109: All Germans are equal before the law.

Men and women have in principle the same civil rights and duties.

Privileges or discriminations in public law based upon birth or rank are abolished. Titles of nobility are regarded only as part of a name and may no longer be conferred.

The state may not confer orders and decorations.

No German may accept titles or orders from a foreign government.

ARTICLE 114: Liberty of the person is inviolable. A restriction upon, or deprivation of, personal liberty, may not be imposed by public authority except by law.

ARTICLE 118: Every German has the right within the limits of the general laws, to express his opinion orally, in writing, in print, pictorially, or in any other way. No circumstance arising out of his work or employment shall hinder him in the exercise of this right, and no one shall discriminate against him if he makes use of such right.

No censorship shall be established, but exceptional provisions may be made by law for cinematographs. Moreover, legal measures are permissible for the suppression of indecent and obscene literature, as well as for the protection of youth at public plays and exhibitions.

SECTION II: COMMUNITY LIFE

ARTICLE 119: Marriage, as the foundation of family life and of the preservation and increase of the nation, stands under the special protection of the constitution. It shall rest upon the equality of rights of both sexes.

It shall be the duty of the state and of the municipalities to maintain the purity, health, and social welfare of the family. Families of many children shall have the right to compensatory public assistance.

Motherhood shall have the right to the protection and public assistance of the state.

ARTICLE 123: All Germans have the right to assemble peaceably and unarmed without notice or special permission.

ARTICLE 124: All Germans have the right to form societies or associations for purposes not prohibited by the criminal code. This right may not be limited by preventive regulations. The same provision applies to religious societies and associations.

Every association has the right to incorporate according to the provisions of the civil code. Such right may not be denied to an association on the ground that its purpose is political, social, or religious.

SECTION III: RELIGION AND RELIGIOUS SOCIETIES

ARTICLE 135: All inhabitants of the Reich shall enjoy complete liberty of belief and conscience. The peaceful exercise of religious worship shall be guaranteed by the constitution and is under the protection of the state.

SECTION V: ECONOMIC LIFE

ARTICLE 151: The organization of economic life must conform to the principles of justice to the end that all may be guaranteed a decent standard of living. Within these limits the economic liberty of the individual shall be assured.

Legal compulsion is permissible only to safeguard threatened rights or to serve the purpose of promoting an overwhelming public interest.

Freedom of commerce and industry shall be guaranteed by national laws.

ARTICLE 152: In economic transactions freedom of contract shall prevail in accordance with the law.

Usury is prohibited. Legal transactions which are contrary to public policy are null and void.

ARTICLE 153: Property shall be guaranteed by the constitution. Its nature and limits shall be prescribed by law.

Expropriation shall take place only for the general good and only on the basis of law. It shall be accompanied by payment of just compensation unless otherwise provided by Reich law.

Property imposes obligations. Its use by its owner shall at the same time serve the public good.

ARTICLE 155: The distribution and use of the soil shall be controlled by the state in such a manner as to prevent abuse and to promote the object of assuring to every German a healthful habitation and to all German families, especially those with many children, homesteads for living and working that are suitable to their needs.

Landed property, the acquisition of which is necessary for the satisfaction of the demand for dwellings, for the promotion of colonization and reclamation, or for the improvement of agriculture may be expropriated.

The cultivation and use of the soil shall be the duty of its owner toward the community. An increase in the value of land which accrues without the application of labor or capital to the property shall inure to the benefit of all.

ARTICLE 156: The Reich may by law, without prejudicing the right of compensation, and with due application of the provisions in force with regard to expropriation, transfer to public ownership private economic enterprises suitable for socialization.

Moreover, in case of pressing need, the Reich may, in the interest of collectivism, combine by law, on a basis of administrative autonomy, economic enterprises and associations, in order to secure the cooperation of all human elements of production, to give to employers and employees a share in management, and to regulate the manufacture, production, distribution, use, and prices, as well as the import and export, of economic goods upon collectivist principles.

ARTICLE 161: The Reich shall, with the controlling participation of the insured, establish a comprehensive scheme of insurance for the conservation of health and of the capacity to work, for the protection of maternity, and for the amelioration of the economic consequences of old age, infirmity, and the changing circumstances of life.

Treaty of Versailles (1919)

Source: "Treaty of Versailles," https://en.wikisource.org/wiki/Treaty_of_Versailles.

Territorial Losses

ARTICLE 80. Germany acknowledges and will respect strictly the independence of Austria; she agrees that this independence shall be inalienable, except with the consent of the Council of the League of Nations.

ARTICLE 81. Germany, in conformity with the action already taken by the Allied and Associated Powers, recognizes the complete independence of the Czecho-Slovak State.

ARTICLE 87. Germany recognizes the complete independence of Poland, and renounces in her favor all rights and title over the territory [defined in the Treaty].

ARTICLE 116. Germany acknowledges and agrees to respect as permanent and inalienable the independence of all the territories which were part of the former Russian Empire on August 1, 1914.

ARTICLE 119. Germany surrenders all her rights and titles over her overseas countries.

Poland

ARTICLE 91. German nationals habitually resident in territories recognized as forming part of Poland will acquire Polish nationality ipso facto and will lose their German nationality.

Within a period of two years after the coming into force of the present Treaty, German nationals over 18 years of age habitually resident in any of the territories recognized as forming part of Poland will be entitled to opt for German nationality.

Persons who have exercised the above right to opt may within the succeeding twelve months transfer their place of residence to the State for which they have opted.

They will be entitled to retain their immovable property in the territory of the other State where they had their place of residence before exercising the right to opt.

ARTICLE 92. In all the German territory transferred in accordance with the present Treaty and recognized as forming definitively part of Poland, the property, rights, and interests of German nationals shall not be liquidated by the Polish Government except in accordance with the following provisions:

The proceeds of the liquidation shall be paid direct to the owner;

If on his application the Mixed Arbitral Tribunal of the present Treaty, or an arbitrator appointed by that Tribunal, is satisfied that the conditions of the sale or measures taken by the Polish Government outside its general legislation were unfairly prejudicial to the price obtained, they shall have discretion to award to the owner equitable compensation to be paid by the Polish Government.

Further agreements will regulate all questions arising out of the cession of the above territory which are not regulated by the present Treaty.

ARTICLE 93. Poland accepts and agrees to embody in a Treaty with the Principal Allied and Associated Powers such provisions as may be deemed necessary by the said Powers to protect the interests of inhabitants of Poland who differ from the majority of the population in race, language, or religion.

Military Restrictions

ARTICLE 159. The German military forces shall be demobilized and reduced not to exceed 100,000 men.

ARTICLE 181. The German navy must not exceed 6 battleships, 6 light cruisers, 12 destroyers, and 12 torpedo boats. No submarines are to be included.

ARTICLE 198. The Armed Forces of Germany must not include any military or naval air forces.

The War Guilt Clause

ARTICLE 231. Germany and her Allies accept the responsibility for causing all the loss and damage to the Allied Powers.

Reparations

ARTICLE 233. Germany will pay for all damages done to the civilian population and property of the Allied Governments.

Occupation

ARTICLE 428. To guarantee the execution of the Treaty, the German territory situated to the west of the Rhine River will be occupied by Allied troops for fifteen years.

ARTICLE 431. The occupation forces will be withdrawn as soon as Germany complies with the Treaty. ■

Concerns about the Treaty of Versailles: German Delegates' Protest against the Proposed Peace Terms (1919)

Source: Brockdorff-Rantzau, Ulrich von. Letter to President Georges Clemenceau on the Subject of Peace Terms, 1919. In *Source Records of the Great War*, vol. 7, edited by Charles F. Horne, 159–65. New York: National Alumni, 1923.

Mr. President:

I have the honor to transmit to you herewith the observations of the German delegation on the draft treaty of peace.

We came to Versailles in the expectation of receiving a peace proposal based on the agreed principles.

We were firmly resolved to do everything in our power with a view of fulfilling the grave obligations which we had undertaken. We hoped for the peace of justice which had been promised to us.

We were aghast when we read in documents the demands made upon us, the victorious violence of our enemies. The more deeply we penetrate into the spirit of this treaty, the more convinced we become of the impossibility of carrying it out. The exactions of this treaty are more than the German people can bear.

With a view to the re-establishment of the Polish State we must renounce indisputably German territory—nearly the whole of the Province of West Prussia, which is preponderantly German; of Pomerania; Danzig, which is German to the core; we must let that ancient Hanse town be transformed into a free State under Polish suzerainty.

We must agree that East Prussia shall be amputated from the body of the State, condemned to a lingering death, and robbed of its northern portion, including Memel, which is purely German.

We must renounce Upper Silesia for the benefit of Poland and Czecho-Slovakia, although it has been in close political connection with Germany for more than 750 years, is instinct with German life, and forms the very foundation of industrial life throughout East Germany.

Preponderantly German districts must be ceded to Belgium, without sufficient guarantees that the plebiscite, which is only to take place afterward, will be independent. The purely German district of the Saar must be detached from our empire, and the way must be paved for its subsequent annexation to France, although we owe her debts in coal only, not in men.

For fifteen years Rhenish territory must be occupied, and after those fifteen years the Allies have power to refuse the restoration of the country; in the interval the Allies can take every measure to sever the economic and moral links with the mother country, and finally to misrepresent the wishes of the indigenous population.

Although the exaction of the cost of the war has been expressly renounced, yet Germany, thus cut in pieces and weakened, must declare herself ready in principle to bear all the war expenses of her enemies, which would exceed many times over the total amount of German State and private assets.

Meanwhile her enemies demand, in excess of the agreed conditions, reparation for damage suffered by their civil population, and in this connection Germany must also go bail for her allies. The sum to be paid is to be fixed by our enemies unilaterally, and to admit of subsequent modification and increase. No limit is fixed, save the capacity of the German people for payment, determined not by their standard of life, but solely by their capacity to meet the demands of their enemies by their labor. The German people would thus be condemned to perpetual slave labor.

In spite of the exorbitant demands, the reconstruction of our economic life is at the same time rendered impossible. We must surrender our merchant fleet. We are to renounce all foreign securities. We are to hand over to our enemies our property in all German enterprises abroad, even in the countries of our allies.

Even after the conclusion of peace the enemy States are to have the right of confiscating all German property. No German trader in their countries will be protected from these war measures. We must completely renounce our colonies, and not even German missionaries shall have the right to follow their calling therein.

We most thus renounce the realization of all our aims in the spheres of politics, economics, and ideas. Even in internal affairs we are to give up the right to self-determination. The international Reparation Commission receives dictatorial powers over the whole life of our people in economic and cultural matters. Its authority extends far beyond that which the empire, the German Federal Council, and the Reichstag combined ever possessed within the territory of the empire.

This commission has unlimited control over the economic life of the State, of communities, and of individuals. Further, the entire educational and sanitary system depends on it. It can keep the whole German people in mental thralldom. In order to increase the payments due, by the thrall, the commission can hamper measures for the social protection of the German worker.

In other spheres also Germany's sovereignty is

abolished. Her chief waterways are subjected to international administration; she must construct in her territory such canals and such railways as her enemies wish; she must agree to treaties the contents of which are unknown to her, to be concluded by her enemies with the new States on the east, even when they concern her own functions. The German people are excluded from the League of Nations, to which is entrusted all work of common interest to the world.

Thus must a whole people sign the decree for its proscription, nay, its own death sentence.

Germany knows that she must make sacrifices in order to attain peace. Germany knows that she has, by agreement, undertaken to make these sacrifices, and will go in this matter to the utmost limits of her capacity.

Counter-proposals

1. Germany offers to proceed with her own disarmament in advance of all other peoples, in order to show that she will help to usher in the new era of the peace of justice. She gives up universal compulsory service and reduces her army to 100,000 men, except as regards temporary measures.

She even renounces the warships which her enemies are still willing to leave in her hands. She stipulates, however, that she shall be admitted forthwith as a State with equal rights into the League of Nations. She stipulates that a genuine League of Nations shall come into being, embracing all peoples of goodwill, even her enemies of today. The League must be inspired by a feeling of responsibility toward mankind and have at its disposal a power to enforce its will sufficiently strong and trusty to protect the frontiers of its members.

2. In territorial questions Germany takes up her position unreservedly on the ground of the Wilson program. She renounces her sovereign right in Alsace-Lorraine, but wishes a free plebiscite to take place there. She gives up the greater part of the province of Posen, the district incontestably Polish in population, together with the capital. She is prepared to grant to Poland, under international guarantees, free and secure access to the sea by ceding free ports

at Danzig, Konigsberg, and Memel, by an agreement regulating the navigation of the Vistula and by special railway conventions.

Germany is prepared to insure the supply of coal for the economic needs of France, especially from the Saar region, until such time as the French mines are once more in working order. The preponderantly Danish districts of Schleswig will be given up to Denmark on the basis of a plebiscite.

Germany demands that the right of self-determination shall also be respected where the interests of the Germans in Austria and Bohemia are concerned. She is ready to subject all her colonies to administration by the community of the League of Nations, if she is recognized as its mandatory.

3. Germany is prepared to make payments incumbent on her in accordance with the agreed program of peace up to a maximum sum of 100,000,000,000 gold marks, 20,000,000,000 by May 1, 1926, and the balance (80,000,000,000) in annual payments, without interest. These payments shall in principle be equal to a fixed percentage of the German Imperial and State revenues. The annual payment shall approximate to the former peace budget. For the first ten years the annual payments shall not exceed 1,000,000,000 gold marks a year. The German taxpayer shall not be less heavily burdened than the taxpayer of the most heavily burdened State among those represented on the Reparation Commission. Germany presumes in this connection that she will not have to make any territorial sacrifices beyond those mentioned above and that she will recover her freedom of economic movement at home and abroad.

4. Germany is prepared to devote her entire economic strength to the service of the reconstruction.

She wishes to cooperate effectively in the reconstruction of the devastated regions of Belgium and Northern France. To make good the loss in production of the destroyed mines of Northern France, up to 20,000,000 tons of coal will be delivered annually for the first five years, and up to 80,000,000 tons for the next five years. Germany will facilitate further deliveries of coal to France, Belgium, Italy, and Luxemburg. Germany is, moreover, prepared to make considerable deliveries of benzol, coal tar, and sulphate of ammonia, as well as dyestuffs and medicines.

5. Finally, Germany offers to put her entire merchant tonnage into a pool of the world's shipping, to place at the disposal of her enemies a part of her freight space as part payment of reparation and to build for them for a series of years in German yards an amount of tonnage exceeding their demands.

6. In order to replace the river boats destroyed in Belgium and Northern France, Germany offers river craft from her own resources.

7. Germany thinks that she sees an appropriate method for the prompt fulfilment of her obligation to make reparations conceding participation in coal mines to insure deliveries of coal.

8. Germany, in accordance with the desires of the workers of the whole world, wishes to insure to them free and equal rights. She wishes to insure to them in the Treaty of Peace the right to take their own decisive part in the settlement of social policy and social protection.

9. The German delegation again makes its demand for a neutral inquiry into the responsibility for the war and culpable acts in conduct. An impartial commission should have the right to investigate on its own responsibility the archives of all the belligerent countries and all the persons who took an important part in the war. Nothing short of confidence that the question of guilt will be examined dispassionately can leave the peoples lately at war with each other in the proper frame of mind for the formation of the League of Nations.

These are only the most important among the proposals which we have to make. As regards other great sacrifices, and also as regards the details, the delegation refers to the accompanying memorandum and the annex thereto.

The time allowed us for the preparation of this memorandum was so short that it was impossible to treat all the questions exhaustively. A fruitful and illuminating negotiation could only take place by means of oral discussion.

This treaty of peace is to be the greatest achievement of its kind in all history. There is no precedent for the conduct of such comprehensive negotiations by an exchange of written notes only.

The feeling of the peoples who have made such immense sacrifices makes them demand that their fate should be decided by an open, unreserved exchange of ideas on the principle: "Quite open covenants of peace openly arrived at, after which there shall be no private international understandings of any kind, but diplomacy shall proceed always frankly in the public view."

Germany is to put her signature to the treaty laid before her and to carry it out. Even in her need, justice for her is too sacred a thing to allow her to stoop to achieve conditions which she cannot undertake to carry out.

Treaties of peace signed by the great powers have, it is true, in the history of the last decades, again and again proclaimed the right of the stronger. But each of these treaties of peace has been a factor in originating and prolonging the world war. Whenever in this war the victor has spoken to the vanquished, at Brest-Litovsk and Bucharest, his words were but the seeds of future discord.

The lofty aims which our adversaries first set before themselves in their conduct of the war, the new era of an assured peace of justice, demand a treaty instinct with a different spirit.

Only the cooperation of all nations, a cooperation of hands and spirits, can build up a durable peace.

We are under no delusions regarding the strength of the hatred and bitterness which this war has engendered, and yet the forces which are at work for a union of mankind are stronger now than ever they were before.

The historic task of the Peace Conference of Versailles is to bring about this union.

Accept, Mr. President, the expression of my distinguished consideration. ▧

John Maynard Keynes, "On Reparations" (1919)

Keynes was the financial representative for the British Treasury to the Versailles peace conference. He tried to prevent reparation payments being set so high that they would traumatize Germans, damage the nation's ability to pay, and sharply limit the ability to buy exports, thus hurting not just Germany's economy but also that of the wider world. He argued that the treaty was a "Carthaginian peace"—one that guaranteed animosity and future conflict rather than following the principles of reconciliation and self-determination laid out in U.S. president Woodrow Wilson's Fourteen Points. *Conservatives in the British government ensured that Keynes was largely excluded from high-level talks. Italics are in the original.*

Source: Keynes, John Maynard. *The Economic Consequences of the Peace*. London: Harcourt, Brace and Howe, 1920.

A capacity of $40,000,000,000 or even of $25,000,000,000 is, therefore, not within the limits of reasonable possibility. It is for those who believe that Germany can make an annual payment amounting to hundreds of millions sterling to say *in what specific commodities* they intend this payment to be made and *in what markets* the goods are to be sold. Until they proceed to some degree of detail, and are able to produce some tangible argument in favor of their conclusions, they do not deserve to be believed.

I make three provisos only, none of which affect the force of my argument for immediate practical purposes.

First: if the Allies were to "nurse" the trade and industry of Germany for a period of five or ten years, supplying her with large loans, and with ample shipping, food, and raw materials during that period, building up markets for her, and deliberately applying all their resources and goodwill to making her the greatest industrial nation in Europe, if not in the world, a substantially larger sum could probably be extracted thereafter; for Germany is capable of very great productivity.

Second: whilst I estimate in terms of money, I assume that there is no revolutionary change in the purchasing power of our unit of value. If the value of gold were to sink to a half or a tenth of its present value, the real burden of a payment fixed in terms of gold would be reduced proportionately. If a sovereign comes to be worth what a shilling is worth now, then, of course, Germany can pay a larger sum than I have named, measured in gold sovereigns.

Third: I assume that there is no revolutionary change in the yield of Nature and material to man's labor. It is not impossible that the progress of science should bring within our reach methods and devices by which the whole standard of life would be raised immeasurably, and a given volume of products would represent but a portion of the human effort which it represents now. In this case all standards of "capacity" would be changed everywhere. But the fact that all things are possible is no excuse for talking foolishly.

It is true that in 1870 no man could have predicted Germany's capacity in 1910. We cannot expect to legislate for a generation or more. The secular changes in man's economic condition and the liability of human forecast to error are as likely to lead to mistake in one direction as in another. We cannot as reasonable men do better than base our policy on the evidence we have and adapt it to the five or ten years over which we may suppose ourselves to have some measure of prevision; and we are not at fault if we leave on one side the extreme chances of human existence and of revolutionary changes in the order of Nature or of man's relations to her. The fact that we have no adequate knowledge of Germany's capacity to pay over a long period of years is no justification (as I have heard some people claim that it is) for the statement that she can pay $50,000,000,000. . . . (202–4).

The Treaty includes no provisions for the economic rehabilitation of Europe—nothing to make the defeated Central Empires into good neighbors, nothing to stabilize the new States of Europe, nothing to reclaim Russia; nor does it promote in any way a compact of economic solidarity amongst the Allies themselves; no arrangement was reached at Paris for restoring the disordered finances of France and Italy, or to adjust the systems of the Old World and the New.

The Council of Four paid no attention to these issues, being preoccupied with others—Clemenceau to crush the economic life of his enemy, Lloyd George to do a deal and bring home something which would pass muster for a week, the President to do nothing that was not just and right. It is an extraordinary fact that the fundamental economic problems of a Europe starving and disintegrating before their eyes, was the one question in which it was impossible to arouse the interest of the Four. Reparation was their main excursion into the economic field, and they settled it as a problem of theology, of politics, of electoral chicane, from every point of view except that of the economic future of the States whose destiny they were handling (226–27). ▨

Documents on Agenda Items
Foreign Affairs
THE YOUNG PLAN AND REPARATIONS

The Young Plan and its predecessor, the Dawes Plan, were highly detailed documents written by and for legal and economic experts. The following is a quick overview.

The Dawes Plan of 1924 modified the original provisions of Versailles to Germany's advantage. Total reparations were reduced to 132 billion RM. Reparation payments would begin at 1 billion RM the first year, increasing gradually over five years to 2.5 billion RM to allow Germany time to adjust. Sources for reparations would include transportation, excise, and customs taxes. Germany would be loaned about $200 million, primarily through Wall Street bonds. The Reichsbank, Germany's central bank in charge of printing the national currency, was reorganized and made independent of the state. In addition, the Ruhr area would be evacuated by foreign troops.

The Young Plan of 1929 was a further revision in Germany's favor. Total reparations would be reduced 20 percent to 112 billion RM. This amount was divided into three sets of bonds (Schedule A, B, and C bonds). Payments would be made over a period of fifty-nine years, making the payments manageable but stretching them out until 1988. The annual payment, set at 2 billion RM, would be divided into two components to ease payments: an unconditional part equal to one-third of the sum; and a postponable part, incurring interest and financed by a consortium of U.S. banks, for the remaining two-thirds. The Allies would release all securities and remove creditors' financial and economic control.

To put the actual burden in perspective, while the total indemnity was large, Germany's actual reparations payments amounted to only a tiny fraction of the total charge. Payment on the schedule C bonds (82 billion RM of the whole amount) was not to begin until the other two had been paid off—which they never were. For practical purposes, then, the tab added up to 50 billion RM, not 132 billion. What is more, Germany paid only a fraction of its annual obligation after the first 1 billion gold mark installment in 1921. As a result, the reparations as a proportion of net national product remained below 5 percent from 1923 on. The actual total payout from 1920 to 1929 had been less than 20 billion RM. Of that, only 12 billion had been cash; the rest was goods such as coal and chemicals, or assets such as railway equipment. Further, the cost of reparations was compensated by the extension of loans, mostly American, that were never repaid. In effect, the United States assumed a large portion of the indemnity. Overall, the reparations had a limited economic impact; the political impact, however, was dramatic.

Hjalmar Schacht, Memorandum on the Young Plan (1929)

Schacht, the president of the Reichsbank, stunned the Müller cabinet in 1929 by releasing a critical memorandum in the midst of the Reichstag debates. Schacht had been a proponent and signatory of the Young Plan draft, but he withdrew his unconditional support when he believed that the German government was not introducing promised financial reforms (i.e., a plan of austerity involving cutting corporate taxes and reorganization of provincial and municipal finances) and that foreign governments were cheating Germany out of surpluses it had acquired since the draft was signed. The memorandum extracts here were collected and edited for English readers from German press accounts.

Source: Schacht, Hjalmar. "Germany and the Young Plan: The Schacht Memorandum." *Bulletin of International News* 6, no. 13 (2 January 1930): 10–12.

The fact that the German Experts did not consider the Young Plan figures as acceptable clearly involves the greatest possible responsibility, which the Experts of the Creditor Powers have assumed by declaring that the figures were within Germany's capacity. When, in the negotiations with foreign Governments concerning the putting into operation of the Young Plan, still further considerable sacrifices were de-

manded from Germany, it became clear that the acceptability of the Young Plan figures was even more doubtful and the responsibility of the Experts of the creditor Powers fell more heavily upon their Governments. In view of the fact that nearly every creditor Power is trying to force fresh financial and economic burdens upon Germany in addition to those of the Young Plan, foreign Governments are violating the agreements which they accepted in the Young Plan as an obligation.

As a result of additional burdens which are being placed upon Germany beyond those incurred under the Young Plan, the promised financial relief will become illusory. There is absolutely no reason for Germany of her own accord, without reciprocal concessions, to renounce in any point the assertion of her right to the promise that Germany's former obligations should be revised by the Young Plan, either with regard to payments or to the relinquishing of claims. If Germany declares herself prepared to follow the unilateral recommendation of the experts of her creditors, she must demand likewise that the recommendations of her own experts should be considered, or else other concessions should be demanded.

Six points under which Germany stands to lose:

1. The renunciation by Germany of the Hague Protocol and the five months' surplus of 400,000,000 marks [£20,000,000] arising through the overlapping of the Dawes and Young Plans.
2. The increase, according to the same Protocol, of the unconditional portion of the German annuity precisely in those early years of the Plan during which facilities are of decisive importance to the success of the whole scheme. This increase amounts in the first year to 40,500,000 marks [£2,025,000].
3. Germany, according to the statements of the British Chancellor of the Exchequer, is to renounce the 300,000,000 marks [£15,000,000] surplus from the past liquidations of confiscated German property in Great Britain.
4. The recent German-Polish Agreement provides for the renunciation by Germany of exception-

ally large property claims, a measure which is bound to compel the German Government to compensate the German owners in full.

5. According to the proposals of the Paris Committee for the Liquidation of the Past, Germany is to renounce a whole series of financial rights involving considerable sums.

6. The losses mentioned do not include the annuity, averaging 19,500,000 marks [£975,000], for 37 years imposed on Germany by the German-Belgian Marks Commission.

In answer to the question as to whether the obligation to agree to such payments and renunciations devolved on Germany from the Young Plan, [I refer] to paragraph 141 of the Young Plan, which states that each concession on the part of Germany must be met by a concession on the part of the other side. On the closing of the account between the Reparations Commission and Germany it was understood that Germany would be able to lay claim to all sequestrated property which had not as yet been liquidated in settlement of reparations. If the German Government, in spite of this, had to renounce such claims, it would be ignoring the clearly declared opinion of the German Experts and would have to assume a responsibility which its Experts had expressly refused.

The intention of the Government to effect a permanent reform of the financial organization of the Reich, the States and the Municipalities, and to make possible the assumption of the heavy burdens of the Young Plan by a measure of internal economic relief to German productions was assumed by the German Experts to be an essential condition of acceptance. In neither direction had the slightest move been made since the signature of the Young Plan. It was already possible to anticipate with certainty that the savings resulting from the Young Plan would not only not lead to a reduction of burdens, but would not even cover the deficit which could already clearly be foreseen. German industry was on the threshold not of a decrease but of an increase of burdens.

The Young Plan was drawn up with all the moral earnestness and sense of responsibility of its authors, not only in the eyes of their own people, but in the eyes of the whole civilised world. We must demand that the Governments shall not endanger this work of peace by the introduction of unilateral interests. For my part I must absolutely refuse to be made responsible for putting the Young Plan into operation if its recommendations and conditions are in any way disregarded, as would seem to be the case judging by present measures and demands. The German people must await the time when the foreign Governments finally abandon their attempt to force further burdens upon and further concessions from German industry beyond those demanded by the Young Plan. They must know that by pursuing such an old policy they are bringing upon themselves the responsibility for subjecting the Young Plan to severe disturbances in the future or for endangering the mobilization of the annuities.

We must demand from the German Government that they do not submit to any further obligations. We must demand, further, that before the Young Plan is finally accepted by them, they must put their house in order both in the Reich and in the States and the Municipalities, and reduce the burdens of the German people to a level which is in accordance with the capacity of German industry. All those who are in agreement with me that the Young Plan is a final instrument of peace, a Plan which is based upon international co-operation and the prosperity of German industry, and which depends upon these two conditions for its success, must demand that everything should be done to fulfil these conditions.

I have energetically opposed the agitation against the Young Plan, I consider the resulting referendum, which that agitation supports, to be a grave mistake, in that it undermines any reasonable and powerful defence of our interests under the Young Plan. But just because I declare myself to be in favour of the acceptance of the Young Plan, I will have no part in its falsification. It would be a self-delusion for the world to believe that we could pay still further indefinite millions and milliards or renounce our right to property. It would be a self-delusion for our people to believe that they were in a position, with the present and possibly even increased burdens on industry, to raise the Young Plan payments and possibly still further charges.

I will not and shall not be responsible for such a deception. ▦

FREEDOM LAW

Law against the Enslavement of the German People (1929)

Source: "Gesetz gegen die Versklavung des deutschen Volkes." 1929. In *Die ungeliebte Republik: Dokumentation zur Innen- u. Aussenpolitik Weimars, 1918–1933*, edited by Wolfgang Michalka and Gottfried Niedhart, 263. Munich: DTV, 1980. Translated by Robert Goodrich.

§1. The Reich Government will solemnly inform the foreign powers without delay that the extorted recognition of war guilt in the Versailles Treaty contradicts historical truth, is based on false premises, and is not binding under international law.

§2. The Reich Government shall endeavor to secure the annulment of the war guilt acknowledgment contained in Art. 231 and Art. 429 and 430 of the Versailles Treaty. It shall also endeavor to secure the immediate and unconditional evacuation of the occupied German territories, without any remaining control commissions, independent of the acceptance or the rejection of the decisions of the Hague conference.

§3. No further financial burdens or obligations based on the war guilt acknowledgment shall be assumed, inclusive of those arising from the recommendations of the Paris reparation experts and the subsequent agreements.

§4. The Reich chancellor and Reich ministers or their plenipotentiaries who lend their signatures to agreements contrary to the provisions of par. 3 shall render themselves liable to prosecution for high treason.

§5. This law enters into force at the moment of its proclamation. ▦

LIQUIDATION TREATY WITH POLAND

German-Polish Agreement (1929)

Source: "Deutsch-Polnische Übereinkunft, vom 31. Oktober 1929." In *Reichsgesetzblatt* (1930), vol. 2, no. 8, 549–51. Berlin: Reichsverlagsamt, 1930. Translated by Robert Goodrich.

I. The Reich government and the government of Poland issue the following statement, which will be presented at the Haag Conference and shall have the power of law with the entry into force of the Young Plan.

II. The German government renounces all claims of a financial or proprietary nature relating to the war or the peace treaty, by the state as well as its citizens—natural and legal persons—which, due to any instance coming from the time before the entry into force of the Young Plan, have been asserted directly or indirectly against Poland, or could in the future be asserted, including the complaints, which have been recognized in special agreements related to such instances.

Regarding the claims of a financial or proprietary nature on the part of Poland, by the state as well as its citizens—natural and legal persons—which relate to the war or the peace treaty and due to any instance coming from the time before the entry into force of the Young Plan have been asserted directly or indirectly against Germany, or could in the future be asserted, including the complaints, which have been recognized in special agreements related to such instances, the Polish government recognizes the determinations in Chapter IX, No. 143 of the Young Plan.

Notwithstanding the determinations of Article V of this agreement, the present declaration represents a complete and final renunciation of the abovementioned complaints, regardless of who is involved.

III. The Polish government declares its renunciation of every liquidation of German properties, rights and interests in Poland, which the Polish government, invoking the determinations of Article 92 and 297b of the peace treaty or in accordance with these determinations, has undertaken or could undertake, so far as these properties, rights, and interests were still in possession of their owners or former owners on 1 September 1929.

All measures for the preservation of existing conditions, which have been taken in connection with the abovementioned liquidation process, shall cease to have effect with the entry into force of the present agreement.

The properties in question shall be released in the actual and legal condition in which they find themselves, together with rights and privileges connected thereto and under maintenance of existing obligations; however, a withholding for the costs and fees of the compulsory liquidation administrators may take place.

IV. Any disputes over the interpretation or application of the current agreement, which cannot be resolved via diplomatic channels, shall be presented to a court of arbitration at the request of one of the contracted parties.

For the purpose, each party shall name an arbiter. Both arbiters shall select a neutral chairman. If no agreement can be reached on the person of this neutral chairman, then the president of the Swiss Confederation shall be requested to select him.

V. Immediately following the signing of the present agreement, both governments shall act to arrange measures, which will be taken in relation to the future activity of the German-Polish Joint Court of Arbitration.

VI. In the execution of Article I, the current agreement as well as its closing protocol shall be ratified by the parties and enter into force simultaneously with the entry into force of the Young Plan. ▨

Military Affairs

THE REICHSWEHR AND ARMORED CRUISERS

Philipp Scheidemann (SPD), "On the Reichswehr as a 'State within the State'" (1926)

Scheidemann's speech picked up on the well-established idea of a "state within a state," what modern Americans would call the "deep state"—any institutional force that operates outside the oversight and control of the formal, public apparatus of the state. Since the Kaiserreich, the Reichswehr had regularly been denounced as such a deep state. Scheidemann's speech was explosive—not because of the basic accusation, which was well known, but because of its specifics. He exposed the ongoing actions of the Reichswehr that threatened not only international relations by flouting the Treaty of Versailles, but democracy itself. Prior to the speech, journalists who reported on the Reichswehr's illegal activities were arrested. The Right denounced the speech as treason; and the SPD entered a vote of no confidence the following day, supported by both the DNVP and the KPD. The center-right coalition of Chancellor Marx (X) collapsed a day after the speech.

Source: *Verhandlungen des Reichstags: III. Wahlperiode 1924: Stenographische Berichte*. Vol. 391, session 252 (16 December 1926), 8577–85. Berlin: Druck und Verlag der Reichsdruckerei, 1927. Translated by Robert Goodrich.

I want to begin the difficult conflict we are entering today with an avowal of our people and our country. The German people have made friends all over the world because of the gravity of their fate, and above all because of the strength with which they endured this difficult fate, but even more because of the determination with which the German people approached the reconstruction. How could it be conceivable that the largest party in the German country, the Social Democratic Party, could be indifferent to this fate? Social democracy is not only committed to the German people to which it belongs, it has also always tried to work for the German people to the best of its ability. It was we who laid the foundations for the resurgence in the democratic Republic, and it was we who also showed the way to the policy of international understanding, for which Foreign Minister Dr. Stresemann recently won the Nobel Prize.

This statement seems necessary to me because in Germany people still exist who consider what they do not understand to be antinational and who still pretend that they have the love of the fatherland as their inheritance. We would be very weak in our love for our own *Volk* if we let the sinkhole of defamation and intimidation hinder us from saying what we think is necessary, what we consider useful and wholesome.

Serious concern about our country compels us today to subject the Reichswehr to political consideration. I will try to do justice to those who oppose our view. We fully understand that officers, who are rooted with all their feelings and thoughts in the past of the earlier system, will find it extremely difficult to get used to the new constitutional relations. We also understand that the reluctance of our neighboring states to follow us on the path of disarmament—that is, to voluntarily do what we have been compelled to do—could give rise to all sorts of concerns in our country. But when circumstances grow out of this complex of ideas and feelings, which we understand, and which appear to us as a threat to domestic peace and a threat to a peaceful foreign policy, then we not only have the right but also the duty to speak. There must be a state power that is strong enough to keep Germany on the path that it has taken to rise again, on the path of a democratic republic and peace. An armed power which, in its essential parts, is pursuing its own policy, which is directly opposed to the policy of democracy and peace, cannot be maintained in the condition in which it is. The new leader of the Reichswehr gave a speech some time ago in which he said: "The Reichswehr is an instrument of the state that has been trained to be obedient." That is a very nice word, and I thank the general for it, but allow me to point out that what he said is only a goal toward which we are striving—that is to say, a state of affairs in the Reichswehr that we want to bring about, but

General Heye is unfortunately mistaken in assuming that this state has already been achieved.

Unfortunately, we are still very far from this state of affairs.

How correct is my assertion that the Reichswehr has developed more and more into a state within a state, a state that follows its own laws and pursues its own policy, I want to prove it to you with facts.

I will say one thing in advance. Ladies and gentlemen, do not pretend that what is being discussed here today comes as a surprise to other countries. I know and expect this objection.

This is how things are, and if you want to be honest, you have to admit it, since every country in the world probably knows exactly what is going on with us. I cannot simply assume that you know that. There are certainly many things that you do not know, so it is still possible that you have no knowledge of them either. The fact is that the people who are least well informed about things in the Reichswehr are the German people.

The complaints that I have to bring forward go in three directions. On the one hand, there is the area of financing many things that are of a bad nature, which I will talk about later, i.e., firstly financial questions; secondly, the relations that the Reichswehr has with certain radical organizations, that is to say, then, more domestic political things that we want to see combated; thirdly, the operations of the Reichswehr, which must seriously endanger our entire foreign policy.

There is great danger for the whole Reich.

If we keep quiet about all these things and thereby give the impression through our silence that we approve of them, the foreign policy that is now being led by Herr Stresemann will be impossible. We must express that the majority of the German *Volk* want nothing to do with such a policy, that we want to honestly uphold the treaties that Germany has entered into.

[*Scheidemann then provided an analysis of clandestine financing for military training and weapons development abroad, particularly in Russia.*]

The connections between the Reichswehr and

right-wing radical organizations is best represented by a report that we have from Rostock and that I want to present to you, omitting everything that is irrelevant. Place—Rostock; Time—December 1924; Speaker—General v. Tschischwitz. Among other things, Tschischwitz said in this lecture:

Our people must be able to defend themselves again, training must be carried out by military experts from the Reichswehr. The backbone of the old army were the district command offices. Unfortunately, we no longer have them. So something similar has to be created. Since this work cannot be done on a part-time basis, full-time employees must be considered. This of course requires money.

And so on. The general further emphasized that his plans met with a positive reception in Pomerania, that no policy could be made without the Reichswehr, only with it. He expressed the hope that in future, replacement of officers would come again from the circles that had provided it earlier. There would always be one or the other cavalry regiment that even a commoner could get into, with great difficulty. [*In other words, only Junkers should be officers.*]

Ladies and gentlemen! In General v. Tschischwitz's speech you actually have in a nutshell everything that comes into consideration for all these things that I am talking about: establishment of district command offices, which we no longer have, with former officers who are on permanent contract, and military training by members of the Reichswehr by so-called sports instructors.

Ladies and gentlemen! Just as the books, the pamphlets, the newspapers, and the instructors at the army technical schools must under all circumstances be completely right-wing extremist—that is, *völkisch* or German-national—the selection of the district officers is also conducted primarily based on this system. One example, which I can add to further, if desired: The Reichswehr representative for looking after weapons stocks in and around Hanover, Lieu-

tenant Voigt, employed on a contract of employment, is on duty in Reichswehr uniform. He is particularly qualified because he was sentenced to six months in prison for participating in the Küstrin Putsch. [*The failed putsch in 1923 by the Black Reichswehr sought to bring down the government of Chancellor Stresemann and create a military dictatorship. Most participants were never punished.*]

Ladies and gentlemen! Conditions are particularly bad in Kiel. There was a cavalry Captain, a D. Lieder, who was paid by the base as an intermediary agent. Who is this Mr. Lieder? He was the head of Organization Consul in Schleswig-Holstein, an organization that later became part of the so-called Viking League, which has since been banned by the Prussian government. [*Organization Consul (O. C.) was the most active right-wing death squad in the early Republic; the Viking League was its successor in 1923.*]

The naval base for the Baltic Sea had the corvette captain Otto Schultze get in touch with Organization Consul for the purpose of joint action in the event of a putsch—that is to say, for any joint action in such a putsch. Cavalry Captain D. Lieder agreed to cooperate under the following conditions—Organization Consul issued its demands to the Reichswehr or the naval base!

1. In the event of joint action, the O. C. retains independent command of the formations formed by the O. C.
2. The Navy shall provide weapons and ammunition for these formations, or it shall provide weapons and ammunition for the day they are needed.
3. The Navy shall provide the money to finance the O. C.

The Navy accepted these conditions!

To secure the deployment of the right-wing associations in East Holstein, the O. C. immediately received twelve light machine guns. In addition, weapons were made available at agreed locations. That was at the time when the former Minister Rathenau was murdered by members of the O. C. The financing was mainly in Danish kroner. The base officers got the Danish kroner from selling nautical instruments abroad. These were exported to the occupied territory and then sold abroad from there. For November 9, 1923—that was the putsch that Mr. Hitler and Ludendorff had arranged—everything was made ready to strike. The right-wing associations were to concentrate on Kiel. The Navy was ready to place its troops under the command of O. C.

[*Scheidemann provided an analysis of the ongoing evolution and persistence of these right-wing organizations and their ties to the Reichswehr.*]

Ladies and gentlemen! What kind of people and what kind of things the Reichswehr is involved with is also evident from the following. In Erfurt on 31 March 1926, the Vikings Laudin and Bartholomäe were sentenced to 214 years in prison and three years loss of civil liberties for desecrating the graves in the Jewish cemetery. During their arrest at the beginning of March in the apartment of the Viking leader Wustmann, a significant arsenal was confiscated. A document was found in Wustmann's coat pocket, according to which these weapons were officially given to the lieutenant colonel by the Reichswehr's 15th Battalion for safekeeping.

I do not want to exaggerate the dangers that arise from the described conditions. So I say that the Republic is not endangered and threatened today, tomorrow, or the day after tomorrow. The Republic has established solid roots among the *Volk*. Its opponents are not in agreement on their goals. One could say of them, they are always quite decisive, they just don't know what they want: a centralized or federalist Republic, under which dynasty, under which monarchy, fascism or whatever—among these ideas there is a fair bit of disagreement. As long as the ship of the Republic has smooth sailing, there is nothing to fear. But who knows when the weather will change! And once turbulent times come over us, then an armed force that is hostile to the democratic Republic becomes a tremendous danger. The Republic needs an armed force that it can rely on under all circumstances. We cannot possibly tolerate conditions that stand in the way of reaching the goal. That would be

a crime against the German *Volk*. That is why we are calling for a reform of the Reichswehr, root and branch. We want a Reichswehr that does not fraternize exclusively with only a part of the *Volk*, and precisely with that part that has not yet come to terms with the new conditions. We want a Reichswehr to which the entire *Volk*, to which, above all, the Republic can look with confidence. That is why the Reichswehr must have a spirit!

We demand strict implementation of the prohibition of any connection between the Reichswehr and the Navy and right-wing extremist organizations, and dismissal of officers who exceed this prohibition. And a fundamental declaration on control of future army replacements by civil commissions with the participation of the lower administrative authorities.

Finally, a word about clandestine armaments and its meaning! Clandestine armaments are of course exaggerated abroad. If we don't say that we don't want them, all the nationalist rabble abroad, which they have there just as much as we have here, draws the conclusion that we will tolerate treaties being circumvented. All military experts agree that a disarmed Germany cannot wage war and that this fact cannot be changed by clandestine armaments. Clandestine armaments, which are incompatible with the peace treaty, harbor the greatest danger; they irresponsibly damage foreign policy; they force people into lies and hypocrisy, and, gentlemen, no cunning can prevent the whole world from saying, if we are someday caught in such a thing: so this is the partner —he is not honest! That cannot be of any use to our German Republic. We want to appear to the world as a decent *Volk* who live up to their obligations. The opponents of disarmament abroad will continue to argue that Germany did not disarm, but only seemingly did it.

That's a fact! If you don't know this, ask Mr. Stresemann, who has to overcome the difficulties. The nationalists and the "Pan-Germans" in France and Belgium are always finding new reasons for a new arms race, in which we would draw the short stick regardless.

What we ask of the Reichswehr is—we know—not

a little. There is a long way to go from the situation now to the situation that we consider necessary. We know that this cannot all be done in a day. We have also agreed to take part in any government where, as we know, the easiest remedy can be provided for, just as we have always been ready to do material work in and outside of government, including with regard to the expansion and transformation of the Reichswehr. In any case, a start must be made, and we believe that this start must be made at the top.

We are convinced, ladies and gentlemen, that a thorough reform of the Reichswehr can be carried out only if the government is made up of truly reliable republicans. A truly republican government could, in any event, act very quickly and do what has to be done under different circumstances. ▪

Otto Wels (SPD), "On Cessation of Work on Armored Cruiser A" (1928)

The speech to the Reichstag presented the SPD's opposition to the Naval Bill when it was introduced in 1928. The SPD based much of its successful election campaign that year—referred to in the text as the results of "20 May"—on opposition to naval funding, demanding instead that the funds be spent on social programs.

Source: *Verhandlungen des Reichstags: IV. Wahlperiode 1928: Stenographische Berichte*. Vol. 423, session 14 (15 November 1928), 325. Berlin: Druck und Verlag der Reichsdruckerei, 1929. Translated by Robert Goodrich.

The Social Democratic faction requests that the construction of armored cruiser "A" cease. The résumé of all the reasons that prompted us to submit this motion ultimately lies in the will of the German voters, which was clearly and unequivocally expressed in [the Reichstag election of 20 May 1928]. On May 20th, the German *Volk* decided in favor of a policy that includes the idea of social justice, the idea of peaceful understanding, and the idea of economic redistribution. May 20th was the rejection of the

power politics embodied in particular by the German nationalists,

If, however, an attempt was made in the German press to see evidence that the relatively small number of signatures for the communist referendum [to end funding for ships] represented approval of the building of the armored cruiser by the majority of the population, it would be a fatal error. This is evident not only from the well-known attitude of my party, which despite your shouting is the largest party of the German *Volk*; it also emerges from the well-known attitude of the broadest circles of Christian workers throughout the Reich, from the attitude of the democratic bourgeoisie, as well as from the internal dislike and disapproval of this armored cruiser by many more right-wing groups of people, especially those among the old officers of the former army.

I am saying again what we have said at our party congresses and also in our program: we are not fighting against, but for the Reichswehr, in order to make it a reliable instrument of the Republic. We also do not fail to recognize the necessity that the Reichswehr must also have an arm that extends to the sea! But above all, for us, the highest commandment is the requirement of the strictest practicality and frugality. The be-all and end-all of frugality cannot consist of throwing hundreds of millions into the laps of the Ruhr industrialists; the needy demand their rights!

In our opinion, the planned construction of armored cruisers first of all violates the principles of practicality and, to an even greater extent, that of frugality.

The duty to be frugal is imposed on us not only by reparation obligations; it is, above all, the social hardship of our people that calls us to do so. Even the *Kölnische Zeitung* [a paper affiliated with the Centre Party] says in its issue of August 1:

In itself one would of course be able to show understanding for the Social Democratic proposal. Even those who emphasize the idea of defense and take the simple, natural point of view that we should not keep our land and sea forces any smaller than the narrow provisions of the Treaty of Versailles allow us—even they will be in doubt about the objective practicality of this shipbuilding. This doubt exists not only in Social Democratic circles, but also in the circles of the bourgeois parties.

As [the defense minister] himself emphasized, the construction of one armored cruiser would not be enough, this would of course have to result in further constructions, so this is not an issue of some 80 million, but 300, 400 million, maybe half a billion.

But is this replacement construction necessary?

The practicality of this building is doubted from various sides. . . . Field Marshal v. Moltke and Prince Bismarck always disdained the fleet and always gave it the cold shoulder. Only under Wilhelm II did the era of naval armament begin, the naval building programs. At that time, the period of German decline began with the naval-building program that led to the isolation of Germany and thus brought about the collapse of the old order.

[The current defense minister] declared in the budget committee on March 3, 1928 that he wanted to make a very honest admission to the committee, namely that he had considered the naval policy pursued before the war to be wrong from a military point of view. He is probably not revealing a secret when he declares that this view was also prevalent in the general staff. The conviction that victory had to be won on land was the reason for this attitude of the general staff.

We are constrained by the Versailles Diktat, and the idea of utilizing all of our armament capabilities within the framework of the Versailles Treaty is not recognized by the Reichswehr Ministry itself.

But if a war with a modern sea power were to arise, then the planned ten thousand–ton ships would not be a defense for our coasts either, but simply targets for those huge ships of the line that would simply sink them to the bottom of the sea. Does it make sense for an imperfect type of ship, which was recently subjected to the sharpest criticisms by the entire Admiralty, against which all who had any understanding or sense in German naval armaments were unanimously opposed, does it make sense at such a time to spend countless millions on an imperfect type of ship just because the Versailles Diktat forced this imperfection on us?

It has been pointed out that the armored cruiser is necessary to prevent a blockade of our coast. I would ask, however: who is the opponent whose blockade we are trying to prevent? We cannot stop the Great Powers from blockading us by using armored cruisers, and we can stop the smaller countries even without armored cruisers. Russia is probably meant here, but the Russians could blockade our Baltic coast if they needed to. They would be careful not to do this, however, because it would be senseless to blockade one part of the country and leave the other part untouched. The freedom of passage to East Prussia has also been mentioned. Allow me to remark that this is an absurd propaganda slogan. For if they are talking about Poland, it should not be forgotten that Poland has plenty of airplanes and some submarines, which we lack, and the armored cruiser would be completely defenseless against them. ▪

PARAMILITARIES

Law for the Protection of the Republic (1922)

Source: "Gesetz zum Schutze der Republik, vom 21. Juli 1922." In *Reichsgesetzblatt* (1922), vol. 1, no. 52, 585–90. Berlin: Verlag des Gesetzsammlungsamts, 1922. Translated by Robert Goodrich.

I. Criminal Provisions for the Protection of the Republic

§1. (1) Anyone who participates in an association or meeting, which includes in its endeavors the murder of members of the Republican government of the nation or the states, shall be punished with not less than five years or with life imprisonment.

(2) If a murder has been committed or attempted in pursuance of this endeavor, anyone who participated in the association or meeting at

the time of the offense and knew of their aspirations will be punished by death or life imprisonment.

§2. Anyone who participates in a secret society will be incarcerated if the society pursues an aspiration referred to in §1 (1).

§3. The participant in an association, meeting, or society referred to in §§1, 2 shall remain unpunished if he informs the authorities or the threatened person of the existence of the association, meeting, or society, and of its known members and their whereabouts prior to a murder or attempted murder by the association, meeting, or society.

§4. Anyone who supports the association or society with advice or deed, in particular with money, or anyone who participates in a meeting referred to in §§1, 2, is considered the equivalent of anyone who carries out the murder.

§5. Anyone who is aware of the existence of an association, meeting, or society mentioned in §§1, 2 or of the plan to kill a person named in §1, will be sent to a penitentiary, or, under mitigating circumstances, to a prison to not less than three months if he refrains from giving immediate notice of the existence of the association, meeting, or society, of the members known to him, of their whereabouts, or of the planned killing and the identity of the perpetrator, to the authority or to the threatened person.

§6. Anyone who aids and abets another who intentionally killed or attempted to kill a person referred to in §1 (1) or who participated in such an act shall be incarcerated.

III. Forbidden Associations

§14. (1) Meetings, marches, and rallies may be prohibited if specific evidence exists that justifies the concern that statements are made during them which constitute an offense referred to in §§1–8.

(2) Clubs and associations in which statements of the kind referred to take place or which pursue aspirations of this kind or which seek to elevate a specific person to the throne can be prohibited and dissolved.

(3) In case of a ban, the organizer is to be issued on request and without cost a statement of the reasons.

§15. The provisions of §14 (1) do not apply to meetings of voters to participate in elections of the Reichstag or the Reich president . . . from the day of the official announcement of voting day until the end of the voting period. The same applies to assemblies for the conduct of balloting and registration which take place in order to ascertain the will of the population on the basis of the Reich Constitution.

§18. In the case of the dissolution of an association or club, the assets of the association or club may be confiscated and used for the benefit of the Reich.

Transcript from the Ulm Reichswehr Trial (1931)

Source: Brügmann, Cord. "Unvergessener Anwalt." *Deutscher Anwaltverlag* 2 (February 1998): 78. Translation at https://en.wikipedia.org/wiki/Hans_Litten.

LITTEN: You said that there will be no violent acts on the part of the National Socialist Party. Didn't Goebbels create the slogan, "one must pound the adversary to a pulp?"

HITLER: This is to be understood as "one must dispatch and destroy opposing organizations."

PRESIDING JUDGE (*reading a question formulated by Litten*): Did Hitler, as he named Goebbels Reich minister of propaganda, know of the passage from his book, where Goebbels declares that fear of the coup d'état cannot be permitted, that parliament should be blown up and the government hunted to hell and where the call to revolution was made again?

HITLER: I can no longer testify under oath, if I knew Goebbels' book at the time. The theme is absolutely of no account to the Party, as the booklet doesn't bear the Party emblem and is also not officially sanctioned by the Party.

LITTEN: Must it not be measured against Goebbels' example, to awaken the notion in the Party, that the legality scheme is not far away, if you neither reprimanded nor shut out a man like Goebbels, rather straightaway made him head of Reich Propaganda?

HITLER: The entire Party stands on legal ground and Goebbels likewise. He is in Berlin and can be called here anytime.

LITTEN: Has Herr Goebbels prohibited the further dissemination of his work?

HITLER: I don't know.

LITTEN: Is it correct that Goebbels' revolutionary journal, *The Commitment to Illegality*, has now been taken over by the Party and has reached a circulation of 120,000? I have concluded that the journal is sanctioned by the Party.

PRESIDING JUDGE: Herr Hitler, in point of fact, you testified this morning, that Goebbels' work is not official Party material.

HITLER: And it isn't, either. A publication is an official Party organ when it bears the emblem of the Party.

HITLER *(shouting, red-faced)*: How dare you say, Herr Attorney, that is an invitation to illegality? That is a statement without proof!

LITTEN: How is it possible that the Party publishing house takes over a journal that stands in stark contrast to the Party line?

PRESIDING JUDGE: That doesn't have anything to do with this trial. ▨

Eugenics and Sexuality

Karl Binding and Alfred Hoche, *Permitting the Destruction of Life Unworthy of Living* (1920)

Source: Binding, Karl, and Alfred Hoche. *Permitting the Destruction of Unworthy Life: Its Extent and Form.* Translated by Walter E. Wright and Patrick G. Derr. In *The Nazi Germany Sourcebook: An Anthology of Texts*, edited by Roderick Stackelberg and Sally A. Winkle, 71–73. New York: Routledge, 2002.

Karl Binding, "Legal Explanation"

Are there human lives which have so completely lost the attribute of legal status that their continuation has permanently lost all value, both for the bearer of that life and for society?

Merely asking this question is enough to raise an uneasy feeling in anyone who is accustomed to assessing the value of individual life for the bearer and for the social whole. It hurts him to see how wastefully we handle the most valuable lives (filled with and sustained by the strongest will to live and the greatest vital power), and how much labor power, patience, and capital investment we squander (often totally uselessly) just to preserve lives not worth living—until nature, often pitilessly late, removes the last possibility of their continuation.

Reflect simultaneously on a battlefield strewn with thousands of dead youths, or a mine in which methane gas has trapped hundreds of energetic workers; compare this with our mental hospitals, with their caring for their living inmates. One will be deeply shaken by the strident clash between the sacrifice of the finest flower of humanity in its full measure on the one side, and by the meticulous care shown to existences which are not just absolutely worthless but even of negative value, on the other.

It is impossible to doubt that there are living people to whom death would be a release, and whose death would simultaneously free society and the state from carrying a burden which serves no conceivable purpose, except that of providing an example of the greatest unselfishness. And because there actually are human lives, in whose preservation no rational being could ever again take any interest, the legal order is now confronted by the fateful question: Is it our duty actively to advocate for this life's asocial continuance (particularly by the fullest application of criminal law), or to permit its destruction under specific conditions? One could also state the question legislatively, like this: Does the energetic preservation of such life deserve preference, as an example of the general unassailability of life? Or does permitting its termination, which frees everyone involved, seem the lesser evil? . . .

So far as I can see, the people who are to be considered here fall into two primary groups with a third intervening in between.

(1) The first group is composed of those irretrievably lost as a result of illness or injury, who, fully understanding their situation, possess and have somehow expressed their urgent wish for release. . . .

But I cannot find the least reason—legally, socially, ethically, or religiously—not to permit those requested to do so to kill such hopeless cases who urgently demand death; indeed I consider this permission to be simply a duty of legal mercy, a mercy which also asserts itself in many other forms. . . .

(2) The second group consists of incurable idiots, no matter whether they are so congenitally or have (like paralytics) become so in the final stage of suffering. They have the will neither to live nor to die. So, in their case, there is no valid consent to be killed; but, on the other hand, the act encounters no will to live which must be broken. Their life is completely without purpose, but they do not experience it as unbearable. They are a fearfully heavy burden both for their families and for society. Their death does not create the least loss, except perhaps in the feelings of the mother or a faithful nurse. Since they require extensive care, they occasion the development of a profession devoted to providing years and decades of care for absolutely valueless lives. It is undeniable that this is an incredible absurdity and a misuse, for unworthy ends, of life's powers.

Again, I find no grounds—legally, socially, ethically, or religiously—for not permitting the killing of these people, who are the fearsome counter-image of true humanity, and who arouse horror in nearly everyone who meets them (naturally, not in everyone)! In times of higher morality—in our times all heroism has been lost—these poor souls would surely have been freed from themselves officially. But who today, in our enervated age, compels himself to acknowledge this necessity, and hence this justification? . . .

(3) I have mentioned a middle group, and I find it in those mentally sound people who, through some event like a very severe, doubtlessly fatal wound, have become unconscious and who, if they should ever again rouse from their comatose state, would waken to nameless suffering. . . .

I do not believe that a standard procedure can be created for managing this group of killings. Cases will occur in which killing seems actually fully justified; but it can also happen that the agent, in the belief that he acted correctly, acted precipitously. Then he would never be guilty of premeditated murder but rather of negligent manslaughter. The possibility must be left open of letting killings which are later recognized as having been unjustified go unpunished. . . .

Dr. Alfred Hoche, "Medical Explanation"

Thus, economically speaking, these same complete idiots, who most perfectly fulfill all the criteria for complete mental death, are also the ones whose existence weighs most heavily on the community.

In part, this burden is financial and can be readily calculated by inventorying annual institutional budgets. I have allowed myself to take up the task of collecting materials bearing on this question by surveying all relevant German institutions, and thereby I have discovered that the average yearly (per head) cost for maintaining idiots has till now been thirteen hundred marks. If we calculate the total number of idiots presently cared for in German institutions, we arrive at a rough estimate of twenty to thirty thousand. If we assume an average life expectancy of fifty years for individual cases, it is easy to estimate what incredible capital is withdrawn from the nation's wealth for food, clothing, and heating—for an unproductive purpose.

And this still does not represent the real burden by any means.

The institutions which provide care for idiots are unavailable for other purposes. To the extent that private institutions are involved in such care, we must calculate the return on our investment. A caretaking staff of many thousands must be withdrawn from beneficial work for this totally fruitless endeavor. It is painful to think that whole generations of caretakers grow old next to these empty human shells, not a few of whom live seventy years or more.

In the prosperous times of the past, the question of whether one could justify making all necessary provision for such dead-weight existences was not pressing. But now things have changed, and we must take it up seriously. Our situation resembles that of participants in a difficult expedition: the greatest possible fitness of every one is the inescapable condition of the endeavor's success, and there is no room for half-strength, quarter-strength, or eighth strength members. For a long time, the task for us Germans will be the most highly intensified integration of all possibilities—the liberation of every available power for productive ends. Fulfilling this task is opposed by the modern efforts to maintain (as much as possible) every kind of weakling and to devote care and protection to all those who (even if they are certainly not mentally dead) are constitutionally less valuable elements. These efforts have their particular importance through the fact that, so far, preventing these defective people from reproducing has not been possible and has not even been seriously attempted. . . .

The next issue to explore is whether the selection of these lives, which have finally become worthless for the individual and for society, can be accomplished with such certainty that mistakes and errors can be excluded.

This concern can only arise among lay people. For physicians, there is not the slightest question that this selection can be carried out with one hundred percent certainty and, indeed, with a much higher de-

gree of certainty than can be found in deciding about the mental health or illness of convicted criminals.

For physicians, there are many indisputable, scientifically established criteria by which the impossibility of recovery for mentally dead people can be recognized. This is even truer since the condition of mental death beginning in earliest youth is of the first importance for our discussion.

Naturally, no doctor would conclude with certainty that a two- or three-year-old was suffering permanent mental death. But, even in childhood, the moment comes when this prediction can be made without doubt. . . .

Goethe originated the model for how important human questions evolve. He saw them as spiral. The core of this model is the fact that at regular intervals a spiral line rising in a particular direction perpetually returns to the same position relative to the axis crossing it but each time a step higher.

Eventually, this image will be apparent even in connection with the cultural question we have been discussing. There was a time, now considered barbaric, in which eliminating those who were born unfit for life, or who later became so, was taken for granted. Then came the phase, continuing into the present, in which, finally, preserving every existence, no matter how worthless, stood as the highest moral value. A new age will arrive—operating with a higher morality and with great sacrifice—which will actually give up the requirements of an exaggerated humanism and overvaluation of mere existence. I know that, in general, these opinions will not even be received with understanding, let alone agreement. But this prospect should not keep anyone from speaking out, particularly a person who, after more than an average lifetime of serving humanity's medical needs, has earned the right to be heard on the general problems of humanity. ▪

Lex Zwickau, Proposed Eugenics Law (1924)

Source: Boeters, Gustav. "Lex Zwickau: Entwurf zu einem Gesetz für den Deutschen Reichstag über 'Die Verhütung unwerten Lebens durch operative Massnahmen' in der Fassung vom 18. Oktober 1925." *Zeitschrift für Sexualwissenschaft* 13, no. 4 (1926/27): 139–40. Translated by Robert Goodrich.

§1. Children who are assessed as incapable of successfully participating in normal primary school lessons due to congenital blindness, congenital deafness, epilepsy, or idiocy when they reach school age are to undergo an operation as soon as possible to eliminate their reproductive ability. The organs important for internal secretion shall be preserved (sterilization).

§2. The mentally ill, the mentally weak, epileptics, those born blind, those born deaf, and the morally unstable, who are cared for in public or private institutions, are to be sterilized before discharge or leave of absence.

§3. The mentally ill, the mentally weak, epileptics, those born blind, those born deaf may marry only after they have been rendered sterile.

§4. Women and girls who have repeatedly given birth to children whose paternity cannot be determined shall be examined for their mental state. If hereditary inferiority is determined, then they are either to be rendered sterile or to be kept in closed institutions until their fertility has expired.

§5. Convicts whose hereditary inferiority is beyond question shall be granted partial sentence remission upon their application after they have voluntarily undergone a sterilization operation. The judicial procedure against criminal sexual offenders shall be regulated by a special law.

§6. The procedures can be conducted only by doctors who are trained in surgery and gynecology and have all the necessary auxiliary equipment at their disposal. The operation and follow-up treatment shall be free of charge to inferior people.

§7. The sterilization of fully normal people shall be punished in the same manner as grievous bodily harm. ▩

"Enough Now! Against the Masculinization of Women" (1925)

This article attacked the physical appearance of the New Woman and explicitly linked it to masculinization. Though the newspaper—the Berliner Illustrierte—*was decidedly liberal, the article clearly expresses the limits of toleration for female emancipation. Mainstream support for women's equality ended with any perceived threat to masculine identity even at the level of fashion. Ironically, the paper had actually helped to promote the flapper image of the liberated woman in the 1920s, but, by 1925, the gender culture war had reached deep into the mainstream, with a strong backlash against women's liberation.*

Source: "Nun aber genug! Gegen die Vermännlichung der Frau." *Berliner Illustrierte Zeitung*, 29 March 1925, 389. Translated by Robert Goodrich.

What was at first a capricious game of women's fashion is gradually becoming an embarrassing mess. At first it looked like a dainty joke: that delicate, graceful women cut off their long women's hair and appear with a page haircut; that you put on clothes that hid the sweep of the female body's lines, the swing of the hips, that fit almost completely flatly; that you shortened the skirts and showed slender legs all the way to the fullest curve of the calves. Even old-fashioned men didn't need to be offended. One would have liked to greet such a being with the lost love word "my angel"—because the angels are sexless, yet, except for the archangel Gabriel, all of them were imagined in female form before they were fully mature. But it had already become offensive to male sentiment when that fashion, that was so well suited to youthful and delicate females, became commonplace among all women. It did an aesthetic disservice to stately and full-figured women.

The movement, however, went even further: women no longer wanted to look sexless like angels, but fashion aimed with increasing determination at masculinizing the feminine appearance. The female custom of putting on male sleeping gowns, even wearing them for the morning toilet, spread ever more widely. And more and more often we see the page hairstyle with its curls disappearing and the modern male hairstyle with the hair brushed smoothly backward take its place. The latest fashion in women's coats is also decidedly masculine; it will hardly be noticed this spring when distracted women put on their husbands' coats. One could speak of a pendulum movement in fashion: with the crinoline came the extreme emphasis of female body shapes, and now it swings just as far in the opposite direction. It is high time that healthy male tastes turned against such wicked fashions whose excesses are transplanted here from America. In the theater we might like, one time, to see an actress, who has enough maturity, playing a man's role, but neither onstage nor in sports should every woman dare to show herself in trousers. And the masculinization of the female face substitutes, at best, an unnatural one for the real charm it takes away: to look like a sweet boy—how disgusting for any real boy or man.

Paula von Reznicek, "The Hand on the Steering Wheel" (1928)

Von Reznicek was a world-class tennis player and author. Her illustrated book Resurrection of the Lady *encouraged full emancipation and active female leadership in society and politics, in large part because of the failure of male leaders. She uses the extremely rare female driver of the time as a metaphor for this emancipation and the male biases she faced. Von Reznicek was from a wealthy family, and her example underscores how much the phenomenon of the New Woman was restricted primarily to the upper classes—cars belonged exclusively to the upper classes, and there was no mass production equivalent of the American Model T.*

Source: Reznicek, Paula von. "Die Hand am Steuer."
In *Auferstehung der Dame*, 128. Stuttgart: Dieck & Co.
Verlag, 1928. Translated by Robert Goodrich.

She has to have a hand in everything, so why not at the wheel too? She didn't ask for long; she reached for it and now wields it like a little scepter. Without batting an eye, her fingers grip iron-hard around the vibrating steering wheel that yields to the slightest pressure and which she masters with the same willpower as a thoroughbred or a bulldog.

We meet her on the road—in the boulevards, along the canals, at the shore, on the sea, and in the air. At first suspicious, with misgivings, testing: Does she have the nerves, overview; won't she lose her head as easily as her heart; are her physical strengths, psychological energy sufficient? It's cute that she tries, brave that she doesn't lag behind, but is she really—good—reliable?

Our qualms are eliminated—experience proves it! She prevailed. It cannot be denied. Her will overcomes miles, her desire for speed gives her perspective. With all speed, she chases down her goals, determined, proud in the knowledge that she is replacing a man without being like him.

The complainers used to groan: "If she only handled the clutch as gently as she would her friends, and were as careful with the curves as she was with her morals"—today you can beg for the opposite: "If only she were so tender with her friends as with her clutch, and in her morality as generous as in her curves. . . ."

Good Friday Prayer for the Jews; Catholic Liturgy (1920)

Catholicism had a strained relationship with Jews—at times protecting and tolerating them, at other times violently persecuting them. The Good Friday prayer dated to late antiquity or the early Middle Ages, and was used every Easter Week as part of intense proselytizing of Jews, often accompanied by violence. The Latin version uses the term perfidis, *which can be translated as "faithless," "perfidious," or "unbelieving," but had only negative connotations.*

Source: *Roman Missal* (1920), 221–22. See https://en.wikipedia .org/wiki/Good_Friday_prayer_for_the_Jews.

Let us pray also for the perfidious Jews: that Almighty God may remove the veil from their hearts (2 Corinthians 3:13–16); so that they too may acknowledge Jesus Christ our Lord.

Almighty and eternal God, who dost not exclude from thy mercy even Jewish perfidy: hear our prayers, which we offer for the blindness of that people; that acknowledging the light of thy Truth, which is Christ, they may be delivered from their darkness. Through the same our Lord Jesus Christ, who liveth and reigneth with thee in the unity of the Holy Spirit, God, for ever and ever. Amen.

Martin Luther, *The Jews and Their Lies* (1543)

As the founder of Germany's dominant Protestant religion, Luther's words mattered. His anti-Jewish extremism went beyond traditional theologically based anti-Judaism and crossed into an early form of antisemitism—an assessment of the Jews as being fundamentally and unalterably different from and hostile to Christians and, ultimately, worthy of nothing but annihilation.

Source: Luther, Martin. *The Jews and Their Lies*. St. Louis, MO: Christian Nationalist Crusade, 1948.

Now what are we going to do with these rejected, condemned, Jewish people?

We should not suffer it after they are among us and we know about such lying, blaspheming and cursing among them, lest we become partakers of their lies, cursing, and blaspheming. We cannot extinguish the unquenchable fire of God's wrath, nor convert the Jews. . . .

I will give you my true counsel:

First, that we avoid their synagogues and schools and warn people against them. . . . Moses writes in Deuteronomy that where a city practiced idolatry, it should be entirely destroyed with fire and leave nothing. If he were living today, he would be the first to put fire to the Jew schools and houses. . . .

Secondly, that you also refuse to let them own houses among us. For they practice the same thing in their houses as they do in their schools. Instead, you might place them under a roof, or stable, like the Gypsies, to let them know that they are not lords in our country as they boast, but in exile as captives. . . .

Thirdly, that you take away from them all of their prayer books and Talmuds wherein such lying, cursing, and blaspheming is taught.

Fourthly, that you prohibit their Rabbis to teach. . . .

Fifthly, that protection for Jews on highways be revoked. . . . They should stay at home. . . . He practices his usury on princes and lords, land and people. High officials close an eye to it. If you princes and masters do not forbid land and highways to such usurers, I would like to assemble a cavalry against you. . . . For you should not and cannot protect them unless you want to be partners of their abominations. . . .

Sixthly, that their usury be prohibited. . . . where they are not lords in their own country over strange lands, and take away all the currency and silver and gold and put it away for safe-keeping. For this reason, everything they have they have stolen from us and robbed through their usury, since they have no other income. . . . (39–42).

Finally: That young, strong Jews be given flail, ax, spade, spindle, and let them earn their bread in the sweat of their noses as imposed upon Adam's children. . . . For it will not do that they should let us cursed Goyim work in the sweat of our brow, while they, the holy people, devour our bread in laziness behind the stove and then boast that they are masters over the Christians, but their laziness should be driven from their back. . . .

Let us apply the ordinary wisdom of other nations like France, Spain, Bohemia, et al., who made them give an account of what they had taken from them by usury and divided it evenly; but expelled them from their country. For God's wrath is so great over them that through soft mercy they only become more wicked, through hard treatment, however, only a little better. Therefore, away with them! (45–46). ◼

Heinrich von Treitschke, "The Jews Are Our Misfortune" (1879)

Heinrich von Treitschke (1834–96) was a politically active and prominent historian of the Kaiserreich. He openly disdained groups of every stripe—women, socialists, non-Prussians, Catholics, Slavs, and Jews. His essay on Jews sparked a national controversy and helped legitimate and define early antisemitism. In particular, he established the trope of the Ostjude *(Eastern Jew)—the Yiddish-speaking, Orthodox poor Jew who, he feared, would eventually swamp the West with their limitless numbers. He also coined the phrase that became a leading motto for German antisemites:*

"The Jews are our misfortune." Nonetheless, his antisemitism called not for exclusion based on race difference but for cultural assimilation, which was possible only on the basis of a common humanity.

Source: Treitschke, Heinrich von. "Unsere Aussichten." *Preussische Jahrbücher* 44, no. 5 (November 1879): 572–76. Translated by Robert Goodrich.

Among the symptoms of a deep change of heart going through our nation, none appears so strange as the passionate movement against Jewry. Anyone is permitted to say unabashedly the harshest things about the national shortcomings of the Germans, the French, and all the other peoples, but any who dared to speak about the undeniable weaknesses of the Jewish character, no matter how moderately or justly, was immediately branded by almost the entire press as a barbarian and a religious bigot. Today we have progressed so far that a majority of the voters of Breslau have sworn under no circumstances to elect a Jew to the state parliament—and this apparently not in wild agitation, but with calm forethought. Anti-semitic leagues are banding together. The "Jewish Question" is being discussed in excited meetings. A flood of anti-Jewish Libelles is inundating the book market. Are these outbreaks of deep, long-restrained anger merely an ephemeral excrescence? No; in fact, the instinct of the masses has correctly identified a serious danger, a critical defect in the new German life. It is no empty formula when we speak today of a German Jewish Question.

When, with disdain, the English and French talk of German prejudice against Jews, we must answer: you don't know us. You live in fortunate circumstances that make the emergence of such "prejudices" impossible. The number of Jews in Western Europe is so small that it cannot exert a palpable influence on your national mores. However, year after year, out of the inexhaustible Polish cradle there streams over our eastern border a host of hustling, pants-peddling youths, whose children and children's children will someday command Germany's stock exchanges and newspapers. The immigration grows visibly, and the question becomes more and more grave: How can we amalgamate this alien people? The Israelites of the West and South belong mostly to the Spanish branch of Jewry, which looks back on a comparatively proud history and has always adapted rather easily to Western ways. In fact, they have become for the most part good Frenchmen, Englishmen, and Italians. This is true to the extent that we can appropriately expect from a people of such pure blood and such pronounced peculiarity. But we Germans have to deal with that Polish branch of Jewry, which has been deeply scarred by centuries of Christian tyranny. As a result of this experience, it is incomparably more alien to the European and, especially, the German essence.

What we have to demand of our Israelite fellow citizens is simple: they should become Germans. They should feel themselves, modestly and properly, Germans—and this without prejudicing their faith and their ancient, holy memories, which we all hold in reverence. For we do not want to see millennia of Germanic morality followed by an era of German-Jewish hybrid culture. It would be sinful to forget that a great many Jews, baptized and unbaptized, were German men in the best sense. Felix Mendelssohn, Veit, Riesser, etc.—to say nothing of the living—were men in whom we honor the noble and good traits of the German spirit. But it is equally undeniable that numerous and mighty circles among our Jews simply lack the goodwill to become thoroughly German. It is painful to speak of these things. Even conciliatory words will be easily misunderstood. Nevertheless, I believe that many of my Jewish friends will concede, though with deep regret, that I am right when I assert that in recent times a dangerous spirit of arrogance has arisen in Jewish circles. The influence of Jewry on our national life, which created much good in earlier times, nowadays shows itself in many ways harmful.

There is no German commercial city that does not count many honorable and respectable Jewish firms. But undoubtedly, the Semites bear a heavy share of guilt for the falsehood and deceit, the insolent greed of fraudulent business practices, and that base materialism of our day, which regards all labor as pure business and threatens to stifle our people's traditional good-natured joy in labor. In thousands of German villages sits the Jew who sells out his neighbors with usury. Among the leading men in the arts and sciences, the number of Jews is not very great; all the stronger do the Semitic talents constitute the host of the third-rate.

Most dangerous, however, is the improper preponderance of Jewry in the daily press, a fateful consequence of our narrow-minded old laws forbidding Israelites entry to most of the learned professions. For ten years the public opinion of many German cities was largely "created" by Jewish pens. It was a misfortune for the Liberal Party, and one of the reasons for its decline, to have afforded too free a scope to Jewry in its press. The present-day weakness of the press is the result of a backlash against this unnatural condition. The little man can no longer be talked out of the fact that the Jews write the newspapers. Therefore, he won't believe them any longer. Our newspaper system owes a great deal to Jewish talents. From the first, the tenacity and acuity of the Jewish spirit found a fruitful field. But here, too, the effect was ambiguous. [They] were the first to introduce a characteristically shameless tone into our journalism. [They wrote] from abroad with no respect for the fatherland, as though not part of it at all, as though scorn for Germany did not cut each and every German to the quick. Add to this the unfortunate bustling intrusion into all and sundry, which does not even shy away from magisterially passing judgment on the innermost matters of the Christian churches. The anti-Christian defamations and witticisms of Jewish journalists are simply shocking, and such blasphemies are put up for sale in its own language as the latest achievements of "German" enlightenment! Scarcely had emancipation been achieved before they brazenly insisted on its pretext. They demanded literal parity in everything and did not want to see that we Germans are still a Christian people and that the Jews are only a minority among us. We have experienced their demands that Christian images be set aside and that their sabbath be celebrated in mixed schools.

Overlooking all these circumstances—and how many others could be added!—this noisy agitation of the moment, though brutal and hateful, is nonetheless a natural reaction of Germanic racial feeling against an alien element that has assumed all too large a space in our life. It has inadvertently performed a useful service: it has lifted the ban on a quiet untruth. An evil that everyone felt but no one wanted to touch on is now openly discussed.

Let's not deceive ourselves. The movement is very deep and strong. A few jokes by Christian Social politicos will not suffice to stem it. Among the circles of highly educated men who reject any idea of church intolerance or national arrogance there rings with one voice: *the Jews are our misfortune*!

There can be no talk, among those with any understanding, of a revocation or even an abridgment of the completed emancipation. It would be an open injustice, a falling away from the good traditions of our state, and would sharpen rather than ameliorate the national conflict that pains us. The Jews in France and England have become a harmless and, in many ways, beneficial element of civil society. That is in the last analysis the result of the energy and national pride of these two ancient culture-bearing peoples. Our culture is a young one. Our being still lacks a national style, an instinctive pride, a thoroughly imprinted character. That is why for so long we stood defenseless against alien essences. Now, however, we are at the point of acquiring those goods. We can only wish that our Jews recognize in time the transformation that is the logical consequence of the rise of the German state. Quietly, here and there, Jewish associations against usury do much good. They are the work of insightful Israelites who understand that their racial brothers must adapt to the morality and ideas of their Christian fellow citizens.

Only one possibility remains: our Jewish fellow citizens must resolve to be German without qualification, as so many of them have already done, to our benefit and their own. The task can never be wholly completed. A cleft has always existed between Occidental and Semitic essences; there will always be Jews who are nothing more than German-speaking Orientals. A specific Jewish civilization will also always flourish, as befits a historically cosmopolitan power. But the conflict will lessen when the Jews, who speak so much of tolerance, really become tolerant and show respect for the faith, customs, and feelings of the German people, who have atoned for the old injustice and bestowed on them the rights of man and citizen. That this respect is wholly missing in a section of our commercial and literary Jewry is the ultimate basis for the passionate embitterment of today. ▇

Leo Baeck, *The Essence of Judaism* (1905)

A German rabbi, scholar, and theologian, Baeck was a leading voice of liberal Judaism in Germany and internationally. He served in the war as a chaplain in the army, and, like most liberal Jews, he was aligned with the DDP as the strongest supporter of civil rights. Originally published in 1905, Baeck expanded his work in 1922 to present a full defense of minorities in general. In the excerpt here, he expresses the notion that treatment of any minority was the ultimate measure of a civilization's morality. He also firmly asserted the idea that Jews were a religious group, not a racial group, and thus came under all the protections against religious discrimination.

Source: Baeck, Leo. *The Essence of Judaism* [Das Wesen des Judentums, 1922]. N.p.: Plunkett Lake Press, 2019. Edited by Irving Howe. Translated by Leonard Pearl and Victor Grubenwieser.

Often it seems that the special task of Judaism is to express the idea of the community standing alone, the ethical principle of the minority. Judaism bears witness to the power of the idea against the power of mere numbers and worldly success; it stands for the enduring protest of those who seek to be true to their own selves, who assert their right to be different against the crushing pressure of the vicious and the leveling. . . .

By its mere existence Judaism is a never-silent protest against the assumption of the multitude that force is superior to truth. So long as Judaism exists, nobody will be able to say that the soul of man has surrendered. Its very existence through the ages is proof that conviction cannot be mastered by numbers. . . . With regard to this fact alone one is often tempted to adapt a well-known phrase by saying: "If Judaism did not exist, we should have to invent it." Without minorities, there can be no world-historic goal.

And just because it was always a minority, Judaism has become a standard of measurement of the level of morality. How the Jewish community was treated by the nations among which it lived has always been a measure of the extent to which right and justice have prevailed; for the measure of justice is always its application to the few. What Israel, which gave its faith to mankind, receives in turn is also a measure of the development of religion. . . .

It requires religious courage to belong to a minority such as Judaism always has been and always will be; for many days will come and go before the messianic time arrives. . . .

Judaism lies open for all to see. We acknowledge the treasures possessed by other religions, especially those which sprung from our midst. He who holds convictions will respect the convictions of others. ▨

August Bebel, "Antisemitism and Social Democracy" (1893)

Bebel, one of the leaders of the SPD in the Kaiserreich, provided the baseline for the SPD's and KPD's relationship to antisemitism. His analysis was generally considered second only to Marx's On the Jewish Question *(1844). Although these works were tinged with generalizations that fit antisemitic views (Jews were seen as materialistic and greedy), the SPD and KPD rejected antisemitism, refused to use it as a political weapon, placed no limits on Jews in their parties, and demanded full equality for Jews in Germany.*

Source: Bebel, August. "Antisemitismus und Sozialdemokratie." In *Protokoll über die Verhandlungen des Parteitags der Sozialdemokratischen Partei Deutschlands, abgehalten zu Köln a. Rh. vom 22. bis 28. Oktober 1893*, 223–24. Berlin: Verlag der Expedition des "Vorwärts" Berliner Tageblatt, 1893. Translated by Robert Goodrich.

Antisemitism springs from the dissatisfaction of certain bourgeois strata, who find themselves oppressed by capitalist development, and by this development partly doomed to economic decline. In misunderstanding the real cause of their situation, they direct the fight not against the capitalist economic system but instead against someone who is also caught up in the same emerging phenomenon but who has become inconvenient to them in the competitive struggle: against Jewish exploitation.

This origin compels antisemitism to make demands that are in conflict with the economic as well as the political laws of development of bourgeois society, and thus are hostile to progress. Hence the support that antisemitism finds mainly among Junkers and priests.

The one-sided struggle of antisemitism against Jewish exploitation must necessarily be unsuccessful, because the exploitation of man by man is not a specifically Jewish form of acquisition but rather one of bourgeois society, which will end only with the downfall of bourgeois society.

Now that Social Democracy is the most determined enemy of capitalism, no matter whether Jews or Christians are its supporters, and since it has the goal of eliminating bourgeois society by bringing about its transformation into a socialist society, by which all man's dominion over man, just as all human exploitation, is put to an end, Social Democracy thus refuses to squander its energies in the fight against the existing political and social order through false and therefore ineffective struggles against a phenomenon that will stand and fall with bourgeois society.

Social Democracy opposes antisemitism as a movement directed against the natural development of society, which, despite its reactionary character and against its will, eventually acts revolutionarily, because the petty-bourgeois and small farming strata, which have been incited by antisemitism against the Jewish capitalists, must come to the realization that not only the Jewish capitalist but the capitalist class in general is their enemy, and that only the realization of socialism can free them from their misery. ▪

CENSORSHIP

German Penal Code §166: Insulting of Faiths, Religious Societies, and Organizations Dedicated to a Life Philosophy

The constitution banned censorship and religious discrimination, which was then regulated by existing laws that allowed certain exemptions. Jews regularly used §166 to sue antisemites for violating their religious rights. Paradoxically, conservatives used this same law to demand censorship of works they deemed insulting, such as All Quiet *for its portrayal of priests.*

Source: §166. *Strafgesetzbuch für das Deutsche Reich vom 15. Mai 1871*. Translated by Robert Goodrich.

§166. Whosoever publicly defames God in a manner that is capable of disturbing the public peace, or whosoever publicly defames a church or other religious or ideological association within Germany or their institutions or customs in a manner that is capable of disturbing the public peace, shall be liable to imprisonment not exceeding three years or a fine. ▪

Carl Zuckmayer, Review of All *Quiet on the Western Front* (1929)

This review, one of the very first, was written by the author and playwright Carl Zuckmayer for the liberal Berliner Illustrierte. *Zuckmayer was himself a decorated front veteran. Politically, he decidedly supported the Republic, but without any particular political affiliation.*

Source: Zuckmayer, Carl. "Erich Maria Remarque: 'Im Westen Nichts Neues.'" *Berliner Illustrierte Zeitung*, 31 January 1929. Translated by Robert Goodrich.

There is now a book, written by a man named Erich Maria Remarque, which was loved by millions and will be read by millions too, now and for all time, and not read as one reads books—rather, as one succumbs to one's fate, to the inescapable in one's time and existence, as one lays hold of it and as one is laid hold of, as one bleeds, as one struggles, as one dies.

This book belongs in the schoolrooms, the reading halls, the universities, in all the newspapers, all the broadcast stations, and all that is still not enough. For it is not concerned with a good cause, as are many war-and-peace novels of the present; it is concerned with the fundamental fact of our life and future being, with the primal stratum, and with the cellular core of centuries. This is the war as we experienced it at the front—we, a very definite generation formed in only a few years, who had had no life before the war, no form, and no content, who were born of the war and crushed by it, and who—along with its dead—live on beyond the war as a singular new beginning.

"All Quiet on the Western Front." An ever-recurring statement from the German military reports. I want, for those born later, to show in a small personal example how it was. One evening in Freiburg, where my brother lay in the army hospital, my parents sat in the dining room of a small hotel. A lady entered with the special edition of the daily military report, which had just come out. My mother asked what news there might be. The lady said, "Nothing new, there is still nothing going on. South of the Somme, an insignificant, bullet-riddled village that no one knows has fallen: Chilly." My mother knew, however, that I had been posted in this village for weeks. For her the unknown village Chilly meant more than if the entire western front had been breached, Strasbourg conquered, Paris conquered, the Czar murdered, and England in collapse. It was 4 September 1916. Nothing new.

Nothing new. Except that for a few hundred thousand people the world was collapsing, along with everything that until then had fulfilled and enlivened them; except that they did not know whether it was now the void, the end, a complete dissolution that would swallow them up—or the whirlpool and obscurity of a new creation. Yes, except that they do not even ask, nor have any idea whether they are the plow or the earth, the axe or the wood, seed grain or carrion.

That is what Remarque offers here, for the first time clearly and indelibly: what went on in these people, what happened inside, in the mines and sap of the soul, in the blood, in the tissue; and that is why it is the first war book that offers truth. We have all repeatedly experienced the impossibility of saying anything about the war. There is nothing more miserable than to hear someone tell his war experiences. So we fall silent and wait. But we do not forget. And it is hardly to be believed and borders on the miraculous that this book has already been written: one always thought two more decades would have to pass before someone could do it. Everything that has been created out of this time until now is patchwork by comparison. And there have already been a few war books that mean much to us: but they derive their momentary value and their present significance precisely from their misrepresentation, exaggeration, or distortion. *The Fire* by [Henri] Barbusse, the novellas by Leonhard Frank, they were so near, were cre-

ated so much in the middle of it all that they could offer only flashes of light and shadows. And Leonhard Frank's most mature and finest novella, *Karl and Anna*, entirely outgrows the war and enters the timelessly human. Then came books that reported and documented: *Soldier Suhren and War* by Ludwig Renn, *1902* by [Ernst] Glaeser. But here, from Remarque, fate itself has become the protagonist for the first time. The whole. That which was behind it, which burned beneath it—that which remained.

And so written, so created, so lived that it becomes more than reality: truth, pure valid truth. The writer preceded the book with a statement: "This book is intended to be neither indictment nor confession. It is intended only as an attempt to report on a generation that was destroyed by the war—even if they escaped the grenades."

The book fulfills this prefatory statement fully and completely.

But it does still more. It draws everyone into the fate of this generation. It shows, without saying it directly, how it lives, along with its dead, how it raises its head, gathers its scattered limbs, slowly, gropingly, unsteadily, stumbling, and how step by step, inexorably, unbreakably, it begins to march. How it retrieves its face from shadows, insane lights, fog, and masks, then retrieves its brow, its will, which it will force upon the century. We are the ones whose lives began with the knowledge of the ultimate and greatest things of earthly existence—of the most terrible: the mortal abandonment of man. And of the highest: comradeship. ▩

Request to Ban *All Quiet on the Western Front* (1930)

This excerpt comes from the request by several states to the board of censors to ban the movie, even though that body had already approved an edited version shown in German cinemas. The declaration of the Reichswehr representative, Captain von Baumbach, claimed that the movie "caricatures, belittles, and scorns" the reputation of the German army, and he stated: "From this fact the armed forces, as the bearer of the glorious tradition of the old army, derives duty here to expressly defend ourselves against unfounded abuse and insult to the honor and reputation of the old army."

Source: "Verfilmung: *All Quiet on the Western Front* (1930)." Erich Maria Remarque—Friedenszentrum. Universität Osnabruck. https://www.remarque.uni-osnabrueck.de /iwnnfilm.htm. Translated by Robert Goodrich.

Such a decidedly one-sided portrayal, which seeks and finds the full crassness of the war and its human weaknesses only and exclusively on the German side and deliberately misses every ethical element on the German side, is perceived as mockery by the broadest circles of the people who participated in the war, regardless of their party membership. Such a representation does so little justice to the emotional life of a generation of the German people who suffered and lost their lives in this war that it seems understandable when it provokes loud protests. In this respect, the supervisory authority is in agreement with the opinion of experts from the Reichswehr Ministry . . . that the present film is not a film about the war, but a film about German defeat. . . . It would not be compatible with the dignity of a people if they allowed their own defeat, filmed by a foreign production company, to be played to them. It would not be understood abroad and would be regarded as approval of the malicious original version of this American film if this film, edited for German consumption, were shown on the screens of German cinemas. ▪

Industrial Relations

Socialization Law (1919)

The law allowed for confiscation of private property by the state (nationalization) and stipulated that such property would then be run as public utilities.

Source: "Sozialisierungsgesetz, vom 23. März 1919." In *Reichsgesetzblatt* (1919), vol. 1, no. 68, Gesetz 6778, 341–42. Berlin: Verlag des Gesetzsammlungsamts, 1919. Translated by Robert Goodrich.

§1. Every German, without prejudice to his personal freedom, has the moral duty to employ his mental and physical powers as the well-being of the community requires.

Labor, as the highest economic good, is under the special protection of the Reich. Every German should be given the opportunity to earn his living through economic labor. Insofar as an employment opportunity cannot be verified, their necessary maintenance shall be provided. The details will be determined by special national legislation.

§2. The Reich is authorized, by way of legislation with adequate compensation

1. to transfer to the public sector through socialization suitable economic enterprises, in particular those for the extraction of mineral resources and the exploitation of natural energy,
2. to regulate for the common good the production and distribution of economic goods if there is urgent need.

Detailed regulations on compensation remain reserved for the special national laws to be issued.

§4. In exercising the power provided for in §2, the use of bituminous coal, lignite, compressed coal and coke, water energy and other natural energy sources, and the energy derived from them (energy economy) shall be regulated by public service principles by special Reich laws. Initially, a law for the special sector of the coal industry shall come into force for the regulation of the coal industry simultaneously with this law. ■

Law on Job Placement and Unemployment Insurance (1927)

The insurance program's resources were calculated to provide relief for an average of eight hundred thousand unemployed, plus a further six hundred thousand from an emergency fund in a temporary crisis. If total reserves were insufficient, the state had to meet the deficit by an interest-free loan or nonrepayable grant. Thus it was a mandate that the state fund all unemployed. When the law was passed, it had the support of both a right-wing coalition government and the SPD. At the time, the Republic was in a prosperous economic phase. The unemployment rate was fairly low (6.2 percent). Politicians calculated that the economic boom that began in 1924 would continue and the scheme would be financially viable. But already in 1928 there were signs of recession, and in the winter of 1928 to 1929 the number of unemployed rose to nearly three million. The state faced a dire liquidity problem due to falling tax revenues and skyrocketing unemployment insurance payments. Since the level of relief was fixed by law and the reserves were insufficient, the government had to take out loans; by December 1929 the debt was 342 million RM.

Source: "Gesetz über Arbeitslosenvermittlung und Arbeitslosenversicherung, vom 16. Juli 1927." In *Reichsgesetzblatt* (1927), vol. 1, no. 32 (1927), 187–218. Berlin: Verlag des Gesetzsammlungsamts, 1927. Translated by Robert Goodrich.

§69. In the event of unemployment, the following are insured:

1. whosoever is compulsorily insured in the event of illness based on the Reich Insurance Act or the Reich Miner's Guild Law,
2. whosoever is compulsorily insured on the basis of the Employee Insurance Act and is not subject to health insurance only because he has exceeded the earnings limit of the health insurance,
3. whosoever belongs to the crew of a German sea vehicle. . . .

§87. Entitled to unemployment benefits are those who

1. are fit for work, willing to work, but involuntarily unemployed,
2. have fulfilled the qualifying period,
3. have not yet exhausted the right to unemployment benefits.

§131. Unemployment is to be prevented and ended primarily through job placement.

§142. The funds which the Reich agency needs to carry out its tasks are to be raised by contributions from employers and employees. . . .

§143.

1. The insured and their employers are obliged to pay the contributions.
2. Insured persons and their employers each pay half of the contributions. ■

Reich Settlement Law (1919)

The National Assembly passed the Reich Settlement Law as a promise for land reform and redistribution to foster a "healthy mixture" of small, medium, and large farms. Reclaimed land and public land were to be provided for farming. More controversially, the law ordered that in districts where estates of at least 100 hectares made up more than 10 percent of farmland, one-third of that land should be made available. This law, dubbed the "Baltic Third," originated in the promise made by the German Baltic aristocracy in 1915 to give a third of their land to the government for resettlement, with modest compensation. However, the power of the Junkers meant that only one-quarter of this land was surrendered to the government. The law did not significantly alter the ownership structure of German agriculture. During the period 1919 to 1933, fifty-seven thousand new farmers were settled on just over six hundred thousand hectares of land. In effect, the law rejected agrarian revolution—the path taken by most countries, in which the economic power of large estate owners was curbed after the World War. Germany chose gradual reform. In practical terms, the Junkers remained entrenched.

Source: "Reichssiedlungsgesetz, vom 11. August 1919." In *Reichsgesetzblatt* (1919), vol. 1, no. 155, Gesetz 6992, 1429–36. Berlin: Verlag des Gesetzsammlungsamts, 1919. Translated by Robert Goodrich.

§1 (1). The states are obliged, where there are no nonprofit settlement operations, to establish them for the creation of new settlements as well as the enlargement of existing small farms at least to the size of agrarian self-sufficiency, insofar as the required land can be established on the basis of the provisions of this law. . . . (1429).

§2. State domains are to be offered at the end of the lease to nonprofit settlement operations (§1) for no more than their earning value, unless their preservation in the state's possession is necessary for teaching, experimental, or other purposes of a public or economic nature. When estimating value, temporary increases in value due to extraordinary circumstances of the war should not be taken into account. . . . (1429).

§3 (1). The nonprofit settlement operation is entitled to claim moorland that is not managed or which is in the process of ongoing burning or peat use, or other wasteland for settlement purposes via expropriation. If the owner undertakes to convert an area corresponding to his economic circumstances into cultivated land within a period set for him, the expropriation of this area can only take place if the period is not met. . . . As compensation, the capitalized net income is to be granted, which the land has in an unimproved state. The expropriation authority only set a higher compensation only if special circumstances make this seem appropriate. There is no legal recourse against expropriation. Furthermore, the regulation of expropriation, including remedies against the setting of compensation, is reserved for the federated states.

§4. The nonprofit settlement operation has a right of first refusal on agricultural land located in its districts that are twenty-five hectares or greater, or parts of such land. The right of first refusal can be extended to smaller properties by determination of the local state central authority. . . . (1430).

§22. Rural communities or estate districts can be obliged, by order of the local state central office, to give those workers who are permanently employed in agricultural enterprises in their district, at their request, the opportunity to lease or use other land for household needs. The obligation is deemed to be fulfilled if up to 5 percent of the leasehold or usable land of the agricultural communal or estate fields is made available. . . . (1434–35).

§24. (1) If the necessary leasehold or usable land cannot be obtained in any other way, the rural community can make use of it by way of forced leasing or expropriation. The employer who employs workers is primarily responsible for giving up the land. The admissibility of compulsory leases or expropriation is declared by the local state central authority at the appropriate place. . . . (1435).

§27. State law regulations for the further promotion

of the settlement system including the procurement of leasehold land for agricultural workers remain unaffected. Agricultural property owned by people whose total property of this kind does not reach 100 hectares may not be expropriated for settlement purposes. . . . (1435). ▨

Fritz Hoffmann, "The Artamans" (1930)

The Artaman League, formed in 1923, was an agrarian völkisch *movement dedicated to a* Blut and Boden *philosophy, emphasizing a "back to the land" component. It linked the basic ideas of agrarian conservativism to the Conservative Revolutionary Movement and racialized social Darwinism. It rejected the West as urban and decadent, and instead looked to the rural East as the only way to save the German race. Lebensraum would be found in the East, but it would require aggressive Germanization and the forced expulsion of Slavs (mostly Poles). Thus the Artamans not only idealized labor service and settlement in the East, they also linked such action to violence. They envisioned a return to the medieval* Wehrbauer *(soldier peasant) who lived on the Germanic frontier. Accordingly, the League sent German youth to work on the land in Saxony and in East Prussia, which relied on seasonal Polish workers, to prevent these areas being settled by Poles. In 1924, two thousand settlers were sent to Saxony, both to work on approximately three hundred farms and to serve as an anti-Slav militia. The Nazi Party embraced these concepts and many Nazi leaders were members of the League, progressively absorbing much of the movement's impetus. By 1927, 80 percent of its membership had become Nazis.*

Source: Hoffmann, Fritz Hugo. "Die Artamanen." *Neues Leben: Monatsschrift für nordisch-deutsches Wesen* 1 (1930): 38–44. Translated by Robert Goodrich.

The Artamans, part of the German youth movement, started six years ago with the cry, "We want to go to the East!" That sound was in large part quite romantic, and many shook their heads. But youth without a goal, without a far-fetched plan and idealistic will, is dead, creeps away to die, is just carried along, sinning against the task of every new generation, which is like that of the son: to become more, to achieve more than the father, than the old generation could. Only such youth, which grab the spokes with all their might to turn the wheel, will acquire historical significance and be able to confront the fateful task of the *Volk*.

What has been accomplished practically?—What the youth movement, the first Wandervogel, was unable to do, the Artamans have done: they no longer went back to the city and the urban manger on Mondays, as most young people still have to do after every Sunday protest; rather, they stayed in the country, created a work community in their Artaman groups, which were held and forged together not only ideologically but much more through objective, practical things; above all, they created a new breath of life so that they could breathe easily, as if in a new Lebensraum. That they were working German soil in place of Polish workers, gathering strength and happiness from it and creating the basis for their own settlement later on (through which the dilettantism of the youth movement will finally be overcome), that they created youth homes out of the filthy and louse-ridden Polish barrack, and made tasty, albeit simple German meals through the cooking skills of the Artaman lasses out of the monotonous Polish supplies (produce from the estate), that they sang German songs while working, filled their evenings and holidays with folk songs, folk dances, homemade plays, and German poetry, that the revival of German customs and traditions, taken from the village youth, became the emanation point of a new will in the countryside, and gained therewith new Lebensraum from the soil where Polish noises had previously been heard—that all just happened as an aside. The decisive factor was that the Artamans provided proof of the power of German youth, who with their strong will are able to take the place of the Poles, whom the prevailing fairy tale once claimed were "irreplaceable."

For six years they have now provided this proof, have proven themselves and triumphed over prejudice.

The first step is taken. The second awaits its fulfill-ment: settlement. Individual settlements of some Artamans have already sprung up, but they still lack the necessary new form: to create a community, each on his own, but from the new experience of the com-munity and, in defense against economic hardship, a more solid standing in the community. What used to be the commons—namely, the collective protec-tion of the cattle herds against wild animals of the forest and against raids—must today be the defense against ever-growing powers and the struggle for a new German land law and labor law that will culti-vate the selection of the hereditarily useful. The Arta-mans cannot achieve this themselves, their number in the population of millions is too small for that, and the echo of their call is still too little heard. It is nec-essary that those who want to go along rally around this work, those who have recognized that this is where the turning point against the West has begun, away from the deathbed of the West and toward the young East. They do that together in the Artaman circle. . . .

And all of this from the basic idea of the renewal of our *Volk*, the connection with the earth, the soil, which gives us a new home.

Now, finally, out of the narrow, bourgeois mouse-holes of care, titles, insurance, foresight and forbear-ance, whining and hesitation! Set a life goal, a life task; look for followers, lads, lasses who join in with-out asking about life insurance, who once again dare to take the first small step with perseverance and tenacity—we first have to learn to walk again: to be able to live in dedication and community for our work! . . .

The East demands different things from us and for those who come after us, our children:

The formation of the new community and *Volk* cell in self-administration and self-help. From such basic cells, the communities, with the lively cooperation of farmers, artisans, workers, merchants, academics, etc., under the unifying idea of rebuilding the East in larger living and economic circles, and giving it therewith a new structure.

Since Versailles, Europe has been in disarray be-cause a hostile law—the exploitation and enslavement of the dying West—has presumed power over Europe.

Protests do not help here—only people who, in accordance with the basic cells of the community, live the new structure and carry it upward, enforce it, fight through with the unifying idea.

The aim of all power groups exploiting the *Völker* is to bring more and more new *Völker* under their control. The young—that is, exploitable—*Völker* are in Eastern Europe, especially in Russia. Russia has rich natural resources (black earth, ores, coal, oil) and many human workers; it shuts itself off against the West—as a result, it is encircled, like its co-fated comrade Germany, which they now want to make into the deployment base against Russia and drive these tried and tested work slaves as a labor and mercenary army to pull their chestnuts out of the fire. ("Crusade" against Russia: "You have to say the Bible when you mean naphtha.")

It is up to us to be able to start the way to the East, formerly as constructive helpers with a superior order and performance, as free Germans, not as slaves. Young people who want this will thwart all devil's pacts and plans of our enemies. Our first task is the preparation on our own ground.

The East confronts us with new practical tasks that can be approached only with the strength of faith and mission if we are to persevere. If we want to save and complete the East, which for the moment is still German, this is possible only if our eyes see the task ahead of us for centuries as generational work, only if to take the first step correctly, to achieve the first little piece.

Artamans, workers, academics, craftsmen, and merchants will have to solve the task together in the new community. No one will accomplish it alone. From the soil of Artam, which today, standing alone, brings together, to form a new type of work commu-nity, young Germans from the most varied of profes-sions, alliances, parties and camps, from the city and rural youth, grows the preparation for this new jour-ney to the East and the renewal of blood and soil. ▪

Notes

INTRODUCTION

1. Erik von Kuehnelt-Leddihn (Francis Stewart Campbell), *The Menace of the Herd, or Procrustes at Large* (Milwaukee, WI: Bruce Publishing, 1943), 183.

2. See "Spelling of Antisemitism," International Holocaust Remembrance Alliance, accessed 20 February 2021, https://holocaustremembrance.com/antisemitism /spelling-antisemitism.

3. "'Great European Statesman': Late Dr. Stresemann; World-Wide Tributes," *The Advertiser* (Adelaide, Australia), 5 October 1929, 21.

4. *The Times* (London), 4 October 1929.

5. Gustav Stresemann, quoted in Martin Broszat, *200 Jahre deutsche Polenpolitik* (Frankfurt am Main: Suhrkamp, 1972), 224.

6. Joseph Goebbels, quoted in Jonathan Wright, *Die Tagebücher von Joseph Goebbels* (Munich: K. G. Saur, 1987), 434. The date of entry in the diary was 3 October 1929.

HISTORICAL BACKGROUND

1. Philipp Scheidemann, "Proclamation of the Republic, 9 November 1918," Deutsches Rundfunkarchiv (German Radio Archive), Frankfurt am Main. Translated by A. Ganse. https://www.facinghistory.org/weimar-republic -fragility-democracy/politics/social-democratic-party -proclamation-republic-november-9-1918.

2. Karl Liebknecht, "Proclamation of the Free Socialist Republic, 9 November 1918," in *Die ungeliebte Republik: Dokumentation zur Innen- u. Aussenpolitik Weimars, 1918–1933*, ed. Wolfgang Michalka and Gottfried Niedhart (Munich: DTV Deutscher Taschenbuch, 1980). Translated by A. Ganse. https://www.facinghistory.org/weimar -republic-fragility-democracy/politics/spartacists -proclamation-republic-november-9-1918-politics.

3. For a summary, see Robert Weldon Whalen, "War Losses (Germany)," 1914–1918-online, International Encyclopedia of the First World War, Freie Universität Berlin, 8 October 2014, https://encyclopedia.1914-1918-online.net /article/war_losses_germany.

4. See Benjamin Ziemann, *Contested Commemorations: Republican War Veterans and Weimar Political Culture* (Cambridge: Cambridge University Press, 2013).

5. Paul von Hindenburg, quoted in *The Great War and Medieval Memory: War, Remembrance and Medievalism in Britain and Germany, 1914–1940*, ed. Stefan Goebel (New York: Cambridge University Press, 2007), 139–40.

6. Ulrich von Brockdorff-Rantzau, letter to President Georges Clemenceau on the Subject of Peace Terms, 1919, in *Source Records of the Great War*, vol. 7, ed. Charles F. Horne (New York: National Alumni, 1923), 164–65.

7. *Verhandlungen der Verfassungsgebenden Deutschen Nationalversammlung: Stenographische Berichte*, vol. 327, session 39 (12 May 1919) (Berlin: Druck und Verlag der Norddeutschen Buchdruckerei und Verlagsanstalt, 1920), 1082–84. Translated by Robert Goodrich.

8. Richard J. Evans, *The Coming of the Third Reich* (New York: Penguin, 2004), 88.

9. Ernst Troeltsch, quoted in Sebastian Haffner, *Der Verrat: Deutschland, 1918/1919* (Berlin: Verlag 1900, 2002), 85. Translated by Robert Goodrich.

10. Rosa Luxemburg, "Der Anfang," *Gesammelte Werke*, vol. 4, *August 1914 bis Januar 1919* (Berlin: Dietz Verlag, 1983), 397. Translated by Robert Goodrich.

11. Theodor Wolff, quoted in Haffner, *Der Verrat*, 95. Translated by Robert Goodrich.

12. Paul Baecker, quoted in Haffner, *Der Verrat*, 96. Translated by Robert Goodrich.

13. Kurt Tucholsky, *Gesammelte Werke* 6 (Berlin: Rohwolt, 1975), 300. Translated by Robert Goodrich.

14. Walter Rathenau, quoted in Bernd Sösemann, *Demokratie im Widerstreit: Die Weimarer Republik im Urteil ihrer Zeitgenossen* (Stuttgart: Klett, 1980), 13. Translated by Robert Goodrich.

15. Erich Ludendorff, *Ludendorff's Own Story, August 1914–November 1918: The Great War from the Siege of Liège to the Signing of the Armistice as Viewed from the Grand Headquarters of the German Army* (New York: Harper, 1919).

16. Oswald Spengler, "'. . . bin vor Ekel beinahe erstickt'—frühe Konturen der Gegenrevolution," 1922, in *Weimar: Ein Lesebuch zur deutschen Geschichte, 1918–*

1933, ed. Heinrich August Winkler and Alexander Cammann (Munich: C. H. Beck, 1997), 57–58. Translated by Robert Goodrich.

17. Adolf Hitler, *My Struggle* (*Mein Kampf*), 1924, trans. James Vincent Murphy (London: Hurst and Blankett, 1939), vol. 1, chap. 10.

18. John W. Wheeler-Bennett, "Ludendorff: The Soldier and the Politician," *Virginia Quarterly Review* 14, no. 2 (Spring 1938): 187–202.

19. Paul von Hindenburg, Testimony delivered on 18 November 1919, in *Stenographischer Bericht über die öffentlichen Verhandlungen des 15. Untersuchungsausschusses der verfassunggebenden Nationalversanurnlung*, vol. 2, 700–701 (Berlin: Norddeutschen Buchdruckerei, 1920.) In *The Weimar Republic Sourcebook*, ed. Anton Kaes, Martin Jay, and Edward Dimendberg (Berkeley: University of California Press, 1994), 15–16.

20. Arthur David Brenner, *Emil J. Gumbel: Weimar German Pacifist and Professor* (Boston: Brill Academic, 2001), 72–73.

21. Joseph Wirth, speech to the Reichstag, in *Verhandlungen des Reichstags: I. Wahlperiode 1920: Stenographische Berichte*, vol. 356, session 236 (25 July 1922) (Berlin: Druck und Verlag der Norddeutschen Buchdruckerei und Verlagsanstalt, 1922), 8054–58. Translated by Robert Goodrich.

22. Müller cabinet communique, 1929, in *Die ungeliebte Republik: Dokumentation zur Innen- u. Aussenpolitik Weimars, 1918–1933*, ed. Wolfgang Michalka and Gottfried Niedhart (Munich: DTV, 1980), 263. Translated by Robert Goodrich.

23. David Hunter Miller, *My Diary at the Conference of Paris, with Documents*, vol. 4 (New York: Appeal, 1924), 224–27.

24. *Frankfurter Zeitung*, 14 June 1924. Translated by Robert Goodrich.

25. Richard Blanke, *Orphans of Versailles: The Germans in Western Poland, 1918–1939* (Louisville: University of Kentucky Press, 1993), 133.

26. Karl Binding and Alfred Hoche, "Die Freigabe der Vernichtung lebensunwerten Lebens: Ihr Mass und ihre Form," 1920, in *Spurensuche: Eugenik, Sterilisation, Patientenmorde und die v. Bodelschwinghschen Anstalten Bethel, 1929–1945*, by Anneliese Hochmuth (Bielefeld, Germany: Bethel-Verlag, 1997), 179. Translated by Robert Goodrich.

27. Alice Rühle-Gerstel, "Back to the Good Old Days?," in Kaes et al., *Weimar Republic Sourcebook*, 218.

28. Joseph Goebbels, "Deutsches Frauentum," 1933, in *Signale der neuen Zeit: 25 ausgewählte Reden von Dr. Joseph Goebbels* (Munich: Zentralverlag der NSDAP, 1934), 118–26. Translated as "German Women," trans. Randall Bytwerk, German Propaganda Archive (Calvin University), 1999, https://research.calvin.edu/german-propaganda-archive/goeb55.htm.

29. Quoted in *The Family in Modern Germany*, ed. Lisa Pine (London: Bloomsbury Academic, 2020), 82.

30. Quoted in Heidrun Holzbach-Linsenmaier, "Dem Führer ein Kind schenken," *Die Zeit*, 6 May 1994. Translated by Robert Goodrich.

31. Oliver Trevisiol, "Die Einbürgerungspraxis im Deutschen Reich, 1871–1945" (PhD diss., University of Konstanz, 2004), 126, 224.

32. See, for example, *Der Stürmer*, Sondernummer 2 (May 1929).

33. Paul von Hindenburg, quoted in *Chronik des 20. Jahrhunderts: 1928*, ed. Brigette Beier (Gütersloh, Germany: Chronik Verlag, 1988), 12. Translated by Robert Goodrich.

34. Gustav Stresemann, *Gustav Stresemann: His Diaries, Letters and Papers*, vol. 3, ed. and trans. Eric Sutton (New York: Macmillan, 1940), 405–6.

CORE TEXTS

1. Johann Gottlieb Fichte, *Addresses to the German Nation* [Reden an die deutsche Nation, 1808], trans. Reginald Foy Jones and George Henry Turnbull (Chicago: Open Court, 1922), 134.

2. Peter Gay, *Weimar Culture: The Outsider as Insider* (New York: W. W. Norton, 2001), 23.

Printed in the USA
CPSIA information can be obtained
at www.ICGtesting.com
LVHW071512161223
766613LV00008B/552

9 781469 665542